Dear Reader:

The book you are about to read is the latest bestseller from the
St. Martin's True  *ork Times*
calls "the leader i you a fas-
cinating account o t has captured the national of peren-
nial bestselling tr SALT OF
THE EARTH is th over life-
shattering violence; Joseph Wambaugh called it "powerful and
absorbing." Fannie Weinstein and Melinda Wilson tell the story of
a beautiful honors student who was lured into the dark world of
sex for hire in THE COED CALL GIRL MURDER. St. Martin's
is also proud to publish critically acclaimed author Carlton
Stowers, whose Edgar Award-winning TO THE LAST BREATH
recounts a two-year-old girl's mysterious death, and the dogged
investigation that led loved ones to the most unlikely murderer: her
own father. In the book you now hold, HUNTING EVIL, Carlton
Smith tells the account of two people with troubled backgrounds
who may have preyed upon the young and the unwary.

St. Martin's True Crime Library gives you the stories *behind* the
headlines. Our authors take you right to the scene of the crime
and into the minds of the most notorious murderers to show you
what really makes them tick. St. Martin's True Crime Library
paperbacks are better than the most terrifying thriller, because
it's all true! The next time you want a crackling good read, make
sure it's got the St. Martin's True Crime Library logo on the
spine—you'll be up all night!

Charles E. Spicer, Jr.
Executive Editor, St. Martin's True Crime Library

THE DOUBLE LIFE OF MICHELLE MICHAUD

Alleged to have raped a number of women with her partner-in-crime and boyfriend James "Froggie" Daveggio, Michelle Michaud led a startling double life. While she sometimes boasted to friends and acquaintances that she was a $1,000-a-night prostitute, Michelle was also a God-fearing mother of two, who volunteered at her local church, and was even employed as a school crossing guard. People who knew her said Michelle had an amazing ability to balance her alter egos, always ready with a smile and a wave behind the wheel of her minivan—the very one that was allegedly rigged to strap down their prey . . .

HUNTING EVIL

EVIL

CARLTON SMITH

St. Martin's Paperbacks

HUNTING EVIL

Copyright © 2000 by Carlton Smith.

Cover photograph by Gregory Urquiaga, *The Contra Costa Times*.

ISBN: 0-312-97572-4

Printed in the United States of America

St. Martin's Paperbacks edition / October 2000

St. Martin's Paperbacks are published by St. Martin's Press, 175 Fifth Avenue, New York, N.Y. 10010.

10 9 8 7 6 5 4 3 2 1

AUTHOR'S NOTE AND ACKNOWLEDGMENTS

This was not an easy book to write, nor will it be an easy one to read. While nearly all crimes are horrible, and many are brutal, it's a reflection of the times we live in that such words have lost their power of impact by frequent use in the news and in our popular culture. But there are such things as truly unspeakable crimes, behavior that leaves one grasping to understand: just how and when and where—and why—did someone who was once a human being sink to such levels of depravity?

As this is being written, James Anthony Daveggio and Michelle Lyn Michaud are facing a trial for their lives in the Superior Court of Alameda County, California, charged with the utterly purposeless murder of a young girl neither knew, nor cared to know, a 22-year-old Pleasanton, California, student selected entirely at random for the sheer unadulterated evil of torturing and killing an innocent victim, simply to enjoy her terror.

But this was hardly the only crime that Daveggio and Michaud were accused of during their four-month odyssey into the abyss; there were also nine separate rapes committed by both Daveggio and Michaud, including at least four of their own children and their friends, as the last restraints of civilized behavior fell away and the pair descended into a living hell of their own making.

All that is necessary for evil to prevail, someone once said, was for good people to do nothing. In this case, there were plenty of warning signs over the years, but no one—not the courts, not the prisons, not the social services agencies, not even the police—took heed in time.

Indeed, even as Daveggio and Michaud were preparing to face a jury for their last alleged crime, authorities were still trying to determine how many others might have died; there was one 25-year-old murder case for which another man may still be wrongfully imprisoned.

Where does it begin? How does an innocent child turn into a monster? Is evil born, or is it made?

There is no simple answer to this, one of the most troubling questions of the last century.

While the notion of sexual homicide is hardly new—the 19th century was marred by several notorious cases, not least that of London's Jack the Ripper—in terms of raw numbers it appears to be one of the fastest-growing categories of crime in America. As recently as twenty-five years ago, such random, sexually oriented murders comprised fewer than six percent of all the murders committed in this country; most murders committed were the result of domestic violence, or were committed in concert with another felony, such as robbery.[1]

But beginning around 1975, the number of random, sexually oriented homicides began to increase; presently, such crimes account for as much as 25 percent of all murders committed in the United States.

Psychologists and sociologists have speculated on the reasons for this stunning increase; some have attributed the rise to the changing nature of sex roles over the past few decades as women have gained greater reproductive freedom, which has caused some men to react violently; others have pointed to the vast increase in sexual imagery contained in popular culture and advertising, which continuously drives home the message that the only true measure of personal validity is sexual success, or even excess.

Still others have pointed to the fracturing of American society over the past quarter-century, the end result of a far

---

1 This and the following statistics about sex murderers are reported in *Sexual Homicide: Patterns and Motives*, Ressler, Burgess and Douglass, (Lexington Books, 1988).

more mobile culture in which the moderating influence of traditional institutions such as churches, neighborhoods, community groups and schools has waned.

Faced with the prospect of a large increase in random, psychologically based murders, law enforcement authorities responded with efforts to, first, understand the roots of this behavior, and second, to develop methods for investigating crimes that were by their very nature difficult to solve.

Between 1979 and 1986, two agents assigned to the Federal Bureau of Investigation's Behavioral Science Unit at Quantico, Virginia, aided by a Massachusetts psychiatric nurse, studied the backgrounds, attitudes and crimes of 36 convicted sex murderers responsible for 105 killings, in an effort to discern just what, if anything, made them different. The study, by agents Robert Ressler and John Douglas, and nurse Ann W. Burgess, showed that the 36 killers—all men, and mostly white—had a significant number of negative commonalities in their childhoods.

Of the 36 men studied, for example, nearly 70 percent lived in homes in which alcohol abuse was a problem; 33 percent lived in homes where drug abuse occurred. More than half grew up in families with some history of psychiatric problems, half had families in which one or more family members had criminal records, and almost half had families that experienced some sort of sexually related problem, such as adultery or incest.

Almost half of the killers experienced physical abuse as children; nearly three out of four were psychologically abused. Sixty-eight percent experienced frequent family moves from community to community as they were growing up; almost half had their fathers leave home before they were 12 years old. In 66 percent of the killers' lives, the mother was the dominant figure in the family; in almost three-quarters of the cases, the killer had a negative relationship with a male caretaker figure. Almost half reported that they believed they had been treated unfairly, both within their family, and in the world at large.

Taken together, these family circumstances could describe

the backgrounds of a substantial portion of the nation's criminal population, and obviously, only a few of those convicted of crimes are serial killers. What made the killers' early lives different from others later convicted of criminal behavior was the far heavier sexual component of their early lives.

More than one-third of the killers, for instance, reported witnessing some form of sexual violence as a child; almost three-quarters reported having experienced some sort of sexually stressful event as children, with almost half reporting that they themselves had been sexually abused. Almost three out of four had voyeuristic experiences as children, and 81 percent had some experience with pornography. More than half experienced fantasies of rape, and slightly more than half had consensual sexual experiences at an early age.

The human mind, of course, is a fantastically adaptable construct. What the researchers came to believe about their study population was that the killers' propensity to commit sexual violence developed from the very way they coped with the circumstances they faced growing up.

"We theorize," wrote Ressler, Burgess and Douglas in *Sexual Homicide: Patterns and Motives* in 1988, "that these men are motivated to murder by way of their thinking. Over time, their thinking patterns emerged from or were influenced by early life experiences."

Faced with unpleasant, even violent surroundings, it is natural for a child to develop an enriched internal fantasy life as a means of relieving psychological stress. In the case of the murderers, the fantasy life diverged into thoughts of violent revenge, often with a sexual component. Indeed, in the minds of the serial killers, the intensity of early, barely articulated sexual feelings somehow became fused with thoughts of fear, anger and revenge into a convoluted mental complex operating on the most basic emotional plane.

"Our study," wrote Ressler, Burgess and Douglas, " . . . suggests that instead of developing peer-related interests and activities, the murderers as adolescents retreated into their own sexually violent fantasy worlds. One begins to see how an early fantasy pattern used to cope with childhood abuse and unsatisfactory family life might turn a child away from reality and into a private world of violence where the child can exert control."

The researchers found that, unlike those children who successfully recover from abusive treatment, the killers did not, in early childhood, escape into creative outlets or fantasies of a better life. Instead, "their energies were funneled into fantasies of aggression and mastery over other people, suggesting a secret, projected repetition of their own abuse and an identification with the aggressor."

As the child grows older, these complex feelings and mental images grow ever more elaborate and detailed; and as the child gains increasing control over his environment as he matures into adulthood, in his fantasies his yearning to control others grows as well—in short, to inflict on others what was inflicted on him; in some primitive, hardly conscious way, the murderer binds the victim to himself through the shared experience of violence.

There are a number of warning signs displayed by the behavior of the sex murderer–to-be as he is growing up, Ressler, Burgess and Douglas found.

For example, almost four out of five of the murderers told the researchers that they were given to excessive daydreaming, a figure that remained steady all the way into adulthood. The same number reported engaging in compulsive masturbation, again from childhood into adulthood. Almost three out of four reported feeling isolated from others throughout their lives.

Just slightly fewer were given to chronic, even unnecessary lying. Almost seven out of ten wet their beds as children, and even 15 percent of the murderers *continued* to wet their beds in adulthood. Over half engaged in stealing as children, a number that rose to 81 percent in the adolescent years, and returned to fully half as adults. More than half reported bullying or assaulting children, a figure that rose to 64 percent in adolescence and that declined only slightly to 44 percent in adulthood.

Two-thirds of the murderers were frequently rebellious as

children, two-thirds suffered from frequent nightmares, and just over half engaged in setting fires. Almost half had temper tantrums, and half had problems sleeping. More than a third assaulted adults, and an equal number reported having irrational phobias. Just over one-third ran away from home at one time or another.

Another third committed cruel acts to animals as children, a figure that rose to nearly half as adolescents, and remained above 25 percent among adults. Significant numbers of the murderers also reported being accident prone, having repeated headaches, being destructive of property, suffering eating problems, experiencing convulsions, and engaging in self-mutilation. Self-mutilation, in fact, actually *rose* among the murderers from childhood to adulthood, from 19 percent of the children to 32 percent among the adults.

More than half reported significant sexual dysfunction, primarily impotency and an inability to have orgasms; this incapacity, resulting from the inability to form trusting and truly intimate relationships, was compensated for by increasingly bizarre forms of sexual experimentation, often including bondage, sado-masochism and, not infrequently, fetishes with rigid objects used for insertion, standing in for the unresponsive organ and representing the notion of sexual control.

Under such circumstances it is hardly surprising that most of the sex murderers were by any conventional measurement failures in real life. More than a third flunked at least one grade in school; more than half had poor performance in high school, and almost half failed to finish. In work, only one-fifth reported ever having a steady job, while over two-thirds said they only worked sporadically. Eleven percent said they had no job at all. In terms of military service, almost a third of those who served had a criminal record while in uniform, and over half received either an undesirable or medical discharge.

"Murder is compensatory in the fantasy world of the murderer," Ressler, Burgess and Douglas concluded. With so much energy devoted to violent fantasizing, the researchers found, the typical sex murderer had little time or interest left over for a productive and healthy life.

One of the most insidious aspects of this internal thought process among serial sex killers is its progressive nature. What begins as an unmanifested but powerful imagining as a child gradually becomes more specific, more detailed, as the years unfold. And as the will transforms acts of the mind to acts in the real world, the violence escalates.

By the time a sex killer has reached adulthood, the fusion of imagination and action is complete, and one feeds the other in a never-ending, downward spiral into greater and greater depravity. As part of this process, other people gradually cease to exist as anything other than objects to be manipulated as part of the fantasy made into reality. For most of the murderers, their first homicidal violence took place after some sort of psychologically stressful event, called "triggering factors" by Ressler, Burgess and Douglas.

"A variety of triggering factors can activate the violence," they reported, "and the murderer's emotional state may leave him especially open to such factors."

In this sense, there is little that is erotic or even lustful (in the conventional sense of the word) about the forces driving the sex killer; instead, all of the normal sexual drive of the killer becomes focused on the compulsive need for control over the victim, and the act of sex becomes almost a symbolic manifestation of the obsessive need to initiate someone else into the dreadful netherworld that preoccupies the mind of the murderer, a sort of psychic exclamation point to the statement of rage.

The case of James Daveggio and Michelle Michaud is particularly unusual in that it is one of the relatively rare situations in which a woman occupies an important and active role in a sex killer's depredations. Michelle Michaud's apparent role in Daveggio's manifested fantasy was to act as the willing enabler, the slavish assistant who would stop at nothing to serve her master's desires. Not surprisingly, it wasn't always a perfect fit—for the simple reason that, just as Daveggio had his fantasies, Michelle Michaud had *hers*.

Since the fantasies are rooted in the internal psyches of each individual, it's not surprising that they do not perfectly mesh. In the end, each realized that the way they saw the other was nothing more than the product of their own imaginations, but by then it was too late.

To this point, there has been comparatively little research into the nature of female psychopathology in the United States, or at least, certainly nothing as ambitious as that attempted with the imprisoned male sex killers by Ressler, Burgess and Douglas. Of course, women are significantly less likely to be murderers than men, and the number of women involved directly or even indirectly in random homicides is statistically insignificant, except, of course, as victims.

Nevertheless, many of the adaptive reactions seen in serial sex killers' psychology have their counterparts among women. In women, just as with men, fantasy plays an important role in thinking and feeling about reality; the studies that have been done suggest that women who become involved in crime do so because of powerful feelings of negative self-worth reaching far back into childhood, and which are very frequently associated with early sexual abuse by older, more powerful figures, usually males. It is highly significant that many of the women who enter the profession of prostitution have had histories of early sexual abuse by fathers, step-fathers, and other powerful male figures in a position to take advantage of a child.

To this end, a woman may build a destructive fantasy around the notion that if she pleases a man with subservience, she may somehow gain control of him. Thus, while male sex murderers may commit violence to validate control over women, female enablers such as Michelle Michaud may assist in the violence, and endure it themselves, to achieve the same over men.

These generalizations aside, Michelle Michaud remains an extremely complex psychological personality, fraught with seeming contradictions, as will be seen. She may best be categorized, inexpertly and seemingly inconsistently, as a rebellious submissive—rebelling against authority in order to gain the attentions of a dominator.

Nothing illustrates this contradiction more than her description as a "dominatrix-type" by some of the police agencies involved in investigating her, and as a "submissive type" by others. In truth, Michelle Michaud was both during the events recounted in this book: dominating others, usually younger women, to serve the pleasure of the one dominating her, Daveggio.

Finally, a word about some of the terms that are often used, sometimes far too loosely, about the sort of events with which this book is concerned: *psychotic* and *psychopathic*. While some people use these words interchangeably, they do so incorrectly. A person who is *psychotic*, a person suffering from a *psychosis*, is a person with a disease of the brain. The cause of the disease may be an injury or an illness, but the general result is that a person who is psychotic suffers from delusions and is, in a legal sense, not responsible for his or her actions.

A *psychopath*, on the other hand, is a person who has no demonstrable brain illness or injury, yet nevertheless exhibits socially unacceptable behavior—in short, a person who has the characteristics of a *personality disorder*. One prominent type of personality disorder may be the *anti-social personality*, in which a person is aware of the difference between right and wrong, but chooses to do wrong for some internal reason. In the 19th century, such a condition was called "moral insanity," but under the present custom and law, such persons are not legally insane.

That they are disturbed, there is no question. Because the vast majority of serial killers are psychopathic rather than psychotic, the question of what causes their development and how they should be dealt with once they are apprehended is a rather crucial issue for our society as we enter the new century.

Unlike other books, in *Hunting Evil* I have made an exception to the usual policy of naming names. In this book, the names of the surviving victims have been changed, along with the names of many others who were innocent of any crimes, even if guilty of bad judgment. Those provided with different names have been marked, on first reference, with an asterisk. I do this to protect their privacy and their reputations. To do otherwise is to commit still another form of violence on those who have already suffered enough.

There has been a tendency over the past several decades to romanticize outlaws, in film if not in books; perhaps it is a reflection of our natural desire to find something appealing in even the most despicable, to look for some sort of human connection in even the worst among us. Although the sentiment might be laudable, there was nothing remotely uplifting or admirable about the criminal activities of James Daveggio and Michelle Michaud, and you won't find anything in here to suggest there was. Although the author invited both Daveggio and Michaud to agree to be interviewed, neither chose to avail themselves of the opportunity, apparently on the advice of their attorneys.

Drawn from numerous interviews and from over 4,500 pages of court and police records, this tale of Froggie and Mickie is a sordid one from start to finish, and stands, if nothing else, as a warning to parents, friends and police alike: all that is required for evil to prevail is for good people to do nothing.

The author owes a large debt of gratitude to a variety of individuals who helped make this book possible under difficult conditions, both legal and otherwise.

First among them are reporters David Holbrook of the *Contra Costa Times*, Mike Henderson of the *Reno Gazette-Journal*, and Ramon Coronado of *The Sacramento Bee*, all of whom took an interest in the story of James Daveggio and Michelle Michaud, and who frequently assisted the author in keeping track of the multiple court proceedings and documents engendered by the case.

Special thanks should also go to a variety of law enforcement officials, including Sgt. Rich Matranga of the Sacramento County Sheriff's Department; detectives Desiree Carrington and Bill Summers of the Placer County, California, Sheriff's Department; Sgt. Jim Ferrie of the Union City, California, Police Department; Assistant District Attorney Rockne Harmon of the Alameda County District Attorney's Office; Sgt. Bea Torres and Lt. Terri McDonald of the California Department of Corrections; Jim Willet of the San Joaquin County, California, District Attorney's Office; Alameda County Assistant Public Defender James McWilliams, and several of his colleagues in the private defense bar; and a variety of federal law enforcement officials who have asked for and been promised anonymity so that they might continue to do their jobs. All of these strove with good heart to explain what happened, despite arbitrary, often whimsical restrictions on critical court records imposed by lawyers and judges that required a constant legal battle to surmount; still, if there are any mistakes in this narrative, they are my doing alone.

Carlton Smith
San Francisco, March, 2000

PLEASANTON, CALIFORNIA
DECEMBER 2, 1997

It was still dark when Vanessa Samson awoke on the last day of her life. The wet fog that seeped over the hills from the bay fell to the lowest places in the valley and hung on tight, an ice-cold blanket that muffled everything, even sound. A cold front had moved in a few days earlier, driving overnight temperatures to just above freezing. It wasn't the kind of weather for walking, but then, Vanessa didn't have a car.[2]

Vanessa pulled on her clothes: a gray sweatshirt with its red San Diego State University lettering across the chest, a pair of blue jeans, and white Nike tennis shoes. She went out into the kitchen, ate a bowl of Cream of Wheat cereal, packed a lunch in her red nylon Safeway Stores lunch box, and put her things into her JanSport backpack. She went to the doorway of her mother Christina's bedroom and said goodbye.

A simple goodbye. That was it, a last word from a beloved child. But that's the way it is with unexpected death. There are no warnings, no omens, no instinctive realization that someone you've cherished for all her life will never come home again. It's just goodbye, a word that will stretch into the silence of eternity.

*   *   *

---

2 Details of Vanessa Lei Samson's last day are contained in testimony by witnesses before the Alameda County Grand Jury, in the voluminous statements provided to the FBI by Michelle Michaud, and in documents contained in reports filed with the Alameda County District Attorney's Office by officers of the Pleasanton Police Department.

At five feet three inches, 120 pounds, with long dark hair flowing down her back, 22-year-old Vanessa Lei Samson was an extraordinarily attractive young woman. After graduation from Amador High School in Pleasanton, Vanessa had taken a series of jobs as an office clerk while she saved money to pay for a higher education. She lived at home with her mother Christina, her father Daniel and her sister Nicole on a quiet Pleasanton cul-de-sac not far from Interstate 680, the multi-lane freeway that tied together the string of communities lying in the long valley east of the Oakland Hills. Vanessa had a regular boyfriend, Rob, who was attending college in the San Diego area, and a wide circle of friends in the Pleasanton area.

Because her old car had broken down irreparably the year before, Vanessa was accustomed to walking to work at SCJ Insurance Services, located in a Pleasanton business park perhaps a mile away. Her route, from her family home in the cul-de-sac to Singletree Way, then down Singletree past the Lucky Supermarket to West La Positas Drive and the insurance office, generally took about twenty to twenty-five minutes.

On this early morning as Vanessa walked, the fog was unusually thick. A schoolgirl neighbor of Vanessa was perhaps 200 feet ahead of her on the sidewalk. The 13-year-old noticed Vanessa walking her usual course behind her, dressed in her tennis shoes, with her black jacket and her backpack. Meanwhile, a host of others living in the homes along Singletree remained inside, preparing breakfast or getting ready to go to school as the fog clung to the ground.

Near the corner of Page Court and Singletree Way, two men were eyeing the roof of a house one of them had recently purchased on the north side of Singletree Way. The roof needed to be replaced. The two men, David Valentine and David Elola, had arrived at the house earlier that morning and had noticed that the roof surface was slick because of the just-above-freezing temperature and the fog. After spraying the roof with water from a hose to get rid of the slippery frost, Valentine and Elola climbed up on the roof and began removing the worn shingles.

Valentine and Elola started at the peak of the roof, ripping the shingles off and throwing them to the ground. Elola was on the side closest to the street. About 7:45 a.m., both men heard a piercing scream that was abruptly cut off, followed by the sound of a sliding car door being slammed shut. Both men looked up and saw a forest green minivan—they thought it might have been a Ford—roll slowly forward down the street, make a stop at the corner, and then turn right and disappear. Both men saw a woman with long dark hair behind the wheel of the minivan. The scream troubled both Valentine and Elola; but because the van was hardly speeding off, neither thought that anything terribly awful had occurred. Elola told Valentine not to worry: it was probably just a mother disciplining a child. They could not have been more wrong.

JIMMY AND CASSIE

James Anthony Daveggio came into the world at 7 a.m. on the dot at Mary's Help Hospital, now defunct, at 145 Guerrero Street, San Francisco, just behind the old headquarters for Levi Strauss & Co., on July 27, 1960.[3] It was a far different world from the one that would swallow Vanessa Samson whole almost 40 years later.

As baby James was taking his first breath, Dwight Eisenhower was still president, the Soviet Union's Nikita Khrushchev had just promised to bury us, Fidel Castro was a young rebel, and the Republican Party was about to nominate young Dick Nixon for president against the Democrats' John F. Kennedy.

On that day, former President Herbert Hoover complained that the United States was in a "moral slump." Out at the Alameda County Jail in Pleasanton, 93 prisoners were testing the latest in fall-out shelters by "volunteering" to spend five days underground. A two-bedroom, two-bath apartment with a deck, garage, swimming pool and a spectacular view from Telegraph Hill rented for $200 a month. Weird people called beatniks were beginning to flourish in San Francisco's North Beach. Four San Francisco cops were on trial for extorting food, drinks and money from the owners of an otherwise ordinary bar that was patronized exclusively by men.[4]

Baby Jimmy was the second child born to his mother *Donna, then 19 years old, and her husband, *Johnny, who

---

3 Birth certificate of James Anthony Daveggio, on file with the San Francisco Bureau of Vital Statistics.
4 *San Francisco Chronicle*, edition of July 27, 1960.

was 23. Jimmy's birth certificate listed his father's occupation as driver for a liquor supply company. It didn't record the fact that little Jimmy was Johnny's second child by his second wife, or the fact that by the time Jimmy was born, Johnny had already left behind his first wife and three other young children. Before another two years would go by, Donna would give birth to a third child, Jimmy's younger sister, *Jodie. Within a year of Jodie's birth, Johnny would divorce Donna and marry yet again, this time fathering two more children, only to get divorced a third time. By the time he reached middle age, in fact, Jimmy's natural father would have married a total of six times. Jimmy would never know the man until he was more than 12 years old.[5]

Jimmy's mother, Donna, was herself the youngest of eight children; her mother, Annie, had married a man named Luther Hance in Missouri just before the Great Depression. Times were hard for Luther and Annie and their brood. Luther, traveling in Texas, died in 1941, and eventually, Annie and the children wound up in northern California, near the small town of Santa Rosa. Years later, Jodie would have the impression that her grandmother Annie had taken up the World's Oldest Profession in order to make ends meet; and that her mother, Donna, had been raped by one of Grandma Annie's drunken paramours when she was just 16. Donna dropped out of high school after the 11th grade.[6]

Jodie never did find out exactly how her father Johnny met her mother Donna, except that it was somewhere near Santa Rosa in the late 1950s; Jodie guessed that they'd met in a bar someplace. Jodie did know that her father's father was named Horace, and indeed, San Francisco telephone books for 1959 show a listing for a Horace Daveggio, a cab driver, but no listing for 1960.

When little Jimmy was born, joining his older sister *Til-

5 Interviews with James A. Daveggio's sister, Jodie, and his former wife, *Dawn.
6 Interview with James A. Daveggio's sister, Jodie X.

lie, the Daveggios lived in Number 5 of 13 units contained in the El Cerra Apartments, a rundown apartment building at 570 Page Street in San Francisco; today the old building has been completely renovated, and stands as one of the upscale residences just west of San Francisco's city center.

The Daveggio family's stay in San Francisco was apparently a short one; the 1961 city directory for San Francisco lists another occupant for Apartment 5. By the following year, when Jodie was born near Santa Rosa, her father Johnny had already moved out and was working on his third family. Like her older brother, Jodie would have no contact with her natural father for almost ten years.

Early in 1964, Donna remarried. With three toddlers to care for and limited job skills, there was little else she could do. Her new husband was *Ron Kerlan, who had recently been discharged from the Air Force; Donna and Ron were married in Carson City, Nevada, in March of 1964.[7]

Ron found a job working for Safeway Supermarkets, and as Jodie later recalled, the family moved frequently in the 1960s, taking apartments in Fremont, Hayward, Newark, and Milpitas, all of them southeast San Francisco Bay area bedroom communities. One of Jodie's earliest memories was one of Jimmy playing with matches in the family apartment while the three children were watching cartoons. Jimmy, four years old, struck off a match and threw it, burning, into the air. The match came down on his shoulder and set his teeshirt on fire. Jimmy leaped to his feet, screaming, and began running around the living room. Grandma Annie, who was in the kitchen, ran in and smothered the flames, but Jimmy suffered extensive third-degree burns to his back, shoulder and armpit that required skin grafts. Jimmy blamed her for the incident, Jodie said later, even though she was barely over two years old at the time.[8]

By 1966, the marriage between Donna and Ron began to

---

7 Alameda County divorce file of Ron and Donna Kerlan.
8 Interviews with James A. Daveggio's sister, Jodie, and his former wife, Dawn.

deteriorate; Ron filed for divorce in Alameda County, citing Donna in those pre–no-fault-divorce days for "extreme cruelty"; the couple separated on Valentine's Day, 1966, and Ron filed for the divorce a month later.

Somehow, though, Ron and Donna patched things up, and Donna later became pregnant with her fourth child, Ron's son *Greg. The family moved to Oakland in the late 1960s, and it was there that two other unusual events happened, both involving Jimmy. In the first, Jimmy and another boy were briefly held captive by a neighbor woman in her basement; the details of the incident never made it to the public record, but it seems to have had some sort of traumatic effect on Jimmy; and in the second, a young black girl was found murdered in a drainage ditch not far from the Kerlan family home when Jimmy was 10 or 11 years old.[9]

By 1971, the Kerlans moved again, this time to yet another East Bay bedroom community, Union City. The family occupied a small tract house on Shield Avenue just to the east of the Nimitz Freeway, the East Bay's north–south link between Oakland and San Jose.

Years later, like many of the East Bay communities and those over the hills like Dublin and Pleasanton, there seemed to be two incarnations of Union City: an older, small town with roots that went far back in the century, which was in turn surrounded by a far newer community made possible by the extension of the freeways. Most of those who moved to the newer parts of town had little in common with the pre-existing residents, or each other, for that matter. Neighbors knew each other, if at all, only in the most superficial way; the sort of social fabric that enforced community mores in older, more established towns was for all practical purposes non-existent.

It was while the family was living in Union City that a third unusual thing happened to Jimmy Daveggio; and it was something that would haunt his sister Jodie for years to come.

---

9 Interview with James A. Daveggio's sister, Jodie.

It was late September, 1974. Cassie Riley was 13 years old, about to be 14. She and her father, Kenneth Riley, and her little brother Kenny, had been living on San Juan Court in Union City for about nine months with her stepmother, Grace, and Grace's daughter, Tammy Moody, 12. Even at 13, Cassie's life had had its share of tragedy: her own mother had died in a car wreck in 1966. Her father had married the former Mrs. Moody a few years later, and now the combined families lived together as one.[10]

After moving to Union City in December of 1973, the Rileys put their two daughters into Alvarado Middle School, in the older part of town about a mile to the northwest of their home in the Casa Verde subdivision of Union City. Cassie was a year ahead of her step-sister Tammy, who was the same age as Jimmy Daveggio's sister Jodie, who also attended Alvarado Middle School. During the previous spring or summer, Cassie had briefly been Jimmy Daveggio's girlfriend. As often happens with young teenagers, the relationship only lasted a few weeks, and now, in the fall, both Cassie and Jimmy Daveggio were freshmen at Union City's only high school, James Logan.

On the afternoon of September 24, Cassie came home on the bus from school around 2:30 p.m. Two days earlier, Cassie had had a tiff with her step-mother about a boy she'd met at school. The pair had words, with Grace telling Cassie

---

10 Information in this and subsequent chapters, unless otherwise noted, was taken from testimony and other court records in *State* v. *Mutch*, 1975 criminal case in Alameda Superior Court.

that if she didn't like the rules of the house, she could always find some other place to live.

Cassie's father, Ken, was an installer for Western Electric, a subsidiary of the telephone company. He had been called to a job in Tahoe City the week before, so it was just Cassie, little brother Kenny, Tammy and Grace at the San Juan Court home. Grace had a job at a market in Hayward.

Around 3:40 on the afternoon of September 24, Tammy Moody came home from classes at Alvarado Middle School. On her way through Casa Verde Park, which ran through the middle of the Casa Verde tract of houses, Tammy saw her step-sister Cassie on the grass of the park with a boy she didn't know. Cassie invited her step-sister to sit down with them, but Tammy didn't stay long; she wanted to get home to get dressed, because her father was coming to take her out to dinner. Tammy's own 13th birthday was five days away. Tammy left Cassie with the boy in the park.

About ten or fifteen minutes later, Cassie also came home. It appears she did not go inside right away, because several neighbors later recalled seeing her lying on the grass in front of the Riley home on San Juan Court. Both Tammy and Cassie's little brother Kenny had the impression that Cassie was sad that day, whether from her tiff with Grace the day before or for other reasons was not later made clear.

Sometime after 4 p.m., Cassie went inside the house, and talked to Tammy, who was getting ready to have dinner with her father. Cassie was hungry. She asked Tammy to loan her some money so she could go to the Quik Stop Market, a nearby convenience store at the corner of Santa Maria Drive and Alvarado/Niles Road. Tammy gave Cassie all she had— 16 cents. About 4:40 p.m., Cassie set off for the store, about a ten-minute walk away.

After this, accounts of events become somewhat murky. A clerk at the convenience store later told police that she'd seen Cassie in the Quik Stop between 4:55 p.m. and 5:15 p.m., which seems like an extraordinarily long time for a hungry 13-year-old girl to decide how to spend 16 cents. The same clerk also told police she'd seen Cassie at the store between 5:15 and 5:30 p.m.

Still another witness, a Union City police cadet, said he'd seen Cassie at the store that afternoon, and a few minutes later as she was crossing Alvarado/Niles Road, presumably on her way home. The girl the cadet thought was Cassie was talking to a dark-haired man in a brown, uniform-type shirt. As the cadet drove through the intersection, he saw the man—the cadet thought he might have been Hispanic— walking west on Alvarado/Niles Road toward a small tidal drainage swale, Alvarado Creek, that paralleled Alvarado/ Niles Road.

But the cadet also told police that he'd seen the girl at the store between 3 and 4 p.m.; further, the cadet had previously worked at the store and knew the clerk who was working there when Cassie came in; the clerk said she hadn't seen the police cadet at any time that day.

Two other witnesses, students Joyce Hiramine and Gena Gloar, were on a bus coming into the Casa Verde tract that afternoon around 5 p.m., and may have seen Cassie Riley in the company of a boy neither girl recognized near the intersection of Alvarado/Niles Road and Santa Maria Drive, just across from the Quik Stop Market. Joyce knew Cassie from school, because she was friends with Tammy Moody. Joyce, who admitted her vision wasn't the best, turned to Gena.

"Look, there's Cassie," Joyce said. Joyce pulled the bus window down and yelled out, "Hi, Cassie," but the girl she thought was Cassie made no response. The boy with her had long hair down to his shoulders, and had his back to the bus.

At almost the same time, two elderly Fremont women, sisters-in-law, were visiting one of the women's sons at San Luis Court in the Casa Verde tract, one street away from the Riley house on San Juan Court. Both saw a young man get out of a large blue older-model sedan, and start walking toward the creek area. About half an hour later, one of the women saw the man return to his car and drive it away.

At about 5:33 p.m., a Union City Police Officer, Joyce Honebein, was on patrol in the Casa Verde tract, and saw a

1961 light blue Lincoln Continental with a dent in its front fender parked near the corner of Santa Maria Drive and San Luis Court, the street between Rileys' house and Alvarado/ Niles Road.

To Honebein, it appeared that the Lincoln was illegally parked in that it was too close to the corner; besides, Honebein said later, she suspected that the car might have been involved in an earlier reported crime. Honebein radioed in the license plate number to her dispatcher.

Honebein later said she looked away for a minute or two, and when she looked up, the car was gone. Honebein drove her patrol car to the corner of Santa Maria and Alvarado/ Niles and saw the Lincoln heading westbound on Alvarado/ Niles Road. She decided to follow it. The Lincoln turned south on Dyer Road, and then turned into a series of u-shaped circles and cul-de-sacs that formed the western portion of the Casa Verde tract. On one of the u-shaped streets, Honebein passed the Lincoln going in the opposite direction. She got a brief look at the driver's face; the driver seemed surprised to see her, mouthing words Honebein thought amounted to "Oh, shit!" to himself as he passed. Honebein made her own turn, planning to pursue the Lincoln, but at that moment the police dispatcher came over the radio and sent her to another call.

That, at least, was one version of the events of the afternoon. But in still other accounts, Cassie Riley may have actually left for the store as late as 5:20 p.m.; at least two witnesses saw her in front of the Riley house around that time, heading toward the intersection of San Juan Court and Santa Maria Drive. Still another witness was certain she'd seen Cassie Riley as late as 6:30 p.m. that day, and yet another was to say that he and his wife heard a blood-curdling scream to the rear of their house on San Luis Court sometime after they'd started dinner, which was well after 6:30 p.m.

In any event, sometime around 6:20 or so, Tammy met her mother Grace as she returned from work. The Rileys had a house rule: all three children were supposed to be home when Grace returned from work. Little Kenny was there, and

Tammy was there, but Cassie was not. Tammy told Grace that she'd looked for her step-sister out in front around 5:30, but couldn't find her.

Grace Riley sent her daughter down to the park to look for Cassie once more. Tammy saw one boy playing basketball by himself in the park, but didn't see her step-sister. She returned home, because her father was coming soon to pick her up. Grace now sent Kenny to check the park again, but Kenny couldn't see his sister either.

Grace Riley made dinner for herself and Kenny, fuming a bit about Cassie's absence. After dinner, Grace got in her car and drove to the convenience store to look for Cassie, but Cassie wasn't there. Grace also drove to another park in the neighborhood, but Cassie wasn't there either.

At 7 p.m. Tammy's father arrived to pick her up for dinner, and Tammy left. An hour later, Grace called the Union City Police Department to report Cassie missing; the department wouldn't take the report because Cassie hadn't been gone long enough.

At 8:30 p.m., Grace Riley called Kenneth Riley in Tahoe City, and filled him in. At 10:00 p.m. Grace called the police a second time, and this time the department took a report on the disappearance—a runaway report, since that was the only kind the department took when a disappearance involved a teenage girl who had only been gone a few hours.

Around midnight, Ken Riley checked out of his Tahoe City motel room and began driving back to Union City. He arrived in the early morning hours, and after some discussion with Grace, grabbed a few hours' sleep. Everyone hoped that Cassie had simply gone off with one of her friends for the night, and that she hadn't bothered to tell Grace because of their argument the day before.

The following morning, Tammy went to the school bus stop at the end of San Juan Court and Casa Verde Park, while Ken Riley went to the high school in the hope that Cassie would arrive for class from wherever she had been staying the night.

At the bus stop, Tammy asked if anyone had seen Cassie

the day before. Joyce Hiramine and Gena Gloar both said they had—with a boy they didn't recognize.

Ken Riley returned from the high school later that morning; Cassie hadn't arrived in the company of anyone, let alone a boy. Tammy told her step-father what she'd heard from Joyce and Gena: that Cassie had been seen the previous afternoon with a boy near the entrance to the creek. Riley walked to the intersection of Santa Maria and Alvarado/Niles Road, where Joyce and Gena said they'd seen Cassie walking with the unknown boy toward the creek, and worked his way through the heavy brush and trees toward the creek.

The creek itself was nearly hidden in the brush that ran behind a fence between the houses on San Luis Court. As he made his way along the fence, Riley could see that a dirt path ran along the fence toward the park perhaps one hundred yards away. To his right as he walked west on the path, more bushes, small trees and shrubs covered a small levee between the path and the bank leading down into the creek, which could hardly have been more than a few feet wide before the opposite bank ran up to Alvarado/Niles Road. The foliage was so dense Riley couldn't see the creekbed.

Riley came to the end of the path where it met the park, and looked around. But there was nothing in the park, so Riley reentered the path where it continued west on the other side of the park to Dyer Road. Still Riley found nothing.

When he reached Dyer Road, Riley left the path, crossed the small concrete bridge over the creek, and continued, now eastbound, on the south side of Alvarado/Niles Road. As he made his way down the busy street, Riley glanced over the brush-covered embankment that shielded the creek from the road. He saw a girl's body, apparently naked from the waist down, lying on the south bank of the creek with her head toward the water. Riley knew at once this was Cassie, and that she was dead. He hadn't seen her body before when he was on the path because it was hidden by the bushes.

Riley went immediately home, where he saw Grace in the front yard.

"Call the cops," he told her, and within a few minutes,

Union City Patrol Officer Steven Schwab had arrived. By now the shock had set in, and Riley was barely coherent, Schwab said later. Nevertheless, Riley tried to lead Schwab to the body from the south side of the creek, but the area was heavily overgrown and it was still too difficult to see anything. Riley backed out and led Schwab around to the north side of the creek along Alvarado/Niles Road, where both men could see Cassie's body when they stood on top of the embankment. Schwab called for reinforcements, and took a blanket of yellow plastic from his patrol cruiser. He picked his way down to the body through the bushes from the south side, trying not to disturb anything as he approached. At the body, Schwab made sure the girl was dead, then covered her with the blanket.

Schwab was a rookie patrol officer in Union City; in fact he'd been on his own for only a few months before this call came in. As one of two officers assigned to roving patrol, Schwab had about half of the small city to cover under normal conditions. But this murder was anything but normal; even a rookie like Schwab knew that.

For one thing, it looked as though Cassie had been the victim of a weird sexual attack. Her blue jeans, still fastened at the waist and zipped up, had been pulled down and bunched around her ankles. Her purple, short-sleeved sweater top was pulled up, as was her brassiere. Someone had ripped off her panties and thrown them to the side a short distance away. Schwab noticed that there seemed to be blood on Cassie's face and on her arm, as well as a small pool of blood underneath her. A portion of her body was caked in a thin coating of dried mud. Foliage from the creek was in her hair and on her midsection. A white foamy substance was at her mouth.

But the strangest thing was the way Cassie's body was left, on her back, with her head down near the water and her feet together higher up the bank. To Schwab, as to others, it looked as if Cassie had been in the water, then was pulled out, turned over and left with her head lower than her feet. Schwab noticed a number of shoe prints in the mud around the body, and higher up the bank where it was dustier. He also saw what appeared to be the track of a bicycle tire.

Within a few minutes a number of other police officers had arrived at the scene, including the watch commander, Sergeant Al Guzman. A call was placed to the Alameda

County Sheriff's Department for the assistance of a criminalist to help document the crime scene.

About 11:45, criminalist Laurence F. Harding arrived at the creek. Harding was a graduate student in criminalistics at the University of California at Berkeley. He'd been employed by the sheriff's department the previous May, and had attended only three other homicide cases before this one; in fact, this one was the very first he would handle all by himself. Harding looked the scene over and began taking photographs and making diagrams. After a few minutes, he called his office in Oakland and asked for some additional equipment, including materials to make plaster casts of the shoe prints.

While Harding was talking to his office, the Alameda County contract pathologist arrived. In contrast to Harding, Dr. Allen McNie was a veteran of homicide investigation in Alameda County. As a partner in a private forensic laboratory in Oakland, McNie had performed nearly 10,000 autopsies for the Alameda County Coroner's Office, including at least 125 in cases of death by drowning. After waiting for Harding to finish his call, McNie and Harding went down the bank to look at the body.

Cassie's body was still in full rigor, which meant that she had probably been dead at least twelve hours. McNie recognized the foamy material coming from the mouth: it was consistent with water that had been in the lungs, and was a strong indication that the immediate cause of death was drowning. However, McNie could see a number of scrapes, bruises and cuts over various portions of the body, particularly the head and neck; from these, McNie concluded that Cassie had almost certainly been attacked by someone, and held under water. A more exact assessment of the sequence of injuries could be made only after an autopsy, McNie said. But McNie believed that the body had been in the water for "some time" before it was pulled out and positioned on the bank.

At this point, Harding began noting a number of items of possible evidence in the immediate crime scene, including several cigarette butts near the victim's head. Schwab hadn't noticed the butts, but that didn't mean they hadn't been there. It was also possible that the butts had been dropped by one or more of the police officers since the discovery of the body; while such contamination of a crime scene was a cardinal no-no, it wasn't unheard of. Harding took photographs of the cigarette butts, along with a beer can, a piece of tissue paper, an empty candy box, and two empty match boxes. There was no way of knowing whether any of the items had been there before the murder, or had been dropped there during or afterwards. Harding took more pictures of the scene, including the various shoe prints, and took photographs of the soles of the Keds shoes with their rippled treads while they were still on Cassie's feet.

Sometime that afternoon, Harding supervised as Sergeant Guzman and two other Union City officers mixed the plaster and made the casts of the shoe prints found near the body. What was striking about the prints was the way they intermingled.

There, as plain as day, were at least two different shoe prints: Cassie's rippled Keds print, and on top of it, the distinct imprint from what appeared to be a full-sized sneaker of some sort, exceedingly well-defined, and looking almost new. The fact that the prints intermingled led some officers to believe that the larger sneaker print was that of the killer, and the intermingling of the prints was the record, in mud and dust, of a struggle between Cassie and the person who drowned her. Altogether four plaster casts of the shoe prints were taken; Guzman and the other police officers at the scene believed the unknown shoe prints were vital evidence that would lead to the killer.

That same afternoon, a former Oakland Police Department homicide detective named Jack Richardson came to the scene. The creek area was heavily overgrown, he noticed; in fact, the body was for all practical purposes invisible from the south bank, because of all the small trees and bushes that grew between the path and the wooden fence that formed the rear of the south-facing properties along San Luis Court. The worst thing about the scene, Richardson thought, were all the rats that lived in the creek; they kept trying to get to the body under the yellow plastic blanket, so the cops threw rocks at them to keep them away while the scene processing continued.

Richardson, who had taken a job as an investigator for the Alameda County District Attorney's Office after he retired from the Oakland department, noticed that there seemed to be areas of vegetation in the creek itself that had been torn up, perhaps from some sort of struggle in the water. He suggested the creek be drained so that any evidence under the water might be found.

The following day, after the body was removed, sandbag dams were placed upstream and downstream of the body, and the fire department was brought in to pump the middle segment of the creek dry. Nothing was found.

Meanwhile, Dr. McNie had performed his autopsy, and as he had guessed, the results showed that Cassie had died from drowning. But the injuries about her head, neck and body showed that someone had attacked her; that indicated, McNie believed, that the drowning had been a deliberate act.[11]

Cassie, McNie observed, had sustained a large number of superficial scrapes and bruises—some of them inflicted before death, others contemporaneous with death, and some after death. McNie noted that Cassie's hands showed signs of "washerwoman effect," the sort of wrinkling of the skin that occurs as a result of immersion in water for a substantial period of time; the presence of a mud film on Cassie's panties led McNie to believe that Cassie had been drowned while her panties were still on, and that they had been removed a significant time after death—at least, after a time long enough to allow the mud film to settle and form. Afterward,

---

11 Years later, the report of McNie's autopsy would be lost by the Alameda County Coroner's Office; but it would still be possible to reconstruct most of McNie's findings based on his testimony at the trial of Marvin Mutch.

McNie concluded, someone had removed the body from the creek, disarranged the clothing, and then left it in its odd position.

McNie found no evidence that Cassie had been raped—that is, no chemical residue that might be expected from the presence of semen, nor any tearing of tissues. An examination of her stomach contents indicated that she had eaten some sort of colored sugar candy around two hours before she'd been killed.

McNie found a number of bruises around Cassie's neck and under her chin which led him to believe that Cassie's attacker had had his hands around her throat. Coupled with a number of small hemorrhages in Cassie's eyes, McNie concluded that Cassie's attacker had grabbed her around the neck and choked her, perhaps while holding her head under the shallow water of the creek. But the bruising wasn't distinct enough for McNie to say whether the assailant's hands had come from the front or the rear.

However, McNie noticed a number of other injuries, including a half-inch tear on Cassie's upper lip, an injury to her nose, and scratches under each eye. Scratches and bruises on both of her elbows and a bruise to her right kneecap seemed to suggest that Cassie had been attacked from behind, had fallen forward down the creek bank, and had her head pushed under water by the assailant; the facial injuries were consistent with her face meeting a rock or other such object under the surface of the water. Cassie's body had several other bruises that McNie believed could have been caused by blows from a fist.

While it wasn't McNie's job to theorize about the motive of the attacker, the number and type of injuries suggested that Cassie had been the victim of an assault that was as savage as it was surprising, and that it probably came while her back was turned. The absence of evidence of sexual penetration—and the disarrangement of the clothing well *after* death—seemed to indicate that the motive for the attack wasn't sexual, at least in conventional terms. Instead, the attack had all the earmarks of the work of someone who was furiously angry with Cassie.

While McNie was conducting the autopsy, a Casa Verde area resident, James Hancox, was at home putting his own impressions down on paper. Hancox was a student at Chabot College nearby, and also a cadet with the Union City Police Department. Coming home from class on the morning Cassie's body was discovered, Hancox observed all the police activity near the creek. He stopped to ask one of the police sergeants what was going on. The sergeant told him that a girl had been found murdered in the creek, and showed him the body while it was still on the bank.

Now Hancox grew excited; he told the sergeant that he was sure he'd seen the dead girl the previous afternoon at the Quik Stop market. The sergeant told Hancox to go home and write down everything he could remember.

In his written account, Hancox said he'd stopped in at the Quik Stop the previous afternoon to get something to eat or drink. Instead, he looked at the magazine rack for a while— maybe 10 or 20 minutes, he thought. While he saw the clerk in the store, Valerie Harward, he hadn't talked to her. As he was looking at the magazines, he noticed a young girl come in. The girl smiled at him. Hancox then left the store and got in his car. As he was pulling up to the intersection of Marcia Avenue and Alvarado/Niles Road, Hancox continued, he saw the girl he'd seen in the store crossing Santa Maria where it met Alvarado/Niles Road—in other words, directly in front of him across the intersection. Just at that moment the girl was approached by a young man in some sort of uniform, who said something to her. To Hancox, it appeared the girl abruptly changed direction and headed toward the creek area with the young man. The man, Hancox said, appeared to be around 18 or 19, was darkly complected and had dark hair just below his ear; he appeared to be of Latin descent. The uniform shirt was gray, and it had a gold or yellow patch on its shoulder. This happened sometime between 3 and 4 p.m., Hancox added.

Hancox took the written statement back to the sergeant; within a few minutes, a Union City officer, Mike Shelton, was detailed to get a statement from Valerie Harward.

Valerie told Shelton that she'd been in the store when the girl came in, but it was around 5:15 or 5:30 p.m., not 3 or 4, as Hancox had said. Moreover, Valerie said she hadn't seen Hancox, whom she knew as a former clerk at the store, all day.

Valerie readily identified a photograph of Cassie Riley as the girl who had come into the store; Valerie said she recognized her because she often came in to buy candy. Valerie was busy trying to clean up the store when Cassie came in; her shift was supposed to be over at 5 p.m., but her relief was late, a not-uncommon occurrence. She remembered that Cassie tried to buy three items, but didn't have enough money. Instead, Cassie bought a package of a sugar candy called "Wacky Wafers," and two packets of sunflower seeds, which together totaled 16 cents.

While this was going on, other officers were canvassing the neighborhood in an effort to find out whether anyone had seen or heard anything unusual. Some of the officers went to the park to look for evidence, and it was there that they were met by a man who lived on San Luis Court, Steven Huntoon.

Huntoon told the officers that the previous night, as he and his wife were having dinner, they heard a loud scream from outside. Huntoon immediately got up and went out to the front of his house, thinking someone, perhaps a child, had been dreadfully injured. But the street in front of his house was empty. Huntoon noticed that the sun had just gone down, which made it shortly after 7 p.m. Since there seemed to be nothing out of the ordinary going on, Huntoon returned to his dinner. Now, the following day, as he told his story to the police, Huntoon realized that the scream he and his wife had heard had probably come from the victim.

While Huntoon was relating this story, another Union City officer, Detective Joseph Leon, was assigned to locate and interview Joyce Hiramine and Gena Gloar. Leon found Joyce and Gena at Alvarado Middle School.

The boy she'd seen with the girl who looked like Cassie, Joyce told Leon, was about two inches taller than Cassie (Cassie was five feet two inches), somewhat skinny, with shoulder-length, curly light brown hair. Joyce guessed he was perhaps 14 years old. The boy was wearing a beige- or tan-colored shirt with short sleeves. Joyce didn't notice any shoulder patch on the shirt.

Gena thought the boy with the girl whom Joyce had thought was Cassie—Gena hadn't known her—was as much as four or five inches taller; she also said he had brown hair down to the collar. She thought the boy was about 18. She said that the boy was wearing a shirt that looked like a uniform with a yellow and blue patch on the sleeve.

Still another detective—his or her name remains unknown—began looking for the boy Cassie's sister Tammy had seen with Cassie in the park the day she was killed. Somehow the detective learned that this was a 15-year-old named Monte John Williams. The detective learned from Monte that he'd seen Cassie around 3:30 or so, and that a number of other kids in the park that afternoon had also seen and talked with her.

Who else? the detective asked, and Monte Williams pointed out a number of other kids who also attended the high school. The detective wrote down the names and left; but after he was gone, several of the boys at the high school jumped Monte and gave him a beating for turning their names in to the police. One of those names given to police was almost certainly that of 14-year-old Jimmy Daveggio.

Over the next few days, as Union City Police strove to locate witnesses who might help explain what had happened to Cassie Riley, sheriff's department criminalist Laurence Harding processed the photographs he had taken at the crime scene. By far the most interesting of the pictures were ones that showed the shoe prints.

There were several areas where shoe prints were found. One area, on the path along the fence above the south side of the creek, contained numerous examples of what was probably a basketball sneaker print and Cassie's Keds print. Harding's photographs showed the prints intermingling at three different spots along the trail; it wasn't possible to tell with certainty which way they were headed.

Harding found at least one spot with the Keds print atop the embankment between the path and the creek proper; this print was quite close to an opening in the foliage that led down to the creek. At another spot, perhaps 50 feet downstream from where the body had been found, Harding had photographed a series of prints, all of them looking like boys' sneakers, including one prominent print that matched the tread intermingled with Cassie's Keds along the path. A ruler placed near the basketball-type shoe print showed it was about 11 1/2 inches in length, which in Harding's estimation meant that the shoe was a size 9 or 9 1/2. The photographs also showed what appeared to be the track of a bicycle tire.

And from the area where the casts had been taken, adjacent to the body, Harding's photographs showed a number of Cassie's prints next to some clear impressions of the same nearly new basketball shoe.

All of this seemed to indicate that the person who had attacked and drowned Cassie Riley was someone wearing a basketball-type shoe, and was probably a fellow student of Cassie's who had been in the park on the day she was killed.

Early the next week, Union City Police Detective George Bist—who now assumed overall control of the investigation—sat down with Joyce Hiramine and Gena Gloar to show them photographs. Later, these sessions would provoke controversy, primarily because Bist failed to keep a record of just whose photographs he displayed to the girls. It appeared, however, that Joyce identified at least one and possibly more of the photographs as someone who looked like the boy she had seen with Cassie from the bus. Gena, in turn, looked at a number of photographs which featured men in uniforms; Bist hoped she'd be able to recognize the patch she'd seen on the boy's sleeve.

Meanwhile, officer Mike Shelton—who normally worked as a motorcycle officer but was pressed into duty for the investigation—began interviewing boys at the high school. One of those interviewed, on October 2, 1974, was Jimmy Daveggio, probably based on information provided earlier by Monte Williams.

Years later, Shelton's written report of his interview with Jimmy Daveggio was the only official record showing a possible link between Jimmy Daveggio and the death of Cassie Riley that could be unearthed; that is not to say, however, that other records shedding light on Jimmy's whereabouts and actions on the day Cassie died don't exist.[12]

Shelton's report:

12 The author's request to inspect the Union City Police Department's 25-year-old case file on the murder of Cassie Riley was denied by Union City Police Chief Al Guzman—the same man who a quarter-century earlier had taken the plaster casts of the suspicious shoe prints, and who later played an important role in the arrest and prosecution of Marvin Mutch. Likewise, attempts to locate similar documents from the office of Alameda County District Attorney Thomas Orloff were rebuffed with the explanation that they could not be located. It appears, however, that none of the documents

Daveggio states that approximately six months ago he was involved in a boyfriend/girlfriend relationship with victim for approximately one to two weeks. During that time, there was no sexual intercourse or attempts at same on his part, not that he did not seriously consider same, rather that he did not feel victim would have been receptive to same and he was afraid to initiate any action regarding same. Daveggio has no knowledge of this case, wears size 11 tennis shoes of a variety not consistent with evidence in this case, and since severance of the relationship (mutual) characterizes their relationship as indifferent, as opposed to hostile.

The absence of any information in Shelton's report regarding Jimmy's whereabouts on the afternoon Cassie was killed is a probable indication that still other records relating to Daveggio exist in the Union City police file on Cassie Riley's murder; certainly determining that information would have been a prime objective of any investigator, even before inquiring as to the size of someone's shoes. It is, in fact, likely that Daveggio's name was provided to Shelton through Monte Williams as one of a number of high school kids who had been in the park on the day of the murder.

Twenty-five years later, Shelton had little independent recollection of his interview with Jimmy Daveggio, only that it was one of a number he conducted with high school boys about Cassie Riley; Shelton remembered that he talked to as many as 35 kids about Cassie, "and about all of them claimed she was their girlfriend at one time or another."

Sometime near the end of the week after Cassie's death or the beginning of the next week, Union City Detective Bist was provided with information that a large light blue sedan

---

regarding James A. Daveggio's potential involvement in the death of Cassie Riley were ever provided to the attorney representing the man eventually convicted of the crime, Marvin Lee Mutch.

had been seen in the area around the time that Cassie had been at the Quik Stop Market.

Exactly how Bist came into possession of this information remains obscure 25 years later, but it is likely that the vehicle description came from one or both of the two elderly ladies who had been visiting on San Luis Court the day Cassie was last seen. At some point the two ladies, a Mrs. Sylva and a Mrs. Smith, had seen the light blue sedan parked near the corner; one or both recalled that the car was older, and that it had a dent in the left front fender. One of the ladies recalled seeing it drive away sometime between 5:30 and 6 p.m.

Based on this information, Bist composed an advertisement, which he had placed on the front page of the local Union City newspaper, the *Argus*, on October 7, 1974. In the ad, Bist asked for help in locating a potential witness in the murder of Cassie Riley. He asked anyone who knew of a light blue sedan, maybe a Lincoln Continental, possibly driven by a dark-haired man between 18 and 25 years old, seen near the creek on the day Cassie died, to contact the Union City police. The ad appeared in the *Argus* the following morning. That afternoon, Bist took a call from a 16-year-old Union City girl, Valerie Mutch. Valerie told Bist that the car and driver sounded a lot like her older brother, Marvin.

MARVIN

If it's really true that some people are born to be life's losers, Marvin Lee Mutch is certainly a qualifier. The way his life turned out, he'd barely gotten into the starting blocks before the track officials whistled him off the field, out of the stadium and into state prison for a crime he probably didn't commit.

By all accounts, one of Marvin's biggest problems was that he was both smart and mouthy. It didn't help that he was one of the newest of Union City's newcomers that fall of 1974, when he was just 18 years old, and the police were looking for someone to charge with Cassie Riley's murder.

Like Jimmy Daveggio's, his father left when Marvin was young, leaving his mother, Alice, with the responsibility of caring for Marvin and his younger sister, Valerie. It appears that Alice remarried at some point to a man named Collins, but the marriage didn't last. By the spring of 1974, Marvin, his mother, Valerie, and a little brother were living in Livermore, another small bedroom community to the east of Pleasanton and Union City. It was in Livermore that Marvin first began having serious trouble with the police.

In late May of 1974, when Marvin was 17 years old, a 13-year-old girl in Livermore was accosted by a young man with dark, shoulder-length hair and a leather thong around his neck around 7 p.m.; the young man told her that two girls wanted to talk to her, and bade her come with him. At that point, the young man produced a pocket knife and put the blade of the knife to her throat. The young man forced the girl toward a nearby shack, and told her to do what he said if she didn't want to get hurt.

As the young man backed into the shack, holding the girl by her arm, he put the knife to the young girl's stomach and tried to yank her into the structure. At that point, the young girl broke away and ran. As she looked back, she could see the young man running in the opposite direction.

The girl contacted her mother and brother at a nearby pool hall, who in turn contacted the Livermore police. The police came to the pool hall at 8:55 p.m. and took a statement from the girl, who had a hard time describing the young man; indeed, she couldn't even recall what he was wearing.

Five days later, the girl was contacted again by the Livermore police; this time, the girl told the investigating officers that the young man's name "might be Mutch." The investigating officer returned to the Livermore Police Department and assembled a six-photograph identification spread that included Marvin's photograph. At that point, the 13-year-old girl picked Marvin Mutch's photograph as the person who had accosted her.

Thereafter, the investigating officer attempted to contact Marvin to ask him to come in for a statement. On June 11, Marvin called the investigator; Marvin said he'd hired a lawyer, who told him not to come in, but that he would give a statement anyway that same day at police headquarters after 2:30 p.m. At that point, Marvin's mother Alice got on the telephone line and berated the Livermore Police Department for harassing her son. About an hour later, at 2:15 p.m., Marvin and Alice came to the Livermore department, accompanied by an attorney, John Noonan. Despite having asked Mutch to come in to make a statement, the investigating officer wasn't there. Mutch, his mother and their attorney left.

Subsequently, the Livermore investigating officer attempted "continually" to induce Marvin to come in and answer questions, to no avail.

This Livermore incident was curious for a variety of reasons, not the least being the fact that Marvin Mutch was never charged with a crime in connection with it until *after* he'd been arrested by the Union City Police for Cassie Riley's murder. But there were several other anomalies about the report that should give rise to suspicions about its authenticity.

First, the girl's inability to initially offer any sort of description of the young man who accosted her tends to make the tale a bit suspect. The fact that she reported the incident almost two hours after it happened is another red flag; in most genuine assaults against 13-year-old girls, especially in small towns the size of Livermore in 1974, police were usually contacted immediately. The delay suggests that something else might have been going on between the girl, her mother and her brother at the pool hall where the police contact was made.

Next, the fact that the 13-year-old girl learned five days later that the perpetrator's name "might be Mutch" makes the provenance of this information suspect. In the absence of any showing as to how the girl knew the name "might be Mutch," the possibility exists that the people who told her it "might be Mutch" could in fact be the police themselves. The girl's identification of the photograph of Mutch under these circumstances is likewise suspect. The fact that the Livermore Police Department apparently didn't bother to seek Mutch out rather than wait for him to come to them suggests that even the police didn't take the girl's claim all that seriously.

Finally, the fact that no charges were immediately filed against Marvin Mutch in connection with the incident seems to suggest that the allegation was indeed a part of a pattern of harassment against the Mutch family, as complained of by Alice Collins; it's noteworthy that shortly after the incident, the Mutch/Collins family left Livermore and relocated in Union City.

Why would the Livermore Police be harassing 17-year-old Marvin Mutch? Twenty-five years later, with so many records destroyed and institutional memories depleted by retirements and similar changes, there's no way to say for sure. But Mutch's eventual Alameda County Public Defender in the Cassie Riley case, James McWilliams, suggests that several parents in the Livermore area were angry at Mutch for his consensual sexual involvement with their daughters. Indeed, Mutch seems to have had an interest in the occult to go along with his snappy mouth and limited bank balance; together, the traits might indeed have made him seem the boyfriend a parent would love to hate.

In any event, by early September of 1974, Marvin, Alice, Valerie and the younger brother had moved into a townhouse in Union City, an accommodation that was located perhaps half a mile southwest of Casa Verde Park. Marvin had an old Ford Mustang to get around in, and a girlfriend in Pleasanton. On Friday, September 13, Marvin took a job as an armed, uniformed security guard with a private company called Hayward Patrol. Hayward Patrol was owned by a woman named Mrs. Daly; the strawboss was a man named William Christ.

Today, giving a kid barely 18 years old a holster, gun, badge and uniform, and putting him to work without any real training would be legally impossible in California, to say nothing of being utterly dangerous, at least litigation-wise. In fact, it doesn't happen anymore. But times were different in 1974, and soon Marvin was out standing guard, six-shooter on his hip, at a variety of locations, including a potato chip factory and a supermarket.

Almost immediately the bad luck of Marvin Mutch struck: his car, the old Ford Mustang, threw a rod and was rendered into useless junk on his second night on the job, September 14.

Marvin began walking toward the Union City townhouse from the security company's headquarters in Hayward; the trek would be at least three or four miles before he got home, well after midnight. At that point, another Hayward Patrol employee, guard Mervin Velasquez, saw Marvin walking down the street, and stopped to offer him a ride. As Velasquez said later, he'd never met Marvin Mutch before that night, but recognized the Hayward Patrol uniform.

Marvin got in Mervin's car, and told him about the Mustang's engine blowing up. As it happened, Velasquez' mother owned a 1961 Lincoln Continental. Velasquez offered to sell the old boat to Marvin for $50 down and $50 a payday. Marvin agreed. The following day, Sunday, September 15, Velasquez' wife signed over the title to Marvin, and Marvin signed a note, composed by Mrs. Velasquez, that accepted all liability for operation of the car. As it turned out, the note Marvin signed was undated.

Less than two weeks later, Cassie Riley was murdered in Alameda Creek, and the car sold to Marvin Mutch was identified as having been at the scene about the time the murder was believed to have happened.

At the time she made her call to Union City Detective Bist, Valerie Mutch, Marvin's younger sister, was on juvenile probation; years later, the records no longer existed to show what the offense might have been. But this juvenile trouble may have been just more of the Mutch bad luck, as was the fact that Alice Collins had been hospitalized in September, thus leaving the two Mutch children home alone with their younger half-brother.

In any event, when Valerie Mutch called, Bist had a ready-made way of inducing Valerie to cooperate, even if she wasn't already feuding with her older brother.

The sequence of Bist's next moves remain unclear after 25 years, in part because the trial record of the case against Marvin Mutch was itself muddled by incorrect and occasionally contradictory testimony.[13] But it appears that by the time Valerie Mutch called, Bist might already have known about the car. That was because Union City officer Joyce Honebein—on patrol in Casa Verde the day Cassie was last seen—had also read the ad, and remembered calling the license plate of the Lincoln she'd seen into the police dis-

---

13 Detective Bist, who eventually left law enforcement and became director of personnel for the city of Stockton, California, could no longer recall many details about his investigation of the Cassie Riley case. Bist acknowledged, however, that because the evidence in the case was entirely circumstantial, it was possible that Marvin Mutch was wrongfully convicted. He offered to assist in an effort to clear Marvin Mutch's name if evidence could be developed demonstrating his innocence.

patcher. She called Bist, and told him about the car she'd
thought was illegally parked. The dispatch log showed that
Honebein had radioed in with a request for a warrant check
on a 1961 blue Lincoln with a license plate of BLB 184.

It seems likely that Bist then obtained the name of the
registered owner of the car, which would have led him to
Mervin Velasquez if Marvin hadn't reregistered it yet, which
appears to have been the case. Velasquez in turn would have
led Bist to Hayward Patrol, and to Mrs. Daly and William
Christ, Marvin's immediate supervisor. Bist talked to both
Mrs. Daly and Christ. Christ told him that Marvin Mutch had
been scheduled to work that day, October 8, but hadn't
shown up.

Somewhere along the line of his inquiries on Marvin, Bist
learned that Marvin and his family had moved to Union City
from Livermore; Bist contacted officers at the Livermore department, who told him that Mutch was a suspect in the reported attempted assault there of a 13-year-old girl.

The Livermore officers also told Bist that Marvin Mutch
had been previously arrested on juvenile charges of battery,
burglary, forcible rape, brandishing a weapon, assault with
intent to commit rape, and crimes against children, which
certainly made Marvin seem like he was right up there with
the young John Dillinger. The Livermore officer, however,
failed to tell Bist that none of the arrests had ever made it
to court, which suggests either that the Livermore police
were less than competent in putting away a dangerous felon,
or that there was little merit to the allegations.[14]

About 4:30 that afternoon, Bist, accompanied by Sergeant

---

14 Today, more than 25 years after these events, Marvin Mutch maintains
not only that these allegations were untrue, but that the Livermore police
knew they were untrue when they communicated them to Bist. According
to Mutch, the allegations stemmed from a Santa Clara, California, rape
case in which a resident of a group home that then 12-year-old Mutch was living
in was subsequently convicted. Although the resident was the only person
involved, all of the other residents of the group home were made to partic-
ipate in a police line-up as potential suspects. All of the others were cleared,
including Mutch.

Al Guzman and Detective Leon, arrived at the Mutch–Collins home in Union City. Valerie Mutch let them in. The three officers then made a search of the house, and located a wad of papers that Valerie identified as belonging to Marvin. The papers included several Union Oil Company credit card receipts signed by an employee of Hayward Patrol, and a number of other scraps of paper. The paper looked as if it had once been wet—the ink had run, and the pieces were stuck to one another.

Valerie told Guzman and the detectives that her brother had come home, either shortly before or possibly shortly after the day Cassie had been murdered. His security guard uniform was wet and streaked with mud, as were his pants. Marvin had stripped off his shirt and had given it to her to wash, not before taking the papers from his breast pocket and putting them on the top of a rolltop desk in the living room.

Valerie told the detectives that Marvin seemed nervous, excited when he arrived. Marvin told her, she continued, that someone had taken his keys and had thrown them in a mud puddle, and that he'd fallen trying to get them back. Marvin made a joke about it, she said. Then he'd taken a shower. Afterward, Marvin had gone out, taking his pants with him, but leaving his boots behind in the bathroom. Valerie noticed that Marvin's hard leather boots had tiny flakes of mud on them.

Over the next two weeks, Valerie added, Marvin continued to be nervous; once he'd begged her to go with him to the Quik Stop Market, because, he said, he didn't want to go alone. Twice so far, he said, the police had stopped him to ask him questions, and he didn't like it.

At some point during the search, one of the officers located some of Marvin's writings, which included some poems and documents about witchcraft. These were also seized.

Guzman looked throughout the house for a pair of basketball shoes, but didn't find any. When asked, Valerie Mutch said her brother didn't own any sneakers; he only had two pair of shoes, and both were made of hard leather, she said.

Still, Bist thought he had enough to arrest the person who'd killed Cassie Riley. Here was a suspect who'd probably been in the area on the day Cassie Riley died, who'd apparently gotten soaked, who had a possible track record for accosting young females, and who'd become nervous after Cassie's death. The clincher was the patch on the sleeve of the Hayward Patrol uniform: Valerie said Mutch wore the shirt constantly, and the patch was blue and gold, just like the one described by witnesses Hancox and Gloar.

Bist put out a request for all law enforcement agencies to be on the lookout for Marvin and his dented Lincoln. Then he sat down to write an application for a warrant to search Marvin's car and Marvin's mother's house, even though he'd already conducted the search of the house. Bist finished the affidavit in support of the warrant at 9:51 p.m. that night.

Just as Bist was preparing to take the warrant to a judge for approval, two Alameda County sheriff's deputies on patrol in Sunol, a small community located between Pleasanton and Union City, spotted Marvin's car parked in front of a bar on Main Street.

The deputies pulled their cruiser up to block Marvin off, and turned their spotlight on. One deputy drew his revolver and aimed it and the spotlight at Marvin, while the other pointed a shotgun at him. Marvin was sitting in the front seat with a Pleasanton girl. The deputies ordered Marvin to get out of the car with his hands up. Marvin did so. After seizing their prisoner's security guard's holster and gun, the deputies handcuffed him and put him in the back of their patrol car. Another deputy sheriff came by and took the Pleasanton girl to the Pleasanton police station so her parents could pick her up. Then the deputies notified Bist to come and get his suspect.

It took Bist almost an hour to get to Sunol. When he got there he put Marvin into the back of his own car and drove him to the Union City police station. There Marvin was made to strip everything, including his shoes, and was given a jail coverall. Bist put Marvin in a windowless holding cell and told him he'd be back to talk with him later.

Just what Bist was up to for the next few hours remains unclear; it may be that he simply wanted to give Marvin time to get scared, and that he used the time to brief the Alameda County District Attorney's Office on the case, and perhaps others. In any event, Bist did not return to talk to Marvin until just before 2 a.m., almost four hours after he was arrested. Marvin was removed from the cell and taken to a small interrogation room, which contained a table, three chairs, and a tape recorder. Bist read Marvin his Miranda rights, but didn't tell him he could ask that the questions be stopped so he could consult a lawyer.

Almost from the outset, Marvin admitted that he'd been in the area of the creek on the day Cassie Riley had last been seen, and even that he might have seen her, among other people in the area. Marvin told Bist that he'd lost one of his hubcaps in the creek, and that he'd gone down into the small channel to look for it. And Marvin admitted that the police in Livermore had wanted to question him about the 13-year-old girl who claimed he had accosted her with a knife.

But Marvin denied being the young man in the Livermore incident, and adamantly denied killing Cassie Riley, or, indeed, committing any act of violence toward her at all. Moreover, Marvin said, he was represented by a lawyer in the Livermore case.

Bist wasn't buying Marvin's denial. He tried to convince Marvin to confess to Cassie's murder. He showed Marvin photographs taken at the scene of the crime, and suggested that things would go much easier for Marvin if he admitted the crime, but claimed it was an accident or a mistake. In that case, Bist told Marvin, the police would help him.

Still Marvin denied killing Cassie Riley. Bist told him that the evidence against him was overwhelming.

"All I want," Bist said, "is a straight story, so I don't have to bug you, Marvin. I don't want you to look like a heavier guy than you are. You look like a nice guy. I think you made a mistake, Marvin. I think the best thing for you to do, when you've made a mistake, hang onto it like a man. Only a man can make mistakes."

But Marvin persisted in his denials. Bist got mad, and insisted that Marvin tell him the real story.

"I just gave you my story," Marvin said. "You wanted a statement. I gave you a statement."

Marvin and Bist continued to go back and forth, with Marvin telling Bist it didn't matter what he said, Bist had already made up his mind not to believe him. Bist denied this.

"We don't want to take a case to court and prosecute it . . . we care, here. Otherwise I wouldn't be here. I wouldn't be taking my time to find out your side of the story."

Marvin wanted to know what Bist had done with his clothes and his wallet. Bist said Marvin wouldn't be needing his clothes, and wouldn't get them anyway, because the police had taken them as evidence. He wouldn't need his wallet, Bist indicated.

"No," said Marvin, "I imagine I'm going to need my wallet so I can contact an attorney, because I think as soon as I get my attorney on it, I'll be out of here, because there is no reason I should be held here, no reason at all, because you can't tie me—I didn't do—"

Later, this remark by Marvin was considered to be evidence that Marvin had formally invoked his right to speak to a lawyer, as guaranteed by the Miranda decision; as a result, everything that Marvin said after this point could no longer be used against him at his trial. Bist apparently didn't recognize this as Marvin's demand to speak to an attorney, because he continued with his questions for more than an hour. At some point, in fact, Assistant District Attorney John Taylor came into the interrogation room and asked questions, as did a consulting psychologist who'd been contacted by the police. Both Taylor and the psychologist asked Marvin about his feelings on witchcraft and a variety of other matters hoping to gain some insight into his mental processes. The still-uncharged Livermore case was brought up, despite the fact that Marvin was represented by an attorney in that case, which was improper conduct by the police.

Finally just before 4 a.m., Marvin was permitted to make his first telephone call. By that time the authorities had decided to charge Marvin with Cassie Riley's murder despite his denials, and despite the fact that there was no way they could link Marvin Mutch to the plain-as-day basketball shoe prints that had been found next to the body.

Marvin's trial began the following April. By then, charges had been filed against him in the Livermore case, which gave the authorities the right to hold him in jail pending the filing of formal charges in Cassie Riley's murder. That didn't take place until February of 1975, despite Bist's insistence that the evidence against Marvin was overwhelming.[15]

Marvin was assigned a young lawyer from the public defender's office, James McWilliams. When he looked over the case, McWilliams was shocked: in his view, there wasn't nearly enough evidence to justify bringing a murder charge against Marvin Mutch. Not only was there no way to prove that Marvin had even seen Cassie Riley, let alone attacked her, there was the evidence from the basketball shoes, which seemed to clear Marvin of involvement in the crime.

But when McWilliams asked the court to dismiss the case against Marvin for lack of evidence, he was rebuffed; by this time the case had received extensive publicity in the East Bay area, and feelings against Marvin were running high. In fact, Marvin claimed that a jail guard, calling him a child molester, had beaten him after one of his court appearances. And the Union City police, apparently proud of their quick solution to the murder, refused to allow McWilliams or his investigator to interview any of their officers.

Since the case was going to trial, McWilliams concentrated on trying to knock out some of the evidence that might

---

15 All of the information about the trial of Marvin Mutch is contained in the Alameda County Superior Court file and trial transcript of *State* vs. *Mutch*, Case #58743, 1975.

be presented against Marvin. He asked that Marvin's statements to Bist, Taylor and the psychologist be thrown out, arguing that Bist had ignored the fact that Marvin was represented by a lawyer at the time of the arrest, and therefore technically shouldn't have been questioned at all. The judge, Gordon Minder, wouldn't go that far, but said that most of the middle-of-the-night interrogation, from the point where Marvin had demanded his wallet to call his lawyer, wouldn't be allowed in. That at least would keep the jury from hearing most of Marvin's ramblings about witchcraft and other damaging irrelevancies.

McWilliams also tried to get the results of the search of the Mutch–Collins house suppressed, contending that Bist's warrant failed to establish any reasonable nexus between the crime and Marvin; it was like going from A to C without stopping at B, McWilliams argued. But Judge Minder refused, and allowed in the evidence about the wet papers. It wasn't all bad, though; McWilliams would be able to use the search to establish the fact that no one could put Marvin in a pair of basketball shoes.

After selection of a jury of seven men and five women, and an opening statement by Assistant District Attorney Taylor—McWilliams reserved his opening until after the end of the state's case because he was confident that Minder would order the case dismissed for lack of evidence—testimony began.

Tammy Moody testified that Cassie was in the park with Monte Williams on the afternoon she was last seen, and that Cassie borrowed the 16 cents to go to the store. Kenny Riley told his story, about looking for Cassie, but when McWilliams asked Kenny if he knew why Cassie had been sad that day, Taylor objected. He also objected when McWilliams tried to find out who Cassie's boyfriends were, and was sustained by the judge both times.

McWilliams said he was only asking because the coroner's report showed that Cassie had argued with her stepmother about a boyfriend the day before she was last seen, but Minder ruled that the whole line of questioning was irrelevant.

Grace Riley then testified about Cassie's apparent disappearance and her attempts to find her; when asked if she'd given a runaway report on Cassie to the police that night, Grace said she had, but only because the police told her it was the only way they would take the information.

Ken Riley now took the stand and described how he had discovered his daughter's body the morning after Cassie went missing. He only went to the creek to look because Joyce Hiramine had told Tammy that was the direction Cassie was heading.

Following Ken Riley's testimony, Taylor moved into the details of his case. He called Union City Patrolman Schwab to establish the crime, and McNie to establish the cause of death: drowning accompanied by trauma from a beating. After McNie, Taylor called Richardson, the former Oakland homicide detective, whose only useful contribution seemed to be his observation that the next witness, criminalist Laurence F. Harding, "was a very young man."

Harding was a crucial witness for both sides; by having the veteran Richardson describe him as a relative youth, Taylor was attempting to signal the jury to be wary.

Harding described taking his photographs, and making his diagrams of the crime scene. Harding said he'd also been given a wad of papers by the Union City police, and after prying them apart and inspecting them closely, had found a small leaf between two of the papers that appeared to match vegetation that was normally found in the creek. Harding told of supervising Guzman and two other Union City police officers in taking the plaster casts of the various shoe prints.

The shoe prints, of course, were what McWilliams was most interested in, since they strongly suggested that someone other than Marvin Mutch had committed the crime. Harding admitted that he hadn't taken a cast of every shoe print at the scene; that wasn't directly helpful to Marvin, but it did seem to suggest that any prints that may have belonged to Marvin's hard leather boots weren't obviously present near the body, as the basketball shoe prints were. McWilliams tried another way:

"Did you see any footprint in that area that was not a sneaker type?"

"I don't remember," Harding said.

McWilliams directed Harding's attention to one of the plaster casts that showed two different prints, one of the basketball shoe and one of Cassie's Keds, and asked him to describe the print that wasn't a Keds shoe. Harding responded by describing the basketball shoe's tread pattern, a mix of diamond-shaped protuberances and straight lines crosshatching the bottom of the shoe.

"Was it a sneaker?" McWilliams asked.

But before Harding could answer, Taylor objected. The witness, Taylor said, was hardly an expert on shoes.

"Was it a flat-soled shoe?" McWilliams persisted.

"Yes, it was. There was no separation between heel and toe," Harding replied.

"Ever see a shoe with such a pattern?"

"Yes."

"And what kind of shoe was that?"

Taylor objected again. He wanted to prevent the jury from focusing too much on the presence of the basketball shoe prints, because they didn't fit the case against Marvin Mutch. This time, however, Minder overruled the objection.

"It is what I would call a basketball shoe," Harding said, "a canvas-top, rubber-soled shoe."

McWilliams asked if the basketball shoe print and the print from the Keds shoe overlapped. Taylor renewed his objection, again contending that Harding wasn't an expert on shoe prints; this time Minder upheld Taylor's objection.

McWilliams asked where the casts had been taken. Harding pointed to an area on his crime scene diagram that corresponded to a dug-out spot of mud approximately 18 inches from Cassie's head. Two of the casts contained impressions of the basketball shoe only, while a third contained both the basketball shoe and the Keds. A fourth cast of the basketball shoe was taken from the end of the path near the entrance to the park, Harding said.

McWilliams wanted Harding to state that it was apparent from the casts that the Keds print was under the basketball shoe print, meaning that it had come first, but again Taylor objected to Harding's qualifications as a shoe print expert. He wanted the jury removed so he could question Harding's qualifications.

Minder agreed, and the jury trooped out of the courtroom. When they were gone, Harding admitted that he hadn't yet received his master's degree in criminalistics from the University of California at Berkeley because he hadn't finished his thesis, and that his undergraduate degree was in mechanical engineering; before taking up criminalistics, in fact, he had worked for the Lockheed Missile and Space Company as an engineer. His only experience with shoe prints, Harding admitted, was as part of a class project at the university, in which students had taken casts of known shoe prints to make sure they understood how to do it.

Minder was in a hurry to get out of the courtroom, in part because it was the lunch hour. When McWilliams persisted that even with such limited experience, Harding was qualified to say which print had come first—after all, it was obvious by the fact that the basketball shoe print was on top of the Keds print—Minder cut him short.

"I can tell you, Mr. McWilliams," Minder said, "right now he's not qualified as an expert . . . he's not an expert in the identification of footprints." With that, Minder declared the court in recess and went off to lunch.

That afternoon, Taylor brought on a series of witnesses in an effort to link Marvin to Cassie's disappearance. Valerie Harward, the Quik Stop clerk, testified that Cassie had come into the store just before 5 p.m. and spent about 15 minutes looking at candy before leaving at 5:10. Under cross examination, she admitted that she'd first told the police that Cassie had been in the store from 5:15 to 5:30. She also said that James Hancox, the police cadet, had never been in the store the day Cassie was last seen.

Hancox was called to testify. He claimed he was looking at the magazine rack when Cassie came in the store, and that they had made eye contact. Hancox said he didn't talk to the store clerk. He recollected seeing Cassie and a man in a tan shirt with a gold patch on his sleeve walking in the direction of the creek.

Hancox described coming home from school the following day, and finding all the police activity at the creek. One of the officers had told him to go home and write down his statement, Hancox said.

Under cross examination by McWilliams, Hancox admitted that he'd seen the clothes of the victim before writing his statement; in fact, he said, he'd been around the crime scene for about 40 minutes before going home to record his impressions from the day before. Then Hancox made a curious assertion that should have caught McWilliams' attention, but did not.

He testified that he worked as a cadet on Sunday, Monday and Tuesday, each day from 4 p.m. to midnight. Of course, if that was the case, Hancox couldn't have seen Cassie at the store around 5 p.m., because he would have been at work. And indeed, Hancox had originally told police that his encounter with the girl he thought was Cassie was around 3 to 4 p.m., which meant that the man he'd seen in the uniform couldn't have been Cassie's killer, since everyone else agreed she was alive and well between 4:30 and 5 p.m.

"When did you first feel the girl you had seen was Cassie?" McWilliams asked.

"When I saw the picture in the paper," Hancox said.

McWilliams brought out still other details that damaged Hancox' testimony. Hadn't he told Valerie Harward, the Quik Stop clerk, during the court's afternoon recess that he was sure he'd seen Cassie, because she'd gotten a cold drink at the store?

Hancox thought she had, even though Cassie only had 16 cents.

Didn't Valerie Harward tell you that she was sure you weren't in the store at all that day? McWilliams asked.

Hancox said Valerie must have been mistaken.

The next day, Taylor called Joyce Hiramine, who said she'd seen a girl she thought was Cassie heading for the creek with a boy she thought might be 14 or 15. This was about 5 p.m., Joyce added, when she was riding the school bus with Gena Gloar.

Under cross examination, Joyce said she'd told police that the girl she'd seen had something in her hands, like a newspaper; she appeared to be reading it with the boy who was walking with her.

Had she ever seen Marvin Mutch before? McWilliams asked, and Joyce said she hadn't. And in fact, in her initial statement to the police, hadn't she said that the boy's shirt was blue, and that she never mentioned any sort of uniform?

Yes, Joyce said.

And hadn't she been called to the school principal's office to look at photographs shown to her by the Union City police after Cassie was found murdered?

Yes, Joyce said. And hadn't she picked out some of those

pictures as people who looked like the boy she'd seen with Cassie? Joyce agreed that she had picked out some pictures.

As soon as the jury was out of the courtroom for the noon recess, McWilliams asked Minder to order Taylor to provide the defense with copies of the photographs shown to Joyce; without them, he couldn't adequately cross-examine a witness who might be able to show that it hadn't been Marvin with Cassie Riley.

Taylor, McWilliams went on to complain, kept insisting that the photographs of other potential suspects had been destroyed.

"What's your response to his motion?" Minder asked Taylor.

"Same response I made to him every time," Taylor said. "My understanding is that within one or two days of the death of Cassie Riley, when these witnesses, such as the one who just testified and said she didn't notice anything about a uniform on the man, were contacted first . . .

"That sometime in the first week or so somebody from the police department went out with some pictures of uniforms to talk to several witnesses and asked—to get an idea of what kind of uniform we're talking about. I don't have any pictures like that.

"I asked at the preliminary [hearing], when he first raised the question, I asked for George Bist to look for them or to try and find out where they are. George Bist is the officer in charge of the case for Union City. He has since—he told me then he didn't think they were preserved. He's since told me he doesn't have them. I've continually told Mr. McWilliams this. I don't see any particular obligation on the part of the police to keep those pictures at a time before, when they're trying to investigate a lot of—"

Minder cut him off. If Joyce Hiramine indeed had identified photographs of boys who looked like the boy she'd seen with Cassie Riley, and it wasn't Marvin Mutch, those boys were possible suspects by exactly the same reasoning that had led police to charge Marvin with the crime. This was potentially exculpatory evidence, and should have been

turned over to the defense in order to make sure Marvin
Mutch was getting a fair trial. But Minder now offered Taylor a way off the hook.

"We're not talking about the obligation of the police,"
Minder told Taylor. "We're talking about whether they're in
existence. If they are, [do] you know where they are?"

"I state on the record," Taylor said, "as I've stated to him
[McWilliams] other times, I know of no such pictures now
in existence. I've never seen any such pictures myself, and
I've asked for them."

"Does that satisfy you, Mr. McWilliams?" Minder asked.

"Yes," McWilliams said. "I'd like to make a motion at
this time based on that, and my offer of proof will go to
another witness who is about to testify.

"I would indicate that both Joyce Hiramine, the witness
who just testified . . . and Gena Gloar, the witness who will
next testify, looked over photographs and made selections of
individuals that they felt resembled closely the male person
that they saw with the person they believed to be Cassie
Riley at the creek. Those photographs I have never seen.
Those photographs could exonerate my client. That's my offer of proof." McWilliams turned to Taylor.

"Do you contest the facts?" he asked.

"You made a motion?" Minder interjected.

"I make the motion—yes," said McWilliams. "I make the
motion to dismiss."

This wasn't an offer of proof, Minder said, but merely a
motion. Not so, said McWilliams; if he needed to, he'd put
Joyce back on the stand and ask her about the pictures the
police had shown her. Both Joyce and Gena would testify
that the police had shown them pictures, and that they had
selected people as resembling the boy they'd seen at the
creek.

Taylor might claim that the pictures didn't exist, Mc-
Williams added, but that was hardly standard police investigative practice.

"As a matter of fact, seems to me it would be an unusual
practice in a homicide investigation to destroy photographs

that witnesses say tend to indicate the person they saw. So I move to dismiss on that ground."

Taylor jumped in, as the prospect of losing his entire case against Marvin Mutch suddenly loomed.

"I never said they were destroyed," Taylor said. "I only said they aren't preserved in whatever state they were shown to the witnesses. If they were pulled out of a number of pictures the police have and put back in, and nobody recording what pictures we're talking about, there's no— they're not preserved as far as I'm concerned."

"Well, what's your response to his motion?" Minder demanded.

"I have no response," Taylor said. "I know of no authority for what he's talking about. He's laid no foundation, nothing by what he's proved, by affidavit or otherwise. Lot of it must be things he knows about that I don't, such as they picked out pictures. If they did that, then that's . . . you know, I don't contest anything he says."

Minder decided to withhold ruling on McWilliams' motion to dismiss for the time being; McWilliams decided that he'd better establish the fact that the police *had* shown pictures of possible suspects to the two girls while he had the chance.[16]

Joyce Hiramine was now recalled to the witness stand. McWilliams asked if she was shown any photographs by the police.

"Yes," she said.

"Did you pick out any photographs?"

"Yes, I did."

"Do you know who the police officer is who showed you the photographs?"

"I think it was Detective Bist."

After Joyce, Gena Gloar was called to the stand. Under questioning from Taylor, she described the person she saw

---

16 In a recent interview, former Detective Bist said he believed that he had shown photographs from various school annuals to the two girls; Daveggio's photograph would have been in the school annuals.

next to the girl Joyce had told her was Cassie Riley.

"He was maybe about four or five inches taller than her, and had pretty hair, about down to his collar, brown. And he was wearing sort of like a uniform, and his shirt was beige, and the shirt was short-sleeved," Gena said.

A day or so later, she said, in answer to questions from McWilliams, Union City Detective Joe Leon had come to school and showed her pictures of people. Gena added that the person she had seen had light brown hair, and it was curly.

Marvin Mutch's hair was dark brown, and it was straight.

Taylor continued to summon witnesses designed to show that a man or a boy in a uniform had been seen near Cassie Riley around 5 p.m. on September 24. None of the witnesses, however, could place the person in the uniform actually in the creek with Cassie. Worse, at least from Taylor's point of view, the witnesses consistently differed in their description of the man (boy) in the uniform, and what time of day it had been. Some witnesses insisted that the uniform shirt was blue, while others said it was green. One witness said the man was Asian. Virtually everyone agreed that the pants worn by the uniformed person were darker than those that belonged to Marvin Mutch, which had been put into evidence.

Under other circumstances, even a zealous prosecutor such as Taylor might have been disheartened by the weakness of his case; but Taylor remained convinced that he had the guilty party; the discrepancies in the witnesses' accounts meant little to him—not when he had an admission from Mutch himself that he'd been in the creek, probably on the day in question, and that he might have seen (or even talked with) Cassie Riley. Given Marvin's bad reputation from Livermore, Taylor was sure he had the right person.

One of Taylor's witnesses was Monte John Williams, the boy who had been sitting in the park with Cassie that afternoon—the same boy who had later given the police information on who else had been in the park that day, and who had been beaten up by his fellow students for his troubles. In his testimony, Monte said that he'd walked Cassie home shortly after 4 P.M.—a statement he'd neglected to give to the police when he was interviewed a second time on October 1. Indeed, McWilliams heard for the first time that Monte had given an interview to the police shortly after the murder, an interview McWilliams hadn't been told about.

Monte said Cassie and he talked to a number of other kids at the park that day, and that Cassie had even played basketball with some of them. Monte mentioned a number of names of those who had been in the park, none of them Jimmy Daveggio. But then Monte made a curious remark: Cassie, he said, had been wearing Converse All Star basketball shoes that day.

This was a curve no one had been expecting. Clearly the size of the shoe print on the muddy bank was far too large to have been made by Cassie; besides, there was no doubt that Cassie had been wearing Keds tennis shoes when she was killed; they were still on her feet the day after the murder.

Regrettably, neither Taylor nor McWilliams followed this up with pointed questions. Just what made Monte think Cassie was wearing Converse basketball shoes when she was killed? Had someone told him about the basketball shoe tracks? Did Monte know someone else who'd been in the park that day who was wearing those kind of shoes? Was this a half-baked effort by Monte to muddy the shoe print issue, so to speak? Whatever possibilities this cryptic remark held for further exploration, both sides ignored it.

In his cross examination, McWilliams tried to get Monte to testify about a rumor he'd heard about Cassie and passed on to the police, but Minder headed McWilliams off on the grounds that it would be irrelevant.

After hearing from the two Fremont sisters-in-law—both said they'd seen the car with the dented fender, and one of them said she'd seen a man in a uniform leaving the car and returning to it about half-an-hour later—Taylor moved to one

of his most important witnesses, Union City patrol officer
Joyce Honebein.

It had been Honebein who had noted the license plate
BLB 184, and had called it in to the Union City police dispatcher; whatever else was going on, this was actual, hard,
documentary proof that the car, at least, had been parked on
San Luis Court at 5:33 p.m. on September 24. Now Taylor
wanted Honebein to identify Marvin Mutch as the person
who was driving the car.

This sparked off another row between Taylor and Mc-
Williams. As it happened, Honebein had come down with an
illness the day Cassie's body had been found; as a result, she
was off work for the last week of September and all of October. It was only when she read Detective Bist's ad in the
newspaper that she remembered calling in the Lincoln's
plate, and as a result, called Bist the day of the night that he
had arrested Marvin.

A month later, Honebein returned to work, and the shift
supervisor, Sgt. Guzman, told her that Mutch had been arrested. By then Marvin's photograph had appeared in the
newspaper, and Honebein had seen it. She told Guzman that
she was pretty sure the man who'd been driving the Lincoln
on the day she'd radioed the plate in was Marvin Mutch.
Guzman then got a booking photograph from the file and
showed it to Honebein. After looking at it, Honebein was
sure: the guy in the Lincoln that day *had* been Mutch.

Now Taylor wanted Honebein to identify Marvin in court,
and McWilliams tried to prevent it. He claimed that the single photo shown by Guzman to Honebein in November was
an improper taint of Honebein's recollection. After a substantial wrangle out of the presence of the jury, Judge Minder
ruled that Honebein's in-court identification of Marvin
Mutch was admissible.

In retrospect, it's a bit difficult to understand why
McWilliams struggled so hard to keep the identity of the
person at the creek an open question to the jury; the fact that
Mutch had admitted having been there was essentially cor-

roborated by the record of Honebein's radio message to the dispatcher.

That in turn made McWilliams' attempts to cast doubt on all the eyewitnesses' varied descriptions of the man in uniform seem like Mutch was trying to conceal something. It would have been much better for Mutch to have admitted to the jury that he'd been at the creek in search of his hubcap, but that he hadn't attacked Cassie Riley. Then the issue would have turned on whether there was evidence that Marvin had made the attack, not on whether he was trying to keep his presence at the creek a secret.

But to get this story before the jury meant putting Marvin on the witness stand in his own defense, and McWilliams didn't want to do that—primarily because Judge Minder had already ruled that if Marvin testified, Taylor would be allowed to ask put on evidence about the Livermore case, under the rather wobbly theory that the two different incidents showed a pattern of assaultive behavior by Marvin.

And that was the last thing McWilliams wanted the jury to hear about; it would have destroyed any chance that the jury would believe his client innocent, even if he hadn't been convicted of anything. In effect, Minder's legally dubious ruling—allowing the prosecution to bring up charges against Marvin Mutch that had never been substantiated—foreclosed Mutch's right to testify in his own behalf; as such, it was probably reversible error, if only Marvin Mutch's poorly paid, publicly appointed appeal attorney had raised it on appeal.

Just a little bit more of this ancient history, and then we can leave the 25-year-old ghosts of Marvin Mutch and Cassie Riley behind and return to the life of Jimmy Daveggio and what was to become of him; the point, of course, is only that when justice miscarries, as it likely did in Marvin Mutch's case, it leaves the guilty not only unpunished, but unapprehended—free to commit still more violence. That there were numerous potential clues that might have led Union City police in a far different direction, had they chosen to follow them, will become apparent; and it is regrettable indeed that many of them led in the direction of Jimmy Daveggio, but were never followed up.

There was also at least one apparent stretcher testified to before the jury, a tale which had the effect of helping to convince the panel that Marvin had to be guilty.

To further cement the notion that it had to be Marvin in the Lincoln that day, Taylor summoned Mervin Velasquez. Velasquez testified about picking Marvin up the night that the old Mustang died, and offering to sell him the Lincoln. Velasquez said he'd never met Marvin before that night, but recognized the Hayward Patrol uniform worn by Marvin as he was walking down the street.

Then Velasquez added that Marvin had told him a curious story that same night. As they approached Alvarado/Niles Road, Velasquez said, Marvin asked him whether he'd heard about the girl who had been found murdered in the creek. This had happened in the first week of September, Mervin added.

McWilliams immediately objected. How come the defense

had never heard of this before? Taylor explained that Mervin Velasquez had only just remembered this the week before.

The effect of Mervin's bombshell was to make it appear that Marvin Mutch had foreknowledge of Cassie Riley's murder—since in the first week of September, the crime was still at least two weeks in the future.

By this time, Hayward Patrol's William Christ had already testified that Marvin Mutch hadn't been hired at Hayward Patrol until "Friday, the 13th," as Christ had melodramatically put it while testifying. How then could Velasquez have picked up Marvin in the first week of September while Marvin was wearing a Hayward Patrol uniform? It simply wasn't possible, because at that time Marvin had never heard of Hayward Patrol, or vice versa. But McWilliams let Velasquez' apparently flawed recollection slip by; he wanted to hammer Vehzquez' testimony in his closing argument, when he would be able to suggest that Valequez had made the whole story up for some reason.

After calling Valerie Mutch to testify that Marvin had come home wet and muddy, Taylor was ready to rest his case. But McWilliams, who hadn't wanted Valerie to testify at all, was successful in getting Valerie to tell the jury that her brother didn't own any basketball shoes, and that she wasn't sure what day Marvin had come home wet. McWilliams was also able to bring out the fact that Valerie was on probation, and that officials from the district attorney's office had been to see her three times while she was lodged in juvenile hall after the murder, thus suggesting that Valerie may have been promised some sort of leniency in return for her testimony.

McWilliams' defense of Marvin Mutch was much shorter, and more direct than Taylor's inferential case. The defense was straightforward: Cassie Riley had been seen alive by neighbors up to an hour after the blue Lincoln left the area.

McWilliams tried to prepare the groundwork for a "the-other-guy-did-it" defense by calling Union City Police Officer Mike Shelton, the motorcycle cop who had interviewed

Monte John Williams and Jimmy Daveggio, among others.

Shelton said he first interviewed Monte on October 1, initially at the school, and then at the Union City police station. Shelton then wrote a report based on his conversation with Monte, in which he admitted that he had paraphrased Monte's exact words.

In the statement, Shelton said that Monte told him he'd asked Cassie to be his girlfriend, but that Cassie had refused. Right after that, she'd left. In this version, Monte didn't walk her home. He also told Shelton that he'd last seen her around 4:30 p.m., but at the park.

"Did you have difficulty talking to him?" Taylor asked Shelton, when it was his turn for cross examination.

"Yes, I did," Shelton said. "At the high school he was rather reluctant to talk to me, although he wouldn't give me any reason as to why he was. At that point—it became obvious I couldn't talk to him there. I contacted his mother and she came to the station, and I brought Monte to the station."

At the station, Monte began to cry when his mother arrived. He was obviously very upset, Shelton said, and reluctant to cooperate.

Why was that? Taylor asked.

"He had been contacted by one of our detectives at the time of the discovery of the victim, and at that time he had accompanied the officer or detective in the car, a police car, and pointed out certain persons in the area. As a result of that, or he felt as a result of that, he was subjected to a battery at a later date and he was concerned of [another] battery occurring."

"He was asked other people that might have seen Cassie that day?" Taylor asked.

"To my knowledge, yes."

Here was an interesting possibility: Shelton interviewed Monte on October 1; Monte also apparently knew about the basketball shoe print, judging from his earlier testimony that Cassie had been wearing "Converse All Stars." Further, someone had beaten him up after he'd named names shortly after the murder. Then, on October 2, when Shelton interviewed Daveggio, Jimmy had a shoe that didn't match the tread found at the park. The question that begged to be asked was whether Monte had told anyone else about the basketball shoe evidence the day after the murder when he was getting his lumps from his fellow students.[17]

It soon developed that Shelton had taped his interview with Monte, but that Monte refused to sign it. McWilliams attempted to have the transcript entered into evidence, but Minder refused to let it in.

With that, the trial broke for another recess.

After the break, McWilliams moved to have Minder dismiss the charges against Marvin Mutch, contending that the state had failed to prove its case. But Minder rejected the motion, so McWilliams continued his defense.

He called Charles Morton, a forensic scientist who *was* a shoe print expert. Morton said he'd examined the casts taken by the police under Harding's supervision, and was able to identify the basketball shoe type. It was, Morton said, a Converse shoe. The Converse print had come after the Keds print, Morton said. Asked to tell what size the shoe was, Morton said it wasn't possible to tell the size from the casts. Then Morton testified to another shocker: of the basketball shoe prints in two of the casts, there appeared to be *two* different Converse shoes.

This seemed to indicate that at some point there may have been two different people wearing basketball shoes treading on the prints left by Cassie's Keds less than two feet from where her head was later found.

Now Taylor tried to let the air out of McWilliams' balloon. It wasn't possible, Taylor asked, to tell just when the shoe prints were placed at the scene, was it? Morton had to say, no, it wasn't possible. The implication was that all the

---

17 The statements of Monte John Williams that might shed light on Jimmy Daveggio's possible involvement in the murder of Cassie Riley were among those withheld from the author by the Union City Police Department and the Alameda County District Attorney's Office in March of 2000.

prints might have been left at the scene at some time prior to or immediately after the murder, and might not in fact have anything to do with it.

While this was certainly possible, it would mean that either the basketball shoe wearers had seen Cassie's body and had done nothing to report it, or alternatively, that Cassie was murdered at the exact spot where she had walked hours before, however unlikely that was. There were no other choices.

McWilliams called two other witnesses, including Susan Lennel, who lived across the street from the Rileys. Susan said she had seen Cassie walking up San Juan Court to the intersection with Santa Maria around 6:30 p.m. She was sure about it, Susan said, because she'd just finished dinner with her sister, and they were going out to collect newspaper subscriptions. She'd told this to John Taylor, the assistant district attorney, but Taylor had never bothered to call her back.

And McWilliams also called Steve Huntoon, who testified about the scream he'd heard sometime between 6:30 and 7 p.m., just as the sun was going down.

"It was one real long scream," Huntoon said.

Taylor tried to suggest that Huntoon had merely heard an overexuberant child, but Huntoon disagreed.

"There's a difference in a playful-type scream and an injury-type scream," Huntoon said. "You can tell the difference."

After a few clean-up witnesses, Judge Minder ruled that the two statements of Monte John Williams would not be admitted as evidence for the jury.

McWilliams then renewed his motion to dismiss the case against Marvin Mutch on the grounds that the police and district attorney's office had failed to provide the photographs of the other potential suspects selected by Joyce Hiramine and Gena Gloar.

Minder wanted to know what case law McWilliams was relying on for such a motion.

"*Brady* versus *Maryland*, Your Honor," McWilliams replied, citing probably the most preeminent federal case on the requirement that police and prosecutors provide defendants with all potentially exculpable evidence. The case was first decided in 1963.

"I'm not acquainted with *Brady* versus *Maryland*," Minder said. "What's the factual situation there?"

When McWilliams said the case required dismissal of charges when the authorities deliberately withhold exculpatory evidence, Minder wasn't impressed. He denied McWilliams' motion.[18]

Then, after closing arguments from both sides, the jury retired to deliberate. McWilliams asked that the judge order the jury sequestered to prevent possible tainting from prejudicial publicity, but Minder refused. Two days later, while the jury was deliberating, *The Oakland Tribune* published a story reporting that Marvin Mutch was a suspect in an attempted assault on a 13-year-old girl in Livermore.

Twenty-five years later, McWilliams remained convinced that the publication of the Livermore allegations sealed Marvin Mutch's fate.

On May 21, 1975, the jury found Marvin Mutch guilty of first-degree murder in the death of Cassie Riley. Judge Minder congratulated them on a job well done.

"And," he continued, "I think you are entitled to know a couple of things that happened, because they're going to be public record anyway."

"During the trial," Minder continued, "or before the trial, as a matter of fact, there were [sic] suppressed some evidence because of the rules of evidence. Part of the defendant's statement was not admitted and in this statement the defen-

---

18 The photographs of potential other suspects apparently were not the only items of evidence not provided to McWilliams for Mutch's defense. In the spring of 2000, Mutch sent the author a number of reports complied by the Union City Police Department, including the statements of at least four other potential suspects in the murder besides James Daveggio. According to McWilliams' own list of discovery materials, none of the statements were provided to the defense, Mutch gained possession of them as part of a parole hearing process years later.

dant admitted, and I'm telling you this because it will probably help you understand perhaps what went on, the defendant admitted that he was in the creek and also that he met the victim, but always denied that he did anything to her.

"Now, the other thing that occurred during the trial, which was also based upon rules of evidence, was the suppression of an offer of proof by the district attorney. The district attorney offered to prove that at some time, I think it was about four months before this incident, he offered to prove by another witness that the defendant threatened another girl about thirteen with a knife."

With these words, doubtless calculated to reassure anyone who still had misgivings about the verdict, Judge Minder sent the jurors on their way.

The fact that the jury had deliberated for more than a week certainly seemed to indicate that its members had at least some doubt about Marvin Mutch's guilt. Apart from the fact that there wasn't a single shred of hard evidence tying Mutch to the crime, there was the vexing question of the basketball shoe prints, which could not have been made by Marvin Mutch.

Whose were they? Who had nearly new Converse All Star basketball shoes that day in the park? What did Monte Williams seem to know that he was reluctant to tell for fear of being beaten up?

Why was Cassie Riley attacked, drowned, and then later removed from the water, which certainly suggested that the killer had stayed in the area for some length of time, if indeed the same person who drowned her had later removed her from the creek?

This was not the action of a sex predator on unfamiliar ground, as the prosecution attempted to paint Marvin Mutch, but instead of a simple vindictive assault. Perhaps the person who had shoved her into the water initially believed she had only been shamming, and returned later only to be shocked to find out that she was really dead as he pulled her body from the water.

If Cassie had eaten the candy she bought at the store at the earliest around 5:15, as the testimony suggested, why did Dr. McNie, the pathologist, testify that the candy had been in her stomach for two hours, which would have put the time of death at 7:15—long after Marvin Mutch had left the area?

How long would it have taken the mud to build up and coat Cassie's underclothing? Certainly that could not have happened in the short time between 5:15 p.m., when Cassie left the store, and 5:36 p.m., when Marvin drove away; in that sense, Union City Officer Joyce Honebein's radio message to the dispatcher was Marvin's best alibi.

The shoes, the shoes—it all comes back to the basketball shoes, just exactly as the Union City police first believed, or did, at least, until Marvin Mutch's head was handed to them on a silver platter by those crack crime-fighters, the Livermore Police Department.

Marvin Mutch went off to state prison to begin serving a life term for murder. Twenty-three years later, Marvin Mutch would still be in prison, still serving his life sentence. By then the law was about to be much more interested in Jimmy Daveggio; but not before a lot more people had gotten hurt.

JIM

The idea that an innocent man might go to prison on the basis of the flimsy evidence presented at Marvin Mutch's trial may shock; but the fact is, for every innocent man imprisoned, a guilty man walks free. That was one of the things that haunted Jodie, Jimmy Daveggio's younger sister, as she grew older.

As the years passed, the events surrounding Cassie Riley's death became ever darker for Jodie; sometimes she wasn't sure what she remembered, and what she had simply imagined.

At times she could recall very clearly being at home when the police came to the house to question her brother Jimmy about—*what?* Sometimes Jodie thought it was about Cassie. She remembered her mother Donna telling the police that Jimmy had been home at a time the police were asking about. Jodie knew Jimmy hadn't been home, but her mother had lied for Jimmy.

Jodie knew Cassie; not very well, because she'd been older. But Jodie knew Tammy Moody, who was in her class. And then Cassie had been murdered, found in Alameda Creek, raped, they said; it was all anyone could talk about for a while, at least in Union City.

And Cassie had been Jimmy's girlfriend, or one of his girlfriends, anyway; and the police had come and asked questions, and Donna had lied and Jodie had a bad feeling about her brother and Cassie Riley, because Jimmy was just *mean* . . . and there was the black girl who'd been found in the ditch in Oakland when Jodie was seven or eight, another ditch, another girl, and it didn't feel right to Jodie but there

wasn't any point to thinking about it because it would be
wrong to think Jimmy might have . . . and her mother would
get mad at her if she knew what Jodie was thinking, so it
was best to put those thoughts aside, they didn't exist, and
try to pretend they were just like anyone else, because they
were . . . weren't they?

Jimmy and Mom: there was something there that Jodie
never quite grasped. Jodie had heard Donna criticize Jimmy
viciously, telling him to his face that he was worthless; but
let anyone else say anything bad about Jimmy, and Donna
would be all over them. Either Donna was attacking her children for their failures, or defending them against others who
attacked them for their failures. There seemed to be no middle ground, and certainly no praise for their successes.

In their family, Donna was the main force, the aggressive
one; probably, if times had been different when Donna was
growing up, she would have ended up being one of those
ruthless businesswomen television was always using as char-
acters. As it was, she held a night job as a waitress at a biker
dive in Hayward, where the female help was required to wear
hot pants and skimpy halter tops. Still, Donna was sharp—
both smart and mentally agile, always ready with an answer.
She ran things in the Kerlan household.

Ron was simply there, nice, quiet, and largely passive.
His idea of a good time was a can of beer and the television.
For a real good time, Ron liked going to Reno or Lake Tahoe
to gamble. It was as if Ron had decided long before that
Tillie, Jimmy and Jodie were Donna's kids, that they belonged to *her*, not the two of them as parents, and it was up
to Donna to do whatever had to be done when it came to
whatever Donna's kids needed. For all that, Jodie liked Ron;
after all, he was the only father she'd ever known, even if,
in Jodie's opinion, he let Donna boss him around too much.

Each of them was different. Tillie tended to be quiet, almost passive; Jodie sometimes thought Donna intimidated
her. Jimmy was wild, self-destructive, really. It was as if he
went out of his way to get into trouble; the more he was
punished, the wilder he became. It was like living with a

stick of burning dynamite and you never knew how long the fuse was. Jodie herself was something of a mix, she thought, sometimes quiet and watching like Tillie, and at other times explosive like her brother. She often felt herself in emotional turmoil, and longed to be part of an ordinary family, like all the others she went to school with. Or as she believed the others to be.

But there was always Jimmy. From the time he was a teenager, Jimmy had always attracted women. His startling blue eyes commanded attention, and when he wanted to, Jimmy could charm anyone. He seemed to know just what women were thinking, and even when he was wrong, he could seem just impish enough to be forgiven.

Sometimes Jodie thought Jimmy was the center of her mother's life, the most important person in the world to her. And Jimmy seemed to know that without being told. That was why, Jodie believed, Jimmy kept getting into trouble— to get Donna going, to make her do something to get him off the hook. And Jimmy was *always* in trouble.

There was the time, for instance, when Jimmy had stolen some girlfriend's mother's car, and had driven it, along with the girlfriend and some friends, to Lake Tahoe; there was another time when Jimmy had gotten someone pregnant, and Donna had to take the girl for an abortion.

Or the fights: Jimmy was always getting into a fight with someone. It was one crisis after another in the Kerlan household. And there was that something about Cassie . . .

It was some time after Cassie was murdered but before Marvin Mutch went on trial that someone—either her mother or Ron or someone, Jodie was never sure who—decided it was important for Jimmy to finally get to know his real father. Somehow Donna got in touch with Johnny, and Johnny, then between wives, agreed to take Jimmy for a while.

By now Johnny was living in Pacifica, a small community just south of San Francisco. Johnny had become a big pro football fan. To Johnny, football was a man's game, something that built character, and he thought playing football was just the sort of thing Jimmy needed to get himself straightened out. So Jimmy moved in with his natural father in Pacifica, and transferred to a high school there. Johnny helped him get a part-time job at a local fast-food franchise, and tried to get to know one of his by-now eight children.

In the meantime, the Kerlan family relocated to Pleasanton, over the hills to the east of Union City.

In 1960, the year Jimmy Daveggio was born, Pleasanton was a sleepy little town of fewer than 3,000, known mostly for being the location of the annual Alameda County Fair. It was one of a number of similar small towns east of the series of ridges running northwest to southeast behind the city of Oakland and its entourage of southern bayfront communities like Hayward, Fremont and Union City.

But where the bayfront towns provided housing for workers who found jobs in shipping and manufacturing, the valley towns were agricultural, at least in the beginning. Starting with Walnut Creek and proceeding south on a line behind the ridges, the communities of Danville, San Ramon, Dublin, Pleasanton and, on the far south, Sunol, made their livings on fruit and livestock and garden produce.

To the immediate east was the cattle town of Livermore, and over another range of hills, through the Altamont Pass still farther east, came the broad central California valley with the towns of Tracy, Stockton, Modesto and Manteca. Across the broad valley of the San Joaquin River came the ramparts of the Sierra Nevada, Lake Tahoe, and, on the other side of the snowcapped barrier, the self-proclaimed "Biggest Little City in the World," Reno, Nevada.

For itself, Pleasanton—named for Union Civil War General Alfred Pleasonton—had so much in common with the fictional Hill Valley of the movie *Back to the Future* that it might have been cast as the movie's stunt double. Pleasanton began as a Wild West crossroads, a hangout for outlaws who used the hilly canyons to the east and west as hideouts, and slowly grew into a more bucolic environment with a rail stop, a picturesque downtown complete with a Main Street and a number of fashionable Victorian homes adorning leafy streets laid out in a sensible grid pattern; the small hamlet was surrounded by square miles of farms providing food for an emerging nation's dinner tables.

All this began to change in 1960, the year of Jimmy Daveggio's birth. Driven by the nearly insatiable demand for housing and spurred by the expansion of the interstate highway system into the area, houses began springing up almost overnight in most of the valley communities. Pleasanton had just 345 housing units before World War II; by 1959, the number was just over 1,100, encompassing a population of less than 10,000.

Between 1960 and 1970, however, more than three times as many houses were built as had previously existed, a number that then more than quadrupled in the twenty years from 1970 to 1990, when the population was nearing 60,000. Just as in Union City, the new town was built up around the old, and soon swallowed it up as if it were a quaint relic from an unfathomable past. It was in the middle of this second wave of housing expansion that the Kerlan family first arrived in Pleasanton in 1975.

Jodie and Tillie enrolled at Pleasanton's Foothill High School, and for once in their lives, the Kerlans began to enjoy a year free from Jimmy's destructive crises. Things were going so well, in fact, that the Kerlans decided to buy a nice, two-story house in Pleasanton in a tract just west of the Interstate 680 Freeway on Clovewood Lane—as it happened, a house that was almost directly across the freeway from another, similar house on Sierra Court in Pleasanton, a house that would one day become the home of Vanessa Samson and her family.

Whatever hopes the Kerlans might have had for Johnny to straighten Jimmy out were fairly quickly dashed: Jimmy was fired from the fast-food joint for stealing. Then Jimmy took to lifting things of Johnny's, and that was it—Jimmy was out. Jimmy came to live with the Kerlans in the Clovewood Lane house, and enrolled with Jodie for his junior year at Foothill High School.

Something happened at the high school, Jodie wasn't sure

what, but soon Jimmy was feuding with one of the high
school administrators, the assistant principal for attendance
and discipline.

"Jimmy called him a baldheaded mother-fucker," Jodie
recalled, years later. That was Jimmy: always challenging
authority, bringing the wrath of the establishment down on
his own head to get attention. By now Jimmy had changed
his name to Jime, almost like Hendrix. He posed for his
junior photograph for the Foothill High School annual, a
good-looking kid with long, curly brown hair and a sardonic,
knowing grin. But after cursing the assistant principal, Jime
was suspended from school; years later he would blame the
administrator for ruining his chance at a football career.

By now Jime had an old car, a bright blue 1957 Thunderbird. One day Jime and a friend decided to rob a gas
station in Pleasanton. With Jime acting as the wheelman, the
pair pulled into the gas station. The friend jumped out and
pulled a gun on the service station attendant, demanding the
money. The attendant complied, Jime's friend jumped back
into the car with the loot, and Jime peeled out—just as the
attendant wrote down Jime's license plate number.

For his role as an accomplice in the armed robbery, Jime
was sentenced to a short term at the Alameda County boys'
detention camp. Donna, Jodie and little Greg visited him
every day until he was released.

Once he was out of the juvenile lock-up, Jime was placed
in Valley Continuation School in Dublin for the rest of his
junior and senior years. From then on, Jime just seemed to
drift, not finishing high school.

It was around this time, Jodie said later, that her brother
tried to rape her.

Years later, talking about this still upset Jodie; it appears
that the 14-year-old Jodie tried to tell her mother about the
attack, but that either Donna didn't believe her, or *wouldn't*
believe her. Somehow, Jodie got the idea it was *her* fault.
But this was when Jodie first became aware of the intense
hatred she felt for her brother: it wasn't just the attack, it

was the fact that Jimmy could get away with it and no one would believe her.

For all of her life from then on, Jodie's feeling for her brother would be balanced between rage and guilt: rage over what he had done and the way her mother had responded to it by blaming her, and guilt for hating her brother. But Jime's sexual behavior didn't seem to carry any consequences, at least as far as Donna was concerned.

There were others in Pleasanton, however, who would not have been at all surprised to learn that Jimmy had attacked his own sister. One was *Mike Brown, who had known Jimmy when both attended Logan High School in Union City, and who met him again after the Brown and Kerlan families moved to Pleasanton. Years later, when police were trying to assemble information on Daveggio's background, Mike Brown contacted the Pleasanton police to tell them what he knew of Jimmy Daveggio from their years together in Union City.

Even as a youngster, Brown told the police, Jimmy was wild. Once, when they were 13, Jimmy had taken an 11-year-old girl into the bushes and had sex, Brown remembered. At Logan, Jimmy was nicknamed "Froggie," because his raspy voice reminded people of the character of that name on the Little Rascals reruns on television.

"Froggie" was soon involved in using marijuana and LSD, Brown recalled. In the afternoons and evenings, Brown, Froggie and others used to hang out at a bowling alley in Hayward; years later, a young girl would be abducted from the same area, which, in light of the crimes Daveggio would eventually be accused of, made Brown wonder whether Daveggio had been involved. He was easily capable of it, Brown assured the police.

Later, after they'd both moved to Pleasanton, Brown had met "Froggie" Daveggio at Foothill High School. Brown said Jimmy had boasted of raping a Castro Valley girl. Jimmy had bragged that the girl had liked it, Brown said, and had asked him to "call her sometime." Brown said Jimmy never called her, because he'd also stolen her wallet with $60 in it. Daveggio thought this was funny, Brown added. But one thing was sure: "Froggie" Daveggio was a very violent personality.

By the summer of 1979, when Jimmy was 19, he had begun seeing an 18-year-old Pleasanton girl named *Arnelle Carter; Arnelle had a brother, *Joe, among her several siblings. In the 1970s, the Carter family had become friends with a teenager, Mike Ihde, whose father worked as a carpenter at the Alameda County Jail in Pleasanton; Ihde grew close to Arnelle, her mother *Abbie, and Joe. It appears that Ihde, Joe Carter and Jimmy Daveggio all attended Valley Continuation School around the same time in 1977, and became good friends.

On December 15, 1978, Ihde was in Jackson, California, a small town in the Gold Rush country foothills of Amador County, when he begged a ride from a woman in the parking lot of a local supermarket. Somehow Ihde forced the woman to drive down a deserted road, where he tied her hands and raped her. After this he tried to beat her head in with a rock. The woman survived the attack. Ihde was soon arrested and convicted of rape and attempted murder, and sentenced to a term in the California State Prison at San Quentin. One of his first visitors was Arnelle Carter.

By the time Ihde was sent to prison, Arnelle was pregnant by Jimmy. He married her on September 29, a date that would eventually have significance in his life. Arnelle's daughter *Joanie was born in April of 1980.

Three months later, in July of 1980, Jimmy—now calling himself by the more mature nickname of Jim—left Arnelle and the baby, unable to stand up to the responsibilities of being a father.

In a very real way, Jim was replicating his own father's behavior 18 years earlier; the month he chose to abandon his family—July, the month of his own birth—was to loom larger and larger in Jim Daveggio's life the older he got; somehow, when July rolled around each year, you could bet

Daveggio would get into trouble, almost as if he was punishing himself for having been born.

That same month he abandoned Arnelle and Joanie, July of 1980, the 20-year-old Jim met another Pleasanton girl, 17-year-old *Dawn, at a swimming hole along the creek running through Niles Canyon, a lightly traveled but scenic shortcut between Pleasanton and Union City. Dawn's parents had just divorced, and she was living on her own, while working for a lawyer. She was immediately impressed by the good-looking boy with the startling blue eyes.

"He was very nice," Dawn recalled, years later. "Very personable. Well, he's a great talker. It's only that, when it comes to backing it up, he can't."[19] But it would take Dawn nearly six years to learn that about Jim.

Still, Dawn should have gotten a clue about her new boyfriend's character when he had to go to court in early September on charges of burglary and offering stolen property for sale; he'd been arrested by Pleasanton police the previous July 1, just before leaving Arnelle and Joanie. Both charges were eventually dismissed when Jim's accomplice pleaded guilty and took all the responsibility.[20]

According to Dawn, though, this didn't stop Jim from burgling; it only made him more careful. The criminal justice system had its first swing against the adult Jim Daveggio, but missed.

Dawn and Jim moved in together sometime that winter. Dawn came to work one morning at her lawyer's office, only to discover the man dead in his office chair from an apparent heart attack. Once Dawn had notified the authorities, she knew she was out of a job, so she found work as a waitress at a Denny's Restaurant in Pleasanton. Jim had a job in sheetmetal work in San Jose. As far as Dawn knew, Jim had never been married before; he'd never told her about Arnelle or Joanie.

---

19 From a private interview with Dawn by the author in the fall of 1999.
20 Records of the Superior Court of Alameda County.

All that changed in July of 1981, when Dawn was at home getting ready to go to work. The telephone rang, and a woman who identified herself as Arnelle asked to talk to Jimmy. When Dawn wanted to know who was calling, Arnelle told her she was Jimmy's wife, and that she was going into labor.

On July 13, 1981, Arnelle gave birth to her second daughter by Jim Daveggio, *Astrid. Dawn was angry with Jim for withholding the fact that he'd been married to Arnelle for the whole time he'd been living with *her*, and not saying anything about it. Not only that, it turned out that Jim had fathered two children by Arnelle, and he hadn't told her that, either. And Dawn could calculate as well as the next woman: when Jim had been seeing her, he'd still been sleeping with Arnelle. Dawn decided to move out.

Jim was very upset about Dawn's decision to leave him. He pleaded with her to come back, saying that he couldn't live without her. Eventually Jim convinced Dawn to return; once they were back together, Jim made Dawn promise never to leave him again. Dawn promised, a vow she would eventually come to regret.

That fall, Arnelle filed for divorce from Jim, and asked for $650 a month in spousal and child support; at the time, Jim was unemployed, and Arnelle and the babies were living on welfare.

It wasn't too long after Arnelle sued for divorce that Jim's mother Donna decided to step in to straighten out her son's life once more. Donna decided—perhaps listening to her husband Ron, the Air Force veteran, for once—that what Jimmy needed was a hitch in the military service to help him settle down.

"It was Donna's idea," Dawn remembered later. "She thought going into the Army would be good for him." So Jim signed up as a U.S. Army recruit at the age of 21, and Dawn moved in with the Kerlans, and took a new job at a pizza parlor.

While subjecting Jim to the organization and discipline of

the armed services may have seemed like a good idea on paper, with someone as wild as Jim it was a disaster.

"He didn't even make it through boot camp," Dawn recalled. "He hated it. He hated people always telling him what to do and where to go."

After three months in the Army at some installation in New Jersey—Jim later referred to it as "Fort Lost-in-the-Woods"—Jim obtained a medical discharge.

"He stared at the sun until he couldn't see," Dawn recalled. That spring he telephoned from the East Coast to tell Dawn he'd been let out of the armed forces.

After Jim returned from the Army, he and Dawn continued to live with the Kerlans; meanwhile, Donna tried to talk Dawn into leaving Jim.

"She told me he was no good, a bum," Dawn said.

Soon Dawn developed a strong dislike for Donna.

"She was a witch," Dawn put it later. "She loved embarrassing Ron. She called him 'stupid,' and told him he couldn't do anything right, that if something had to be done, she was the one who had to do it."

It was while they were living at the Kerlans' that Dawn saw a side of Jim that she'd always known existed, but simply hadn't thought much about, at least until she was confronted with its causes.

"He was the man of the house," Dawn said. "Ron was nice, but he was just there. It was Jim who was the only one who counted. One day Jim got mad at me for not making the bed. I said, Why don't *you* make the bed, for once? He threw a fit. Later, Donna told me that it was my job to make the bed, it was my job to do whatever Jim said.

"He always thought he was great, and that women were here to do what he wanted them to, period," Dawn said. No matter what went wrong, to both Jim and his mother, it was never Jim's fault; it was Donna's job to get him out of trouble.

"She made it easy for him," Dawn said.

But Dawn didn't heed the warning of her prospective

mother-in-law, or of her own eyes; on May 7, 1982, the couple were married.

"I thought that I could change him," Dawn said, in the same famous last words used by many who learned to know better.

Once he'd established who was in charge—Jim was the boss, Dawn the bossee—Jim apparently decided to live the sort of life a little king was entitled to. After they were married, the couple moved to first one apartment, and then another; Dawn worked as a waitress, again at Denny's, while Jim spent his days sleeping and his nights committing burglaries or hanging around two downtown Pleasanton beer parlors. Occasionally Jim filled in behind the bar; at one point, he obtained a security guard's license, a choice whose irony would have bewildered Marvin Mutch, had he known about it.

Apart from burglary and drinking, Jim's next favorite pastime appeared to be getting into fights with people in bars. Soon he had sustained a broken nose, a laceration on the top of his head from a broken beer bottle that caused a horrible scar, and had lost many of his teeth.

"He wanted everyone to think he was a tough guy," Dawn recalled. "He was always getting into fights."

When Dawn brought home her paycheck, Jim would cash it and head for Lake Tahoe or Reno to gamble.

"All my money went to him," Dawn said. "He spent money like a drunken sailor." The last part was right, anyway. Jim developed a prodigious capacity for alcohol, along with an appetite for cocaine and marijuana.

Dawn recalls that Jim committed commercial burglaries regularly during this period. Once Jim burgled the local Ace Hardware store, and made off with a lawn mower and video equipment; the stuff later wound up at the Kerlans' residence, Dawn said.

When Dawn asked Jim where he'd been all night, Jim

wouldn't say. "I don't want to get you into trouble," he told her.

No matter how much he stole, Jim's appetites always seemed larger than his capacity—in part because he lost money gambling almost as soon as it came in. When he was short of money, and Dawn was tapped dry, he'd call his mother. When Donna wouldn't give him any, Jim would throw a fit.

"He'd yell and curse me, then curse his mom, then he'd leave, slamming the door." Sometimes he'd be gone all night, and never tell Dawn where he'd been when he returned the following afternoon.

But Donna hadn't given up on straightening out her son. In the summer of 1983, Jim's mother arranged for Jim and Dawn to go to Oklahoma City, where one of Donna's relatives owned a business. The plan was for Jim to take a job there, and settle down, away from all the bad influences that had caused him to drink, fight, gamble and rob.

Not surprisingly, the move to Oklahoma didn't work out. The truth was, Jim didn't like working, and he was incapable of taking direction from anybody. He quit. After only a month in Oklahoma, Jim and Dawn returned to Pleasanton, where Donna again worked at Denny's, and Jim returned to his favorite haunts in the downtown saloons.

Jim took a job supervising the ragwipers at an automatic car wash in Dublin, just down the street from the continuation school he had attended with Mike Ihde after getting kicked out of Foothill High. It didn't pay much, but then, it didn't demand much either.

By this time, Jim had grown into a barrel of a man; at five feet nine inches, and 210 pounds, with his missing teeth, broken nose and tattoos, Jim Daveggio was scary to look at. He'd found a tattoo parlor in Alameda that catered to sailors and bikers, and sported an eagle on his chest, a lion head on his left shoulder, a rose on his back, and a skull on his right bicep, which now swallowed up his first tattoo, a single name—Cassie.

*   *   *

Meanwhile, Mike Ihde had been released from prison on parole, and was living in San Lorenzo, a small town on the bay side of the hills. For a while, things were quiet; but then women started getting hurt again. One was Kellie Poppleton, who was last seen in Fremont on December 1, 1983. Kellie was 14 years old, five feet five inches, and 123 pounds. On the afternoon of December 2, a passerby noticed her body along the side of a lightly traveled road near Sunol; the road paralleled a watercourse called Sinbad Creek.[21]

Whoever had killed Kellie had beaten her badly, probably with his fists, and had tied a necktie around her neck; a plastic bag had been put over her head. Her pants had been pulled down and her shirt pulled up to expose her chest. She had been raped so viciously that she was still bleeding when she was found. The case would remain unsolved.

On July 8, 1984, while Dawn was working at her job at a dairy products facility in Pleasanton, Jim got off work at the car wash and headed to the Black Angus Restaurant near the junction of Interstate 580 and 680 in Pleasanton for an evening of drinking. Sometime that night near closing, Jim left the bar of the restaurant with a young woman, driving Dawn's old Datsun.

When they returned to the restaurant parking lot some time later, the woman was hysterical. She claimed Jim had kidnapped and raped her.

The police came to sort the matter out.[22] Dawn, meanwhile, was waiting at her job for Jim to come pick her up. When he didn't show, she finally decided something must be wrong. She called the Pleasanton police, who told her that Jim had been arrested.

Dawn got a ride to the Black Angus, but when she arrived, Jim had already been taken to jail. The police wouldn't let her take the car; it was being impounded for evidence.

The next day, Dawn talked to Jim in jail.

---

21 Alameda County Coroner's Report #83-2337.
22 Records of the Pleasanton Police Department, case #84-3125.

"He swore he didn't do it," Dawn said. Jim told her that he'd been drinking in the bar with some other people when he'd noticed a young woman having a fight with her boyfriend. He'd offered to give the woman a ride, and she'd accepted. Once in the car, the woman had come on to him, Jim said. There was no kidnapping, and certainly no rape.

The Pleasanton police weren't buying it. They charged Jim with one count of kidnapping, one count of oral copulation, and one count of rape by means of a foreign object, which in California can include the fingers. Together, the offenses charged required as much as $18,000 bail.

At the time, Jim gave the Kerlans' address as his home address, and Dawn's name and the number of a motel room in Tracy where the two were staying as the place to reach her. But in the morning, Jim was released on his own recognizance, and returned to work at the car wash.

More than two months later, the Alameda County District Attorney's Office dropped all the charges against Jim, citing a lack of evidence necessary to prosecute; apparently the victim's state of inebriation at the time of the incident, coupled with her fight with her boyfriend, caused the prosecutors to feel that proceeding against Jim would be fruitless. The police told Dawn that the woman had refused to press charges.

Still, by this time, Dawn was beginning to get the idea: her husband just couldn't seem to stay out of trouble. The worst of it was, no matter what he did, Mother Donna continued to insist that Jim wasn't to blame. The Black Angus incident was the woman's fault, Donna insisted, first for having a fight with her boyfriend, then for going for a ride with Jim, then for leading Jim on, and finally for calling the police.

Dawn was now 21, and beginning to understand that living with Jim was going to be one crisis after another; no matter how much he swore he loved her and that he couldn't live without her, the central fact was that he was going nowhere, and he was taking her with him. Dawn didn't like it; this wasn't what she wanted in her life.

Perhaps because of Jim's arrest, Dawn for the first time

began to realize that she was going to have to take responsibility for her own future, because Jim wasn't going to do it.

Three months after Jim's arrest and release in the Black Angus incident, Mike Ihde was busy once again. The victim this time was 18-year-old Lisa Monoz, the niece of an Alameda County sheriff's deputy. Lisa was five feet four inches, weighed 144 pounds, and had blond hair and blue eyes. She was found dead six days after Thanksgiving near a freeway overcrossing in San Lorenzo, beaten and raped, with her blouse and bra pushed up over her breasts.[23]

---

23 Alameda County Coroner's Report #84-2271.

Sometime after Lisa Monoz' death, Mike Ihde decided to leave the area. He went to Vancouver, Washington State, just across the Columbia River from Portland, Oregon. Whether Ihde did this mainly to evade the scrutiny of police isn't clear; however, the Vancouver area was then one of the nation's major distribution centers for the manufacture of methamphetamine—"crank," as the bikers called it; it seems likely that Ihde had gotten involved in the crank business through contacts he made while in San Quentin.

Meanwhile, Dawn realized she needed to get a better job; she was hired by the telephone company, a first step out of her treadmill existence with Jim. Then Dawn got pregnant. She found out just before Jim's 25th birthday in the last week of July, 1985.

"I just got off the telephone with the doctor," she recalled. "I told him I was pregnant."

"That's fine," Jim said. "We're going out." Then he and a drinking pal he'd just met headed out the door of the Tracy apartment he shared with Dawn "to go fishing," as he put it. It was about three in the afternoon.

But Jim and his friend, Jonathan Huffstetler, didn't go fishing. Instead they went drinking.

By ten that night, Jim and Huffstetler were in a Tracy dive called Joey's, drinking at the bar. A little after 11 p.m., a woman named *Brenda came in and went to the cigarette machine, only to discover she needed more quarters. A man at the bar offered to give her some change, and Brenda accepted. After getting her cigarettes, Brenda sat down at the bar next to the man, who was Jim; Huffstetler was on Jim's right.[24]

Jim was "very nice," Brenda said later, very polite as well as friendly. Brenda ordered a beer. In the conversation that followed, Brenda indicated that she was on her way to another bar, Bill's, across town. Jim and Huffstetler asked how to get there, and Brenda said she'd show them. After half-an-hour, the trio left Joey's for Bill's, with Brenda leading the way in her car.

At Bill's, all three sat at the bar once more. Jim began buying Brenda large brandy-and-Kahlúa drinks, perhaps three or four, in Brenda's recollection. At length, Brenda decided to go home. She realized she was in no condition to drive, so she left the bar and went to her car to make sure it was locked. She intended to walk home, which she'd done before.

After this, things became a great deal hazier for Brenda. She remembered that Jim offered to drive her home, and that she declined the offer, since she lived only six blocks away. Then Jim told her to shut up and get in the car. Brenda again declined. He grabbed her by the shoulder and shoved her into the car.

The next thing she knew, she was sitting on the front seat between Jim and Huffstetler. Jim was driving. Brenda realized the car was headed out of town, going toward the San Joaquin River. She got scared and started crying. She asked Jim to stop the car and let her out, but Jim refused. She noticed that Huffstetler was holding a gun.

Jim told her to shut up and stop crying.

After a while Jim stopped the car. He told Brenda to fellate him, but Brenda wouldn't do it.

"If you don't do what I want," Jim told her, "I'll beat the shit out of you." But Brenda still refused, so Jim began slapping her head and pulling her hair. He forced her head down into his lap, while Huffstetler laughed and told her to shut

---

24 Details of this incident are based on Brenda's testimony reported in *State vs. Daveggio*, San Joaquin County Superior Court case #37227A, 1985.

up if she didn't want to get hurt even more. He ripped off her blouse and brassiere and threw them in the back seat.

Afterward, Brenda felt sick. She asked for her blouse back, and said she wanted to go to the bathroom. Huffstetler let her out of the car.

As Brenda began moving toward the rear of the car, thinking about running away, Huffstetler fired a shot from the gun. Brenda fell to the ground. Huffstetler grabbed her and told her to get up, and then started arguing with Jim, who was furious with Huffstetler for firing the gun and making so much noise. Jim told them to get back in the car so they could get away before someone came. There was an arrest warrant out for Huffstetler, who was wanted in Santa Monica, California, for driving under the influence.

As Jim drove back into town, a Tracy police car passed in the opposite direction, then made a u-turn and came in behind them, flashing its red lights for them to stop. Jim pulled over. The patrol cop, who had stopped the car because Daveggio had his high beams on, immediately noticed that Brenda was upset. The cop made them all get out of the car, and Brenda told him that she'd been kidnapped by the two men and raped.

That wasn't so, Jim told the cop; Brenda had gone with them voluntarily. The cop made Jim and Huffstetler put their hands on top of the car, and called for assistance. Early on the morning of July 26, Jim and his drinking buddy were booked into the Tracy jail on charges of kidnapping, two counts of forcible oral copulation, assault with a firearm, and carrying a loaded firearm in a vehicle.

Dawn got the call from Jim from jail, collect. She thought he was drunk. The next morning he called back, and wanted her to pick up his car. Jim said he would get his mother to post bail. He'd already talked to a lawyer, who said the fee for getting Jim out of this mess would be $10,000, which he hoped Donna would put up as well.

"I knew he did it," Dawn said, because she and a friend of Jim's went down to pick up the car, and saw Brenda's bra still in the back seat.

When she confronted him at the jail, Jim told her that he hadn't forced anybody. He said the woman making the accusations had been drunk. The next day, his 25th birthday, Jim made bail and was released.

A month later, after a preliminary hearing, Jim and Huffstetler were bound over for trial in Superior Court. The criminal justice system would get yet another try at putting Jim Daveggio away where he could do no more harm, but it would flub this chance, too.

After Jim bailed out, life went back to normal—if that's what to call it—for Dawn and Jim. Jim's trial was postponed repeatedly as his $10,000 lawyer worked his magic. Jim's defense would be that Brenda had agreed to go with them, and that the sex had been consensual. The defense was helped considerably by the fact that Brenda's recollection of the events was somewhat clouded by alcohol.

In March, Dawn gave birth to a girl, *Dulcie; and almost from the moment of Dulcie's arrival, Dawn realized that her time with Jim was coming to an end; Jim was no longer the main person in her life.

Even while he was waiting for his trial on the kidnapping charges, Jim continued to get into trouble. At one point Jim was arrested by the Walnut Creek police and charged with indecent exposure; the details of that incident and its outcome have been lost to time, in part because the municipal court in Walnut Creek routinely destroys its files ten years after a case has been decided. In Pleasanton on his 26th birthday, July 27, 1986, Jim was arrested for contributing to the delinquency of a minor by furnishing alcohol to a 16-year-old girl.

In mid-September of 1986, Jim agreed to plead guilty to one count of assault with intent to commit forcible oral copulation for the attack on Brenda; all of the other counts against him were dismissed, including the kidnapping, because of the haziness of Brenda's testimony. Huffstetler pleaded guilty to one count of sexual battery.

Following his guilty plea, Jim was referred to the probation department for a sentencing recommendation. In early October the probation officer, Henry Ledden, completed his report and forwarded it to the judge.[25]

After summarizing the incident involving Brenda in Tracy, Ledden gave a sketchy account of Jim's background, including the fact that his natural father had left the family when Jim was two, and noting the fire that required skin grafts.

"The defendant acknowledged that the divorce affected him," wrote the probation officer, who also noted that Jim admitted to getting into a lot of fights at school. Jim admitted resenting Ron Kerlan, but still considered Ron his father. Jim claimed to have graduated from "Valley High School" in Dublin, and asserted that he'd been active playing football and baseball. Jim also claimed he'd received an honorable discharge from the Army. He said that while he'd experimented with illegal drugs, he didn't have a drug problem.

His main problem, Jim said, was that he drank too much. He made no mention of the death of his onetime girlfriend, Cassie Riley, nor of his teenaged friendship with the convicted sex predator Michael Ihde.

"On the surface," Ledden concluded, "the defendant appears to have functioned reasonably well within the community. Defendant has completed high school, is married and employed [at the Dublin car wash]. Upon closer look, there have been three incidents involving sexually aberrant behavior between July, 1984 and now. The defendant was arrested on July 8, 1984, for an incident which closely resembles this current offense. However, that matter was handled informally and never reached the courts.

"Secondly, we have this defendant involved in this serious offense. The complexion of the case changed dramatically when authorities learned the victim was quite intoxicated on July 25, 1985." (The third instance of sexually aberrant behavior was the 1986 Walnut Creek indecent exposure charge,

---

25 San Joaquin County Superior Court records.

which was still awaiting resolution in court at the time of the probation officer's report.)

Based on this prior behavior, Ledden had it right when he offered his conclusion: "Psychiatric evaluation is imperative to determine whether the defendant has the potential for similar behavior in the future," he wrote.

The following month, San Joaquin County Superior Court Judge Stephen Demetras ordered Jim to be sent to the California State Medical Facility at Vacaville for a psychiatric evaluation before pronouncing a final sentence.

Among other things, the headshrinkers of the Department of Corrections were supposed to decide for the court whether Jim Daveggio had the characteristics of a mentally disordered sex offender. But as it happened, the professionals at the prison were hardly able to scratch the surface of Jim Daveggio's seriously disordered mind, let alone decide how dangerous he actually was.

Located behind high, barbed-wire-topped chain link fences, surmounted by concrete guard towers, and surrounded by olive groves, the California Medical Facility at Vacaville was one of the most crowded of California's many overcrowded prison facilities in the fall of 1986. Its primary mission was to provide medical care for the prison system's inmates who suffered from serious illnesses. It also served as one of three initial evaluation centers for inmates newly arriving in the prison system who required classification in terms of their required security level. On top of that, the facility was also used to house long-term inmates who, for whatever reason, couldn't be accommodated at any of the state's other prisons.

The law that Judge Demetras relied upon in sending Jim Daveggio to Vacaville was one of those penology ideas that looked good on paper, but which suffered in execution. As indeterminate sentencing—in which judges decided how long a guilty person should serve, based on the defendant's background and the facts of the offense—fell out of favor in the 1960s and 1970s, to be replaced by more definite terms, the state's Department of Corrections was pressed into service to perform the assessment function previously performed by judges. The idea was that the department's professionals—its psychologists, psychiatrists and corrections counselors—were better qualified to determine whether a person should get hard prison time, or probation.

That it didn't work very well was the result of the sheer numbers of prisoners that came flooding into the system, which in practical terms meant that few if any of the prisoners received anything like an adequate evaluation. The system had up to 90 days to decide what to do with the new committals; in practice, however, the evaluation was usually performed within three weeks, in order to make room for still more new prisoners.

Jim arrived at the prison in late October of 1986, on a Department of Corrections bus, one of several dozen "greenies" who arrived daily. The bus pulled up to a sally-port, the steel doors of the prison clanged open, and the "new fish" filed into the institution's reception area, a long narrow room with a processing counter.

There the new arrivals had their identities verified, were questioned as to their current health, made to strip, directed to an open-sided shower area, cleaned up, and issued green coveralls for uniforms—hence the name "greenies." Each was given a "fish kit"—plastic comb, toothbrush, soap, a pencil stub and a few pieces of paper. Then they were marched into one end of the three-tiered prison complex that was painted entirely green, assigned bunks in four-by-eight-foot cells, and locked in. The color scheme was used to make it obvious to the guards whenever one of the red-suited and presumably more hardened inmates wandered into the neophytes' area, where they were apt to prey upon the new arrivals.

When Jim arrived, however, the facility was nearly 2,000 inmates above its maximum capacity. That meant each cell was double-bunked, two men to every cell; more, there were so many prisoners, an overflow of other inmates was sleeping on foam mattress pads in the corridor that ran between all the tiered wings, while others were assigned to space on the floor of the institution's gymnasium. The entire prison was noisy and dangerous for staff and inmates alike; it was, in short, hardly a setting conducive to penetrating analysis of an inmate's inner soul.

There was no attempt made to sort out the new prisoners on the basis of their offenses. Sex offenders like Jim were mixed with drug offenders, murderers, burglars and con artists, without rhyme or reason. All were given a standard educational achievement test, to measure an inmate's math and

reading skills, followed by two psychological tests designed
to give the prison staff some idea of the inmate's emotional
and cognitive state.

Afterward, an inmate met with a psychologist for a short
interview, and then with a corrections counselor. Once a
week, under the supervision of a staff psychiatrist, the psychological staff and the corrections staff met to make their
assessments of the prisoners, preparatory to compiling a report that would be sent back to the sentencing judge. The
reports by law remained secret, available only to the sentencing judge and the probation officer assigned to the case
back in the county where the inmate's offense had occurred.

Years later, one of the psychologists who was on the
prison staff during the time of Jim's stay commented real-
istically on the utility of the exercise. All they had to go on,
she said, in making the evaluations asked for by the court,
was the probation officer's report, which gave some of the
details of the offense, the mental tests given by the prison
staff, and the interviews, which usually took no more than
an hour. There was no effort made to burrow deep into an
inmate's past, to see what made him tick; an incident like
the death of Cassie Riley would have remained known only
to the inmate if he chose not to bring it up.

And the worst of it was, the psychologist added, there
was never any feedback from the system: no way to know
whether the shrinks had guessed right, or wrong, on those
who were recommended for probation. The inmates simply
went back to the county where they had come from, and no
one ever let the psychologists know what happened to
them—unless, by chance, they were returned to Vacaville on
another commitment after doing something else.

A little over a month after he arrived, Jim was returned
to San Joaquin County, along with the recommendations of
the prison staff. The staff found that Jim had no psychological illness (at least as defined by the generic tests for mental
illness given); Jim blamed his troubles on his problems with
his father, Johnny, and his addiction to alcohol. He was
found "marginally qualified" to receive probation. Among

the conditions of probation were requirements that he "totally abstain" from alcohol and that he stay away from places where alcohol was sold, that he get mental health counseling as required by his probation officer, and that he keep in frequent contact with the probation officer.

After his return from Vacaville on December 10, 1986, it appears that Jim was allowed to be free through Christmas. Then, after the turn of the New Year, Judge Demetras sentenced Jim to serve a year in jail, and five years of probation. With credit for time already served and time off for good behavior while in jail, Jim would be out in six months.

While Jim was serving this time in the San Joaquin County jail at French Camp, just outside Stockton, Dawn was coming to a decision: in spite of her earlier promise never to leave Jim, she served him with divorce papers at the jail on their fifth wedding anniversary. She met him in the visitors' area while accompanied by an ex-boyfriend.

"When he first saw me he had a big smile on his lips," Dawn recalled. But when Dawn gave him the papers without a word, he grew sullen. Dawn remembered his insistence that he never leave her, and was suddenly a bit afraid of him.

A month later, Jim was released from jail. He called and left a message on Dawn's answering machine. When Dawn got home from work, she heard Jim's voice.

"Just wanted to let you know I'm out," came the familiar voice. Jim identified himself as James.

James? Dawn was nonplussed. Jim had never called himself James before. She called an acquaintance in the Pleasanton police. The acquaintance assured her the department would be keeping an eye on her ex-husband.

Jim—now James—moved back in with his mother and Ron at the house on Clovewood Lane in Pleasanton. He enrolled in a school for diesel mechanics, tuition paid for by Donna. It was in the mechanics school that James met the woman who was to become the third Mrs. Daveggio.

While James was finishing his jail term and attending diesel school, his onetime pal Mike Ihde was facing his own legal troubles. In Vancouver, Washington, Ihde was on trial for murder.

In what looked to be a reprise of his earlier *modus operandi* in Jackson, Ihde accosted a 68-year-old woman outside a Safeway supermarket in Vancouver. After cadging a ride, Ihde raped and murdered her. The crime had gone unsolved until August of 1986, when—just weeks before Jim Daveggio was facing his own trial in the Tracy case—Ihde met a woman in a Vancouver tavern, and invited her to go for a ride with him. Outside, in the car, Ihde choked the woman into unconsciousness before a passerby intervened. It wasn't long before the Clark County authorities matched Ihde to the rape-murder of the woman at the Safeway; and in April of 1987, as Daveggio was finishing his jail term, Ihde was convicted of first-degree murder, as well as the attack on the second woman outside the tavern. At that point, no one had any notion of whether or how many Ihde might have killed in the past, and it would be years before anyone found out.

JAMES

Now James entered into what would be, for him, probably the longest stretch of domestic tranquility of his adult life. Having taken up with his fellow mechanic, *Diane, James soon moved in with her and her 8-year-old daughter, *Brittany, in a house in the southeastern Sacramento suburb of Carmichael.

In many ways, this was a chance for a new start for James—away from the Pleasanton bars he had frequented and worked at, away from his drug-consuming, business-burgling friends, away from the scene of all his prior failures: Arnelle, Joanie and Astrid; Dawn and Dulcie; away from Mike Ihde, who was now serving a life sentence at the Washington State Penitentiary in Walla Walla; and most of all, away from the Pleasanton police, who had marked him down as a bad actor, as a rapist, drunkard and all-around troublemaker.

True, James had to keep in touch with his probation officer for the next five years, and register as a known sex offender under state law; but this seemed a minimal intrusion compared to the long stretch in prison if he hadn't been found qualified for probation. A year went by, and then another. In July of 1989, James established a car repair business, Smog Enders, just across the American River in north Sacramento. To James' mother and sisters, it began to seem as though James had finally settled down. Then, in August of 1989, Diane got pregnant.

Two months later, on September 30, 1989, James was arrested by Sacramento police not far from his business for picking up an undercover cop posing as a prostitute, offering

her money for sex, and for disorderly conduct. James was
arrested just before lunch, booked into jail before 1 p.m., and
was out by 2:30 p.m. James apparently had been drinking,
because when the case went to court in December, he was
given drinking-and-driving diversion as was usually provided
for first-caught offenders, fined $292, and ordered to undergo
HIV testing, routine for all prostitution arrestees.

Coming as this did when James was still on probation
from the Tracy sex crime—probation which required him to
abstain from all alcohol, not to mention requiring him to
maintain registration as a sex offender—it's difficult to guess
why the court treated James as leniently as it did. After all,
his parole could have been violated and he could have been
sent to prison for the drinking alone; that a known sex offender would be caught in a sex offense and not been found
in violation of probation seems strange.

Of course, it may have been that the court didn't know
of James' sex offender status; certainly the court record
doesn't show it. And it may have been that James' probation
officer was unaware of his arrest, because there's no reflection in the court record of James having been on probation,
either, which would have been the case if the probation officer had contacted the court. One possibility is that the Sacramento court people simply didn't bother to notify the
probation authorities for what was essentially a routine, non-
violent offense; another is that James' probation officer was
so pleased with his charge's progress so far in getting married and starting his own business that he decided the minor
transgression of attempting to pick up a hooker wasn't worth
ruining James' new life.

What does seem clear—admittedly in retrospect—is that
James' penchant for getting into sexual trouble was still very
much a part of his personality.

But for the most part, James stayed clean and out of trouble. The following May, James' first and only son was born
to Diane. Afterward, in the last contact she would ever have
with the boy she'd known as Jim, Dawn and her daughter

went to Carmichael to meet James, Diane, Brittany and the new baby.

Dawn thought Diane was proud of James, even fiercely protective.

"I was trying to let her know about James," Dawn recalled, but Diane wasn't listening. She told Dawn that she would always be with James, that nothing could ever happen that would make her leave him. *That sounds familiar*, Dawn thought.

While James was settling into his new life in Sacramento, his old friend Michael Ihde was also growing accustomed to his, inside the sprawling Washington State Penitentiary at Walla Walla—colloquially known as The Walls.

One night in 1988, while exchanging reminiscences with a cellmate, Ihde confessed to committing three murders of young girls while in Alameda County, after having been paroled in 1982 on his rape and attempted murder case in Jackson. Four years after this cellblock heart-to-heart, Ihde's cellmate experienced a religious conversion. The cellmate wrote a letter to the Alameda County Sheriff's Department, imparting the gist of Ihde's admissions.

Since Ihde had been paroled in 1982 and had apparently gone to Washington State in 1985 or 1986, the number of unsolved murders that might be attributed to Ihde was relatively small. An examination of the evidence in the Lisa Monoz case showed that biological evidence, semen, had been recovered and stored. The evidence was subjected to a DNA analysis.

The following month a sheriff's department detective went to Washington State and obtained a court order to test Ihde's blood for its DNA pattern. When the two samples matched—a one-in-13-billion occurrence, according to the state's DNA experts—Ihde was indicted for murder in Alameda County. By 1994, Ihde was on his way back to Alameda County to stand trial for Monoz' murder. In November of 1996, Ihde would be convicted of that crime, and sentenced to death a month later. But Alameda County authorities would always wonder: who were the other two victims of Ihde? And, had he acted alone?

Sometime after the birth of his son, James began to cultivate a new circle of friends in Sacramento—the Devil's Horsemen.

As outlaw motorcycle gangs went, at least in the Sacramento area, the Horsemen were fairly far down on the biker food chain. As in most areas of the country, the outlaw biker culture was almost feudal in its hierarchy.

At the top of the heap in Sacramento were the Hell's Angels—perhaps a half-dozen or so bona fide members of the notorious gang, along with a number of associates and others called "hang-arounds." The Hell's Angels contingent was in effect the lord of the realm, with the sole authority to charter other, lesser clubs, such as the Devil's Horsemen.

These lesser groups were legitimized based upon their willingness to subordinate themselves to the more powerful Angels, who alone had the power to authorize a lesser club to wear "colors," usually a leather jacket with a "patch" on the back, running from the shoulders to the waist, and denoting the club's identity. Anyone wearing unauthorized outlaw colors was severely dealt with by the Angels, usually through violence perpetrated by one of the loyal subordinate clubs. In return for the charter, the lesser clubs pledged loyalty to the Angels, and made themselves available to them for favors or tasks the Angels didn't want to undertake themselves.

The Devil's Horsemen had about a dozen members, all white men mostly in their mid- to late thirties; about half had records as small-time criminals—for such things as burglary, driving under the influence, illegal drug use and sales, and assault. Others had no criminal records at all.

The Devil's Horsemen's "patch" consisted of a red horse's head outlined in blue, facing left. Across the top—a separate, curved patch called the top "rocker"—came the club name, Devils Horsemen (apparently bikers could care less about proper possessive punctuation). On the bottom rocker was the club's hometown, "Sacramento."

The club members called each by their monikers: "Big Bill"; "Little Bill"; "Stick"; "Smash"; "Bub"; "Cowboy"; "Strollin' "; "Fester"; and of course, "Froggie," for James. The club had a headquarters of sorts—"the clubhouse"—on Franklin Boulevard in south Sacramento, with a sign over the door, DHMC. The club was next door to a business that sold religious supplies, for accidental irony.

When he became a member of the Devil's Horsemen, James acquired a motorcycle, the requisite Harley-Davidson; in fact, it wasn't possible to be a member of an outlaw biker club without one. Later, there would be some confusion over the origins of the Harley. Some of James' relatives believed that he had won the bike in a raffle; others said it was given to him by the other members of the club. Part of the confusion seems to stem from the fact that club members were required to sign over the titles to their motorcycles to the club as a condition of joining; as a result, the registrations of various motorcycles used by the club members appear to flit from member to member as various circumstances dictated.

In the club, James achieved for perhaps the first time in his life some measure of social acceptance. The fact that the members were in many ways very much like him—given to drinking, fighting, roaming and tattooing, and many with jail experience behind them—meant that James at last had a peer group to identify with. The fact that the club members called and considered themselves "outlaws" shows something of their state of mind: anti-social personalities taking pride as social pariahs, the sort of long-haired, bearded, tattooed rumblers encased in leather who run in packs to drink and fight, loyal first to one another and above the norms of ordinary society. In this group, James' past was no disadvantage, but rather a badge of distinction.

The club members went on "poker runs"—essentially, motorcycle rallies where members drew a single playing card upon reaching designated checkpoints; when the rally was

completed, each member had a poker hand. At the end of
the day, the poker hands were bet against one another and
against the members of other clubs. Winnings from the poker
run pots were accumulated in a safe in the clubhouse for
future runs.

As the first years of the 1990s rolled by, James rose in
stature among the Devil's Horsemen. Having named his hog
"the Ball of Purple Thunder," James soon followed suit by
dyeing his hair purple; his tattoos begin to proliferate until,
by the mid-1990s, he had a mini–art gallery on his arms and
chest: a heart with a knife through it, topped by the old eagle
and now accompanied by a rising sun, with "Joanie" above
on his left chest; a pair of wings with the letters "HAAH"
on his right chest; the old lion's head on his shoulder, with
"Astrid" underneath; a pair of tragedy and comedy masks on
his left forearm, with the words "Smile now, cry later"; the
old rose on his left shoulder blade, now accompanied by a
heart and a bird, and the word "forever"; the old skull on his
right bicep, now metamorphosed into an intricate design,
completely obscuring the one-time "Cassie"; the word
"power" on his right tricep; a skull with five aces in its mouth
and the words "dead man's hand" on his right shoulder; and
another obscure design on the left bicep.

Together, these ostentatious displays marked James as one
of a group, giving him a sort of connectedness with others
that he had never had before. The Horsemen drank together,
partied together, and fought together; in their minds, it was
them against the world, including the law.

As James became more immersed in the outlaw biker
world, his business began to take a lesser role in his life. In
May of 1993, the State of California obtained a tax lien of
$7,390 against James and Smog Enders; another lien, or per-
haps a reduction of the first, was filed the following January
for $4,732. There was talk that James had been forging smog
certificates. Eventually, he shut the business down.

By then, however, James was deeply involved with the
Devil's Horsemen, and a young woman associate of theirs
named Lizzie B.

Liz was 29 years old in 1995; at five feet six inches, 110 pounds, with long brown hair and brown eyes, she was a very attractive woman who occasionally worked as an exotic dancer. In contrast to many dancers, however, Liz was fairly well off, having inherited two houses in Sacramento from her recently deceased mother, as well as some money from her mother's family.

The way Liz later told the tale, she had been living with a man named Richard in Sacramento in 1994. The relationship was volatile. Early in 1995, Liz was in a bar in Sacramento's south end with Richard when a fight broke out between Richard and his brother and two bikers. James was the bartender at the time.

After the fight, Liz began dating James. Liz soon learned of Diane and James' children, but didn't seem to care. By February of 1995, according to Liz, James had talked her into becoming his mistress, and she often traveled with him on poker runs.

Liz soon discovered that James was sexually dysfunctional; it was very difficult for him to obtain an erection. Soon she began to engage in sadism and masochism with him in an effort to keep him stimulated. In these encounters, James would be the sadist, controlling Liz with both words and simulated violence. It seems that James was quite enamored of Liz; during the first part of their relationship, James added a new tattoo to his collection, this one of a frog mounting a lizard from the rear.

By late April of 1995, James had reached the end of his domestic relationship with Diane, as Lizzie had with her boyfriend Richard; after Richard broke Lizzie's nose in a fight, he moved out and James moved in, into one of the houses she had inherited. But now James began to drink heavily again. While living with Lizzie, James was caught driving his motorcycle under the influence near the Indian casino town of Jackson in Amador County, in the Sierra foothills southeast of Sacramento—the same place where Michael Ihde had first been arrested nearly 16 years before. Because the DUI occurred after James' probation for the Tracy kidnap had ended, it wasn't a violation.

Using some of the money she'd inherited, Liz decided to start her own business, a bar in south Sacramento that was named "Lizzie B's." James became a bartender at the establishment. Not surprisingly, the Devil's Horsemen gravitated toward Lizzie B's to do their drinking—and, it appears, fighting.

It was sometime during this period, or perhaps just before it, that James began using the bikers' drug of choice, methamphetamine, or "crank." The results would eventually be disastrous.

In recent years, methamphetamine has emerged as the worst drug in America's illicit medicine chest, at least if measured in terms of total human wreckage. Because of its attributes of cost and availability, as well as its long-lasting kick, methamphetamine has made serious inroads, from college campuses to the inner city, and from factory floors to faculty lounges.

Indeed, the very cross-cultural demand of "speed," or "meth," or "chalk," or "ice," or "crystal," or "glass"—the actual term depends on where you are and what form the stuff is in—is evidence that the methamphetamine crisis is America's biggest drug problem yet, far bigger than heroin ever was, or even cocaine turned out to be. Even more significant, there are no foreign cartels to blame for importing the stuff; most of it is home-grown, using common chemicals that are easily found on the shelves of your local supermarket.

As a powerful central nervous system stimulant, methamphetamine resembles in many ways all of the worst aspects of the cocaine derivative "crack," which decimated America's inner cities in the 1980s and contributed to the largest upsurge in violent crime in a half-century.

Like crack, methamphetamine takes its user off on a manic high; unlike crack, it can take hours to wear off. And like crack, it is considered powerfully addictive. When used habitually, it can create powerful mood disorders that may result in extreme nervousness, delusions, paranoia and violent behavior.

Methamphetamine was first produced early in the 20th

century as an offshoot of its parent drug, amphetamine. Its normal use is as a component in nasal decongestants and bronchial inhalers, and it may occasionally be prescribed by physicians as a short-term treatment for narcolepsy, attention-deficit disorder, and infrequently, obesity. Because it is a constituent of a number of over-the-counter medical remedies, methamphetamine can be manufactured relatively easily by a marginally competent chemist. Some of these "cookers," as the meth trade calls them, have been known to whip up the drug in self-storage lockers in the dead of night.

While methamphetamine has been around as an illicit substance for a number of years, particularly among blue-collar workers appreciative of its energy-inducing, painkilling properties, its popularity as a recreational drug has grown substantially over the previous decade, and indeed has made its way into high schools and even junior high schools. It is a little-noted fact that in many of the high school shootings that took place between 1997 and 1999, methamphetamine was frequently used by the teenaged shooters in the days, weeks and months before they committed their violent acts. When junior high school students in such relatively rural states as Arkansas and Oregon acknowledge that methamphetamine is easily available in their social circles, that's evidence of a widespread problem.

According to statistics collected by the Drug Abuse Warning Network, an organization that collects information on emergency room admissions for drug-related episodes in 21 metropolitan areas, hospital admissions for methamphetamine use increased by 237 percent between 1990 and 1994, then took a downturn, only to rise again in 1996. Altogether, according to one survey, the number of people in the United States who have tried methamphetamine at least once rose steadily from 3.8 million in 1994 to 4.9 million recently.

The drug can be snorted like powdered cocaine or heroin; it may be smoked in the form of a burnable compound like crack cocaine or heroin; and it may be injected, just like either of the two better-known drugs. A person who snorts the drug may experience a powerful "rush" or "flash," an intense nervous reaction, within five minutes; the same person who smokes a "rock" of methamphetamine may experience the same sort of rocket-blast rush as a crack user, which means within 10 to 20 seconds; however, unlike the crack user, the meth user runs along on an energy high for as long as five or six hours.

One of the principal effects of the drug is to release high levels of the neurotransmitter dopamine into areas of the brain that regulate sensations of pleasure. But it comes at a cost: according to tests done with animals, the drug has been shown to damage nerve endings in parts of the brain. High doses can foul up the body's temperature-regulating mechanism, so that users may break out in a large sweat, and may even go into convulsions and die of overheating.

And because of its roller-coaster–type ride—in which the user goes up, peaks, and glides back down—habitual users may succumb to a form of bingeing, in which the user tries to keep the high longer by ingesting more methamphetamine. At the end of that time, the user either crashes into a depressive state, or uses still more methamphetamine. The usage pattern is therefore progressive: the more one uses, the more one crashes; the more one crashes, the more one uses— a so-called "run."

For an addicted user, the pattern is only broken when the user either runs out of methamphetamine or, in the words of one expert, "becomes too disorganized to continue."

Prolonged use of the drug over a period of weeks or even days can cause radical changes of personality—in fact, there is some scientific data suggesting repeated use of methamphetamine may cause molecular changes in the brain's cellular structure. It is not uncommon for habitual users of methamphetamine to display "twitchiness," a sort of catchall term for jangling nerves, acute reactions, momentary delusions, and an underlying feeling of anxiety, dread, and suspicion, all leading to woeful lapses in judgment, including sudden outbursts of manic violence.

Unlike heroin, which was in its inception an import from the Mideast via the Mediterranean, or cocaine, which came from South America initially through Florida, the illegal manufacture and distribution of methamphetamine was originally a profit-making venture of outlaw motorcycle gangs; thus, some of the language of the meth trade reveals its biker roots: the "run," as in a biker run, or "crank," from when the substance was said to have been smuggled in bikers' crankcases (also because it "cranked" up the user). As a result, as far as the police are concerned, the members of outlaw motorcycle gangs such as the Hell's Angels, the Banditos, the Outlaws and the Pagans, the nation's biggest and best organized outlaw motorcycle gangs, remain one of the primary sources of methamphetamine. It also suggests one of the main reasons that, sometime in 1996, James Daveggio became a meth dealer.

The pull of methamphetamine—with its rush, followed by the long period of glide in which the senses were heightened and confidence and aggression soared, it was the perfect chemical to accompany a throaty, dangerous run on a heavy motorcycle—quickly ensnared James with both its addictive power and its potential for profit. The bars James worked at provided good locations for distribution. Soon James assembled a network of users and couriers, a number of them women, connected by pagers. Customers came in and had drinks, money and drugs changed hands, and the good times rolled. But fueled by speed, the bars began attracting a rowdy element. Charged up on booze and crank, James fell back into his old Pleasanton pattern of picking fights with the customers. Soon the only people who came to Lizzie B's were James' drug customers, or people who wanted to fight.

According to Liz, as 1996 unfolded, James' use of methamphetamine grew, along with his belligerent outbursts at the bar. To come down easier, James also increased his drinking. Neither substance was beneficial to his stunted sex life. By the spring of that year, he and Lizzie were feuding; as far as Lizzie could tell, James was driving away all her bar's customers and ruining her investment. When matters came to a head in the middle of the summer, Lizzie fired

James and evicted him from her inherited house.

James soon found a new place to live, with another woman named Sherri. Sherri was so taken with James, she had a frog tattooed on her belly. By now James was using methamphetamine regularly, and giving it away, as well. And as any competent drug dealer knows, once the seller becomes the user, disaster is inevitable.

By October of 1996, James was working as a bartender for another establishment in Sacramento, Bobby Joe's, and it wasn't long before Froggie's coterie of bikers and drug users followed him.

Bobby Joe's was a rather typical saloon for south Sacramento; comprised of a long, narrow barroom with the regulation pool table, a jukebox, electric beer signs and dust and dead flies in the windows, it was the kind of place where working people gathered to have a few brews on their way home from the job. The arrival of the Devil's Horsemen crowd seems to have changed the atmosphere at least slightly; now there was an air of tension in the place, because of the meth transactions, and because of the always present if subtle portent of potential violence.

It appears that James became something of a cult figure at Bobby Joe's. Later, people at the bar would recall a steady stream of women who came in to be around James; they gave them a catch-all nickname: Frogettes. Others recall James boasting of his sex offender status, even of him standing on the bar exposing himself, as the potent concoction of alcohol and methamphetamine lowered his inhibitions and fueled his confrontational nature. It was in this atmosphere and during this time that James first met Michelle Michaud.

MICKIE AND FROGGIE

Afterward, there were two stories as to how this encounter unfolded, both of which illustrate something about the essential Michelle Michaud, but which fail to adequately explain just how complex a personality hers actually is.

One story, told by the patrons of Bobby Joe's and perhaps at least partially apocryphal, has Michelle Michaud swinging into the rowdy bar, taking one look at James and declaring, "I want *that*!"—"that" being James. The patrons recalled Michelle as flamboyant, dramatic, exhibitionistic, and most especially, given to throwing around $100 tips to the help.

The other version, told by Michelle herself, describes a far more ordinary introduction: in this version, Michelle met James when she was attempting to locate a runaway girl from her south Sacramento neighborhood, and community-minded, good-works-doing James offered to help her.

The two different versions almost perfectly encapsulate the dichotomy of personality that ran through everything about "Mickie" Michaud, as she became known while growing up. Indeed, Mickie was whatever you wanted to see in her; and it was her great talent, as well as great misfortune, to be able to divine *how* you wanted to see her, and to take all steps necessary to play that part.

On the surface of things, Mickie Michaud seemed a completely contradictory personality: a dutiful daughter, a loving mother, a church-going volunteer, a neighborhood crossing guard, while at the same time, a working prostitute, a violent whoremaster, an incestuous pedophile, a self-proclaimed hit lady, and one tough cookie. Whether seductress, slave, mommy, ball-kicking bitch or pious church-goer, being somebody she was expected to be was how Mickie had long previously learned how to survive.

To James Daveggio, she became mother, daughter, whore, procurer and enabler, all in one. In Mickie's own eyes, she did it all for "love," even though she was never sure what "love" really was. But it was this desperate desire to have something she could not even define, let alone understand, that did her in.

In the fall of 1996, Mickie was five feet eight inches tall, and weighed around 140 pounds. She had lustrous auburn hair, a fair complexion, and hazel eyes. All in all, she was a very attractive woman, at least in the beginning of her time with James Daveggio. Of course, it was a different story a year later—methamphetamine will do that.

Mickie was born in Casablanca, Morocco, on November 7, 1958. Her father, *Lamont, was in the U.S. Army. Mickie was the first child of Lamont and his wife, *Rowena. When Michelle was four, the Michaud family was transferred to the United States. For reasons not clear, Lamont obtained a certificate of naturalization from a United States Court in North Carolina for Michelle; the accompanying photograph shows a four-year-old peering earnestly into the camera, clearly uncertain about her own immediate future in a new country.[26]

Lamont and Rowena soon added to their family as they traveled around from Army installation to Army installation. There were two sons, one of whom grew up to be a corrections officer at Folsom prison, the other an official with a domestic airline. And finally, in 1973, there was another girl, *Millie, after the family had moved to Sacramento, when Michelle was 15.

By Mickie's own account, she became incorrigible after she entered her teens.[27] She dropped out of a suburban Sacramento high school in the 10th grade, and was soon declared

26 Certificate of Naturalization, United States District Court for the Eastern District of North Carolina, issued June, 1963.
27 *State* vs. *Michaud*, Sacramento Municipal Court, #91M01688, probation officer's report.

a ward of the court, the normal procedure when a juvenile commits a crime. Because juvenile court records in California are destroyed after a ward of the court reaches legal age, it's no longer possible to determine what her offense may have been.

What does seem clear, both from Mickie's own words, and from the observations of those who knew her more than twenty years ago, is that a large part of Mickie's incorrigibility stemmed from her difficult relationship with her father.

One of Mickie's high school classmates, who went on to become a Sacramento County deputy sheriff, recalled visiting the Michaud house one day after school. The future deputy recalled Mickie making a baloney sandwich with two slices of baloney, and then getting a sharp admonition from Lamont for using the second slice.

This was a small thing, but it sheds light on the nature of Mickie's personality: as she grew into adulthood, Mickie began to exhibit attributes resulting from an authoritarian upbringing. In this scheme of things, power flows down, while obeisance flows up. The most powerful figure in Mickie's early life was "Daddy"; and it became Mickie's most urgent goal in life to make her father pleased with her.

In Mickie's view, there was nothing she could do to win her father's approval, and it became the same with the significant men in her life. She simply felt brow-beaten, she once said, and always on the defensive.

"My father can do that to me," Mickie was to tell the Federal Bureau of Investigation, after she was caught. "My father does it to my mother. Makes you feel worthless so nothing just—I don't know how to explain it. It hurts. Sometimes I'd rather my dad just punch me than say the things he does to me because it hurts more. Just like James."[28]

There is something more fundamental involved in this sort of conflict than mere parent-child disagreements. Indeed, it appears that the dynamic of the relationship required Mickie

---

28 From the transcript of the FBI interview of Michelle Michaud, Dec. 5, 1997.

to disobey, her father to respond with disapproval, which satisfied Mickie's desire for attention from her father and unintentionally rewarded the bad behavior. This is the essence of the rebellious–submissive personality.

When Mickie spoke to law enforcement during her interview, both of her interrogators were struck by this aspect of her behavior. Asked whether she had ever seen a counselor, Mickie said no. When it was suggested that often people who have sexual experiences at young ages later, and unfairly, feel significant guilt, Mickie asked to stop the tape to relate something that she had never told anyone other than James Daveggio. From the context of the interview after recording was resumed, it appears that Mickie told the officers that she had been molested by someone when she was ten years old.

In any event, Mickie ran away from home when she was 16; the deputy sheriff who knew her in high school recalls that she moved in with a man who sold drugs, and who also apparently beat her. Mickie herself told of being picked up on the street by a man who threatened her with a gun when she was 17; the man drove her to an isolated spot miles away from her home and raped her repeatedly.

At some point, while still in her teens, Mickie wound up in one of Nevada's legalized brothels, where she worked under the name "Ruby." Later, a number of stories would circulate about this experience of Mickie's, including tales linking her to Joe Conforte, the owner of the Mustang Ranch brothel. According to the legend, "Ruby" was supposed to have been Conforte's favorite.[29]

By the early 1980s, Mickie had returned to the Sacramento area, where she began work in a number of massage parlors owned by a man named Bob Swanger and a second

29 Eventually Conforte's operation was taken over by the U.S. government for failure to pay back taxes, and Conforte fled the country. It was an irony that even as the Daveggio/Michaud case was proceeding through the federal courts in Nevada in 1999, the tax case against the still-absent Conforte was proceeding just down the hall of the same courthouse. Michaud was asked several questions about Conforte during Daveggio's federal trial, but wasn't permitted to answer them by the judge, David Hagen.

man named Charles Sanfilippo. Sanfilippo believed that the massage parlor business was protected by a Sacramento Police Department captain who was cut in on the action as a silent partner. It was while she was working in the massage parlors that Mickie became pregnant by a man who later went on to become a successful Sacramento tire dealer; she gave birth to a son, *Rusty, in 1982, when she was 23.

Mickie soon became connected with a man named *Jose Segovia, whom she later described as a sort of combination musician and pimp who used a lounge in south Sacramento as his headquarters. Segovia, who would later be imprisoned in Nevada for attempted murder, dominated Mickie and a friend of hers. The three lived together for a while, and Mickie became pregnant again, and this time gave birth to a daughter, *Renee, in 1984.

Sometime during this year, according to Sanfilippo, Swanger either gave or sold a piece of one of the massage parlors to Mickie.[30] But the opportunity to move into management was soon thwarted when Sacramento authorities began cracking down on the massage parlors as fronts for prostitution, and the property was ordered seized under the state's Red Light Abatement Act.[31]

Following this, Mickie was tied to a bed and severely beaten by Segovia. Somehow she survived, and when she went to the authorities to complain, Segovia was arrested. The Sacramento District Attorney's Office was eager to convict Segovia, but when Mickie refused to testify against her former lover, the case went south.

Following her escape from Segovia, Mickie applied for welfare, and occasionally worked in massage parlors to pick up extra cash. By the time her sister Millie was 15, Mickie was a seasoned professional sex worker; and while Millie had always looked up to Mickie and was shocked to discover what her sister did for a living, she soon learned to accept it.

---

30 FBI interview of Charles Sanfilippo, Jan. 6, 1998.
31 Records of Sacramento County Recorder.

Late in 1984, Mickie picked up a new client, a man who operated a scrap metal salvage yard. The man later explained to the FBI that he first met Mickie when she was recycling cans for change. He felt sorry for her, he said, and soon was helping her out financially. One thing led to another, and the man became a paying client—one of two "elderly gentlemen," as Mickie later put it, who put an economic floor under her and her children.

But to Mickie, this wasn't love, it came under the heading of work; and like most professional sex workers, Mickie was adept at separating her work from her life. She might turn tricks for a living to pay the rent and support her kids, but that didn't mean she wasn't a good mother, as Mickie used to put it. She arranged for special education for her son, tutoring for her daughter, and made sure to attend church and to volunteer for church activities. She helped the elderly when they needed it, and was generally an upstanding member of the community, as even her parish priest later acknowledged.

In 1989, when she was 31, Mickie had a hysterectomy. As a result, she began taking hormone medication to help keep her moods more stable. In 1991, Mickie was arrested in an undercover bust of a massage parlor, Maxine's Studio, in Sacramento. The arrest outraged Mickie; she thought she'd been entrapped by the officer, and indeed the record shows that the officer probably did go too far in trying to make a case against her. Mickie demanded a jury trial, and got it. After the jury returned a guilty verdict against her, Mickie admitted that she would ordinarily have just paid the fine and taken her lumps but for the outrageous conduct of the undercover cop; she claimed the cop had initiated sexual contact with her, rather than the other way around.[32]

Shortly before this, Mickie and her two children had moved into a tri-level house not far from her parents' home in south Sacramento. As a result, Mickie and her children

---

32 Records of Sacramento Municipal Court, *State* vs. *Michaud*, #91M01688.

were in frequent contact with Rowena and Lamont, as well as Millie. That was how things stood when, in March of 1994, Mickie met the second of her "elderly gentlemen," a retired U.S. Army sergeant named *Bert Rand.

Sgt. Bert, as he later came to be called by the legions of law enforcement people who eventually investigated Mickie, was indeed a kindly gentleman, a man who had been married to the same woman for 49 years. When she died in 1992, Bert Rand was bereft. Then, according to the story he later told law enforcement officers, Rand had a dream in which his late wife had come to him to tell him to take care of Michelle Michaud and her children.

"I don't want to know anything about your past," Rand told Mickie. "We're going to start fresh, one day at a time." For the better part of a year, retired Sgt. Rand saw Mickie on dates, keeping her supplied with cash to help pay the rent and put groceries on the table. Then, in June of 1996, Rand moved in with Mickie at the house in Sacramento, paying $500 a month in rent, and agreeing to make the $480-a-month car payments on the forest green Dodge minivan that Mickie had acquired with her other gentleman friend as a co-signer.

Rand not only paid his share of the rent and for the car, he also furnished the house with a brand new large-screen television set and a collection of living room furniture which altogether set him back nearly $8,000. Rand took Mickie on a trip to the east coast to visit relatives, and on a vacation to Seattle and British Columbia. He began to think about marrying Mickie.

Thus, after a rough beginning in life, it looked as if at the age of 38, Mickie had made it through the dark part of the woods, and was well positioned for her coming middle age.

But it wasn't going to last; Mickie would find a way to screw it up, that was her nature; and she did.

The way Mickie remembered it later, in her conversations with the FBI, she first met James on October 29, 1997, at a neighbor's house.

For almost a dozen years, Mickie said, she'd avoided falling in love with men—after Jose, she just "didn't want to go there again, ever, ever again."

But on this day, one of the neighbor kids had disappeared from home, and there was a meeting at the neighbors' house to decide what to do. The neighborhood kids were always in and out of her house, Mickie said, and they trusted her; so did the neighbors. When the girl disappeared, Mickie decided to prepare a flyer. When it was learned that the girl had run away with a Mexican boy, Mickie got on the telephone and called the Mexican consulate, and had the word put out to watch for the couple if they crossed the border. Mickie's daughter Renee found out that the Mexican boy had threatened to blow up Bobby Joe's, a bar where the girl's stepfather hung out. Mickie went to Bobby Joe's with Renee and a baseball bat; she had the idea that the Mexican boy was a rerun of Jose, and she intended to give him some hefty whacks for fooling around with a 12-year-old girl.

At the bar, Mickie met James, who was bartending. James had long, bleached hair. He was about five nine or ten, and weighed a little over 220 pounds, and was well-muscled, although he was beginning to develop a beer gut. People called him Frog, Mickie said, because his voice was so low and raspy. Mickie was well-dressed, and wearing makeup, cultivating her elegant look to intimidate the Mexican kid.

Mickie told Frog she intended to beat the Mexican kid's

brains in with the baseball bat, because she was going to make sure that nobody harmed the runaway girl. Mickie thought she was being very cocky; she liked to act tough with people she'd just met.

But James talked her out of whacking the kid and then volunteered to go talk to the kid himself, to see what was what. The next day, James did just that, while Mickie watched, baseball bat in hand. After meeting with the kid, James emerged from the pizza parlor where the meeting occurred, laughing. Then the kid came out, looking worried. James took the girl away; Mickie took one look at the kid and knew that James had scared the bejesus out of him.

Afterward, Mickie met James over at the neighbor's house.

"You just couldn't stay away, huh?" James asked.

"No," Mickie said.

Mickie could tell that James was interested in her. He told Mickie he was intrigued.

"That's your first mistake," Mickie told him, interested in spite of herself. "You don't want to know me."

"All right," James said, "why don't I want to know you?"

"Number one," said Mickie, "I don't like men. They generally piss me the fuck off. And number two, I am a ho, a hooker, a prostitute, have been for twenty-two years of my life, and I'm not changing, and you ain't getting nothing out of me." Mickie was doing her best to alienate James, the way she did to armor herself against the rejection she always anticipated.

"And number three?" James asked.

Mickie was stopped short for a moment. "When I get to it I'll let you know," she said. She started to leave, but was stopped by the neighbor.

"Where are you going?" the neighbor asked.

Mickie said she was going to a bar to get drunk and have some fights with men. The neighbor said he'd join her, and invited James to come too.

About half an hour later, Mickie was sitting in the bar with the neighbor when she heard the rumble of a motorcycle. Mickie felt her stomach tighten up, and she realized that she was actually nervous about the prospect of seeing the man called Frog again—and even more surprising, found herself attracted to him.

"All of a sudden I hear this vroom vroom vroom sound, and it gets closer, and my stomach starts, and I'm like, oh, no," Mickie told the FBI. "I didn't want to get that feeling . . . he came in the door and there was this glow around him, it's bright, and I fell in love right there."

James took Mickie back to Bobby Joe's. Mickie, flying on champagne, made an entrance that was later remarked upon by the patrons, in which she made sure that everyone there knew she was a prostitute, but a prostitute who wouldn't take any lip from anyone, as well as a prostitute who had money. She wanted the people at Bobby Joe's to accord her respect so that James might see her with respect as well.

In James, Mickie thought she'd discovered what she had always really wanted in a man. But what she was really doing was investing James with all the attributes her own fantasies had projected: James as a strong, masculine presence, a firm disciplinarian, someone who had the respect of the community.

Mickie was impressed with another aspect of James' personality.

"Man can drink," she told the FBI. "Never seen a man put away booze the way that man could put away booze. And fight, he's a hellion.

"Man, you see him fight the way he did? I tell you, he kicked everyone's ass, too. Nobody kicked his ass. No one, not ever. I'd stand there with an ashtray in my hand in case something happened, you know me. He'd smile about that, turn around, see, 'Where's my backup?' The redhead with the ashtray in her hand, you know, protect your man."

To Mickie, James was gallant.

"Nobody could call me a whore, nobody could look at me like I was a whore, nobody could call me anything but Michelle. Men couldn't pick on me, their little filthy things that they have and their little tricky ways of trying to get you to go out with them. James would jack 'em up.

"And then, [it was] the first time in my life I ever had a man protect me in public. First time I ever had a man stand up to my family [Lamont and Mickie's brothers] and demand respect for me from my family. 'She's your daughter and that's the woman I'm in love with . . .' I never had anybody. Never had anybody stick around long enough, really, and [that] my family couldn't chase away . . .

"I think," she continued, "that the James I knew for the first five months was someone that James wanted to be. I think he really wanted to be this person because we would have [discussions] about the kids [Joanie and Astrid] to live with us. And I did it for him because he needed those kids. He was so guilty that he was never with them when they were little."

This was a mouthful for Mickie, pregnant with psychological meaning: the James she imagined was like "Daddy," as Mickie habitually referred to her own father; as she saw him, James would be there for the children, and somehow, Mickie would have the kind of family that she expected. And James "needed those kids," while feeling guilty about having abandoned them, just as his own father Johnny had left *him* behind so many years before.

This, at least, was James as Mickie saw him on the night he took her to Bobby Joe's. And it was while Mickie was indulging herself in this projection that Lizzie showed up at the bar.

Lizzie had chopped her long brown hair short—"butched up," as Mickie put it. "She looked like she'd been through the wringer." Mickie got the idea that Lizzie had cut her hair to punish James.

Lizzie came to where Mickie was sitting in the bar and gave her the once-over. Mickie could tell that Lizzie was mad at her, and also at James. Mickie thought Lizzie was jealous. Then Lizzie left. Shortly after, Mickie and James went to a motel to spend the night together. That was when Mickie noticed the first crack in the image of James that she had created in her mind: James was unable to achieve an erection.

Mickie didn't think much about this the first night, but as the relationship grew and James still couldn't achieve an erection, Mickie began to think it was *her* fault—an attitude that James encouraged, because it provided a motive for him to be abusive.

But this was still to come on that first night in late October of 1997, when Mickie still had (most of) her fantasy about James intact.

Within a month, James had moved into Mickie's house, and of course, one of the first people he met, even before he moved in, was retired Sergeant Bert Rand.

Rand knew immediately that James meant trouble. He took one look at James and saw him for what he was: "a boy," as Rand put it to the FBI, who was a "deadbeat" who lived off women. Rand couldn't help but contrast the way Mickie acted toward him—"an elderly gentleman"—and the way she looked at James: with stars in her eyes. Within a week, Rand had moved out, leaving his big-screen television, his furniture and his computer behind. Rand still thought Mickie was a good person; it was just that, in Rand's view, she'd been bamboozled by James.

Having wedged himself into Mickie's life, James began to take over; he began to get rid of elements he didn't like. One of the first to go was Mickie's mother, Rowena. Rowena had been in the practice of coming over to her daughter's house across the street to help clean and to assist with the laundry. Now James made it clear to Mickie that he didn't want Rowena coming around any more. Mickie told her mother that she'd been "banned" from the house.

As Thanksgiving arrived, Mickie kept to her own house, not visiting Lamont, her mother, her brothers or her sister Millie. James played on Mickie's long-running resentments toward her own family, and strove to keep her family away from her.

As November turned into December, and then into the New Year, Joanie and Astrid came to stay with James; now the house was filled with children: Mickie's two, James' two from his first marriage to Arnelle, and the two (including Brittany) from his marriage to Diane.

"In the days when everything was good," Mickie reminisced to the FBI, "he'd come home and [I'd] hear the motorcycle, I'd run through the house, 'Daddy's home.' All the kids would gather around, and we'd meet in the garage . . . but I'd run through the house, 'Daddy's home, Daddy's home, Daddy's home.' "

Mickie slid from ball-busting bitch to seductress to June Cleaver with surprising facility, now attempting to create the family fantasy, with "Daddy" James at the head.

"We'd have Thursday night dinner," she said, "it was mandatory. Everybody had to be there, no exceptions, 'in-

cluding you, Frog.' I never called him Frog unless I got mad
at him. And when I'd call him Frog, he'd go, 'Ooooookay,
dear, what did I do?' He was a good man at one time, thought
we were gonna make it. . . . I'd put him at the head of the
table, separate the kids, you know, down the table, and I'd
be down at the foot of the table. I loved how the Waltons
lived."

The interviewing FBI agents laughed at Mickie's semi-
comic description of normal life with James, but Mickie,
while quick to pick up on the humor, was serious: this was
the sort of life she wanted to create to match her fantasy.

"I didn't know how to do all that stuff," Mickie continued.
"Never had it. So I guess I kinda played it by what I'd seen
on TV, and kinda what I thought it should be like, what my
fantasy of it was, and it became a reality. 'And, James, say
grace.'

"He goes, 'Well, "Grace." Who's gonna start first?' 'No,
no, no, James, you're at the head of the table, honey, you
have to do grace.'

"He goes, 'Oh, woman, I'm not—'

" 'James, are you the man of the house? Correct me.'

"Well, 'Grace, Grace.' He'd stand up and everybody'd
grab hands. Damn him. He'd say, 'God, we're grateful for
being here in this house, having these children here, having
this woman love me,' and then he'd start to get choked up,
he'd look across the table [at Mickie] and . . . He'd go,
'amen,' and then sit down, we'd all sit down and eat, and
we'd have this conversation."

On other nights Mickie brought James dinner to Bobby
Joe's, and still later in the evening, she'd bring him sandwiches.

"I guess it got to be too much," she said, later. " 'Cause
I'd make tuna salad sandwiches, peanut butter and jelly sandwiches, ham and cheese sandwiches, and I'd cut all the crusts
off of 'em, and then cut 'em up and put all these different
varieties so he wouldn't have to get tired of eating the same
sandwich all night, if he wanted a snack in a bag, and there'd
be like this big plastic bag, about twenty different varieties

of sandwiches. And he'd put it in the refrigerator and later on I found out that he'd pass some of them out to his friends who were getting too drunk and help sober 'em up, and after a while he just wanted me to quit bringing things down to him because he says they're making fun of him. It kinda hurt because I enjoyed doing it. So I quit."

A week later, James called Mickie at home and wanted to know why she hadn't brought him anything. 'What, you're not taking care of me anymore, Michelle?' I was like, 'James, you told me to quit.' He said, 'No, I wanted you to quit that night, maybe for a couple of nights, but not every night.' I said, 'James, that's not what you said.' Then he started getting ugly that way.

"Now, whatever I did wasn't right anymore, or it wasn't good enough, or I didn't have—I should have anticipated more or I should have been able to know. I've been with him this long, don't I know him by now? And all of this."

It was just before Christmas when someone broke into the home of the owner of Bobby Joe's, and burgled the place, taking all the Christmas presents. A few nights later, someone broke into Bobby Joe's itself, got into the office strongbox, and made off with about $6,000. Bob, the owner, didn't know who did it, but believed it had to be an inside job. Who else knew where the money was, or the fact that there'd been that much in the box?

Bob had his suspicions about James, but didn't confront him over the burglaries; instead, he noticed that the same thing that had happened at Lizzie B's was beginning to happen at Bobby Joe's: James kept getting into fights with customers, even picking on them as if to goad them into a rumble. Soon the customers began to stay away from the place. In February, Bob fired James. James took a new job as a security guard, at least on paper: his business address was Mickie's house.

That there was a gigantic disconnect between her fantasy of James and the reality of living with him should have been apparent to Mickie; the fact that it wasn't stands as proof of the way the dependent psychopathic personality functions: the capacity to hold onto an illusion, to force perceptions to conform to some external image.

In Mickie's mind, James was going to be "Daddy," the head of the household, presiding over dinner at the head of the table, Pa Walton offering grace even while he dealt meth-amphetamines for a living. Nor was that all.

James made frequent trips to Reno or Lake Tahoe to gam-ble; frequently he would lose everything he had, or had been able to siphon off Mickie. He'd call and tell her to wire him some more money. Mickie did it.

Within a month of his taking up residence with Mickie and the kids, James began bringing his girlfriends home. Mickie rationalized this by telling herself that since she loved James, she had to make him happy, and if bringing girl-friends home made "Daddy" happy, who was she to object? She tried to tell herself that if she gave James enough space, eventually he'd get tired of bringing them around.

But when it came to Lizzie, it was a different story. James seemed obsessed with her: what she was doing, who she was seeing. All Mickie could see was that James loved Lizzie more than her.

As the spring of 1997 went on, James became ever more abusive toward Mickie, occasionally beating her, locking her in his room, leaving for days on end without telling her where he was going. Mickie's new life estranged her from Lamont, Rowena and Millie. Normally close to her family, Mickie was now largely cut off from her traditional sources of support.

And it wasn't just love that tied Mickie to James, what-ever she believed. By now Mickie was using methampheta-mines regularly alongside him. It began as an effort to keep her weight down, but soon developed into a full-blown ad-diction. She began to lose weight rapidly, as the chemical suppressed her appetite, even as it robbed her of her inde-pendence.

Money grew tight; without Bert Rand's financial support,

and with James an unreliable source of income, Mickie fell behind on the payments for the forest green Dodge Caravan.

Soon there was another roommate for the menagerie at Mickie's house: a friend of James' who was also heavily involved in the crank trade. As James and the friend continued to deal methamphetamine, traffic into and out of the house increased; that caused some of the neighbors to complain that Mickie's house was a drug outlet.

Sometime in April, the Sacramento police made a visit, looking for James' friend. James and Mickie were in a basement room that James used as an office, and immediately came upstairs to see what the police wanted. The cops took James' friend away because there was a warrant for his arrest.

The Sacramento officer now ran James' name through the computer, but it appeared that there were no wants or warrants out for him. Then the officer asked to look in the office. James told the officer that he'd need a search warrant to do that. Then he reversed himself, and said the room belonged to his friend. The officer soon discovered a stash of methamphetamine and a nine-millimeter pistol. James denied that it was his gun.

The officer now wanted to take James downtown to police headquarters, but Mickie intervened. She said that if anybody needed to go downtown, it was her, not James. The officer asked if Mickie was saying that the drugs and the gun belonged to her. Mickie said she wasn't saying that, but if the police were going to arrest James, she *would* say that.

A few weeks later, the police returned, apparently concerned by his sex registrant status, and his proximity to the crank and the kids. This time they told James that he needed to move. He decided to move back in with Lizzie.

But the cops were not the only ones to serve an eviction notice: Mickie's landlady, a longtime friend, told her that if she couldn't pay the rent anymore, she'd have to move out.

Mickie held a gigantic yard sale. Sold was the large-screen television that Sgt. Rand had bought; gone was the living room furniture. After the sale, Mickie gave all the money to James, who immediately left for Lake Tahoe with Lizzie, where he gambled it all away, and had to hock a gold ring to get out of town.

Mickie spent the rest of July moving out of the house she had lived in for almost seven years, stashing clothes and other belongings at various places around Sacramento, including a storage locker. Her plan was to send the kids to live with her father and mother; whatever else one might say about Mickie's family, they were loyal, through and through. Mickie thought she would live by herself for a while in motels, and investigated some possible jobs in massage parlors.

August 4 was eviction day; by then James had returned from Tahoe with Lizzie, and was at Lizzie's house, along with Brittany, Joanie, and Joanie's young boyfriend. It appears that James was giving the kids crank.

Sometime in the middle of August, Lizzie went to Fresno to attend the funeral of a family member. When she got back, she said later, she noticed that James was acting strange. Then Lizzie learned that while she'd been in Fresno, someone had broken into the Devil's Horsemen Motorcycle Club clubhouse and made off with the club's safe, which held somewhere between $1,500 and $40,000, depending on who was talking. The members of the gang were furious.

It didn't take Lizzie long to suspect that the burglary had been committed by James. James denied it. A fight ensued, with James blackening Lizzie's eyes and leaving various bruises and choke marks around her neck. After the fight, James began paging Mickie to come pick him up; his motorcycle had a flat front tire and was unrideable.

Mickie got the page and tried to decide what to do. She didn't really want to answer it, but she was afraid James would get mad at her. "I knew if I didn't answer it I was gonna be in trouble," Mickie said later. So she got in her van and drove over to Lizzie's.

Lizzie had thrown all of James' belongings out on the front lawn. Mickie was greeted by Joanie and Brittany. Then, in Mickie's version, Lizzie attacked her, shoving her up against the van. James and the girls pulled Lizzie off. The girls threw their stuff in Mickie's van, and then she, James and the girls drove away, pulling James' Harley behind them on a trailer. Mickie took them to a motel on Stockton Boulevard in Sacramento. Lizzie got on the telephone with some of the Devil's Horsemen, and told them that Froggie had been the burglar.

That night, at the motel, James was raging about Lizzie. Mickie was planning to go, but James and the girls asked her to stay. Mickie agreed.

James told Mickie he was going to quit the Devil's Horsemen; then they were all going to move to Idaho to start a new life. Mickie began crying.

"What's the matter?" James asked her. "Didn't you think I would love you enough?"

"No," Mickie said. "I thought you were going back to her." But for that night, anyway, James stayed with Mickie and the girls, and they dreamed of their new life in Idaho.

The next morning, as Mickie put it later, the roof fell in.

That morning, James got up early and called his friend "Doc," one of the Horsemen. James said he was "turning in his patch," that is, quitting the club. In that case, Doc said, James would have to turn over his Harley. James didn't want to do it.

But a short time later, about ten of the Devil's Horsemen converged on the motel room, accusing Frog of having been the clubhouse burglar. Mickie tried to defend him.

"He didn't do this," she told the club members. One, Stick, told Mickie that she was wrong.

"Look, girl," Stick said, "you've given him the world, but he's a piece a shit, get away from him." But Mickie kept insisting that they were wrong, that it was Lizzie who'd taken the safe. Nobody paid any attention to her. The club members marched Froggie out into the parking lot. Mickie thought there was going to be a fight, but Frog didn't resist. Mickie was surprised because James had always sworn someone would have to kill him to get the Ball of Purple Thunder. But the members hitched up the trailer with the Harley on it and rode away.

Afterward, James was beside himself with rage. He cursed Lizzie, and said she had "betrayed" him. But the truth is, James was feeling what for most people would be unimaginable: the indescribable pain of being outcast by the outcasts themselves.

If there is such a thing as a "triggering event," as the researchers Ressler, Burgess and Douglas suggest, this was almost certainly it, for Froggie, anyway.

For James had lost more than just his motorcycle and his patch; gone too was his persona, his very definition of himself. Here was another rejection, the most bitter of all: the notion that all his friends, his brothers of the road, could turn on him was more than James could abide. In James' methamphetamine-addicted mind, his life was over; all that remained was a burgeoning rage—at Lizzie, at the Devil's Horsemen, at the world, for having treated him so unfairly. In James' mind, he was as good as dead—if not from violent retribution from the gang, then certainly in terms of everything that had made him what he was.

Did James really take the safe? At this point, so long after the fact, there's no way to know for sure. In a great many ways, it seems doubtful—primarily because of the tremendous psychological impact the accusation made on James. After all, here was a man who'd spent much of his entire life lying and burglarizing. Being accused of deceit was hardly a new experience for him. But James' extreme reaction to being cast out makes it seem as though, for once in his life, he had been falsely accused. But James' past credibility weighed against him, so that even his closest friends didn't believe him.

And there is a second reason to believe that James was innocent of the burglary: there was no evidence that James had any substantial sum of money in the theft's aftermath. While it's possible that James took every dime and gambled it away, the fact remains that in the aftermath of the fight with Lizzie, James appears to have been almost broke. And there is James' adamant insistence, even to himself, that the accusation was so *unfair*.

But the entire incident was significant not just because of its role in causing James' psyche to collapse in on itself, but also because of how it led to the final reduction of James' last remaining moral fiber. If his life was over, if he was as good as dead, James reasoned, why not go out in infamy? If he was believed to be so rotten, why not *be* rotten? If he was as good as dead, what was to stop him—from anything?

Now James' imagination began to run riot with fantasies of revenge, of robbery, of rape, of murder—whatever it took—to get even with everyone, to take whatever he wanted and to despoil anything anyone held dear.

For some time James had had a fascination with serial killers, especially the most notorious sex killers like Ted Bundy and Gerald Gallego, or the still-at-large Green River Killer, responsible for as many as 50 murders in the Pacific Northwest. Now that he was dead, what was to prevent James from being just as infamous? In the smoldering embers of James' mind, there was now nothing to hold him back.

He began to talk about going out in a blaze of notoriety, Mickie at his side, ever the faithful companion-wife-mother-whore. In James' mind, he and Mickie had become an outlaw couple, desperados on the run.

"He used to call me and him Bonnie and Clyde," Mickie recalled.

And what better place to reveal the new him than at a family reunion? It was almost like the scene out of the movie, when Warren Beatty and Faye Dunaway show up at Bonnie's mother's farm for a last visit before hitting the road to a life of unremitting crime: the day after the Horsemen took the Ball of Purple Thunder, James and Mickie drove to Manteca, just north of Modesto, for Donna Kerlan's 56th birthday.

Afterward, Jodie and her husband would still remember the day James and Mickie, accompanied by Brittany, Joanie and Joanie's young boyfriend, arrived for the family party.

The Kerlans had relocated to Manteca after having sold their house in Pleasanton some years before. It was the first time Jodie had seen her older brother in some time, and she was shocked at his appearance. The last time she had seen him, back when he had first taken up with Lizzie, James had long hair, neatly braided, and was both trim and well-groomed. "He'd cleaned up his image," Jodie said.

But now James looked ratty; it wasn't so much his clothing or his grooming that caught Jodie's attention, but his demeanor.

"Jimmy was angry, intense," Jodie recalled. He was also wired on crank. Even Jodie could see that. His piercing blue eyes were bright, and his mood was snappish. The girls unloaded boxes of stuff from the van and put them in the Kerlans' storage locker.

Later, James sat on the Kerlans' patio with Jodie, her husband and Tillie. He explained that he and Mickie were on the run from the Devil's Horsemen, that he'd been accused of taking the club's safe from the clubhouse. He was so wired Jodie began to get scared.

"You're talking like you've—" she began, but James interrupted her.

"You don't *know* what I've done," he snapped. It was as if James wanted to impress his sister with his notoriety. While they were talking, the sound of motorcycles came from the front of the house. James gave a start and rushed into the house to look through the curtains. A couple of James' friends had just arrived from Sacramento, bringing with them a gun and some more methamphetamine.

The next thing Jodie knew, Joanie and Brittany were in the bathroom. Jodie asked if they were using drugs.

"Why do you think they're in the bathroom?" James asked.

Later, at the end of the day, Jodie realized that James was carrying a gun, and that he seemed ready to explode.

"What is going on?" she asked.

"You know what I'm talking about," James said. He lifted his shirt to display the gun, a .38 snub-nosed revolver.

"What is that?" Jodie wanted to know.

"You never know when you've got to take care of things," James said.

James, Mickie, Joanie, her boyfriend and Brittany spent the next week or so moving around—up to Lake Tahoe, down to the Modesto area to Diane's or James' mother's, back to Sacramento, and over to Dublin, where Joanie lived with Astrid, her mother Arnelle and Arnelle's husband. James was increasingly paranoid: about the club members, who he was sure were hunting for them looking to kill him; about the van, which was on the repossession list because Mickie had failed to keep up the payments; about the police, because the van no longer had a valid registration, which meant they were fair game for any cop who noticed that the tags were expired.

Later Mickie was hazy on where they had been; she recalled staying with various friends, sleeping in the van, getting money and drugs from long-time acquaintances in the Sacramento area, including three of James' friends, Vickie, Fred and Clara. Clara was an older woman who Mickie believed was James' main "cooker," or mixer of methamphetamine, while Fred and Vickie were both dealers.

James was still rabid, still consumed with thoughts of revenge. His talk was filled with references to killing. At one point he took Mickie to an archery store, where Mickie wrote a bad check so James could buy a lethal crossbow—an "Avenger," as Mickie recalled the model name. At one point, James wrote a note to Diane, which he later left at the house of friends.

"I'm sorry it had to end like this," he wrote, telling Diane that his "last wishes" in life were to be buried with "our family." The note ended: "I miss you and the children already, please don't tell them lies at the funeral. I love you, please forgive me." The note was signed, "Your husband, James Anthony Daveggio."

And there was another note, which would eventually be recovered by the police from Mickie's notebook. Although it was unsigned and undated, it matched James' handwriting as well as his mood.

"There is a darkness that has surrounded me. I no longer know good from evil," the note began. James went on to make it clear that, in his mind, he was driven by a compulsion he did not understand, one that had to do with Mickie. "I watch my hand move yet it's not my hand, I see but not with my eyes, something inside me is alive, it has slowly been taking over my body, devouring my soul . . . I'm no longer strong enough to fight it off."

"When they took his bike he was never the same," Mickie said later. "We got guns, money through friends of mine . . . all he wanted to do was kill. That's all he talked about. Killing somebody, killing somebody, he wanted to kill somebody. At first he wanted to kill Big Dog [Big Bill], the [club] president, then it was Rick, Stick. Then it was Little Dog [Little Bill]. We went by Little Dog's house."

James fired a crossbow bolt at Little Bill's house, Mickie recalled. He shot a bolt at the clubhouse door with a note on it. He shot one at Big Bill's house. And he talked about shooting Lizzie. Once, after James had been gone overnight with the van, Mickie heard of another club member who'd taken a nighttime spill on his motorcycle and had broken his back. Mickie thought James might have been responsible. She checked the van to see if it had any damage.

Mickie and Froggie

James A. "Froggie" Daveggio and Michelle "Mickie" Michaud, awaiting justice at the Alameda County Courthouse. Daveggio and Michaud were accused of raping women—some barely in their teens—across three states, and of taking the life of 22-year-old Vanessa Lei Samson.
GREGORY URQUIAGA, *THE CONTRA COSTA TIMES.*

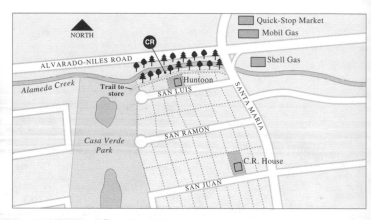

The Cassie Riley Murder

On September 25, 1974, 14-year-old Cassie Riley was found dead on the south bank of Alameda Creek in Union City, CA. Footprints found on the bank suggest that her killer may have been someone other than Marvin Mutch. Nevertheless, Mutch was convicted of the crime. Evidence that Cassie dated James Daveggio did not come out at Mutch's trial. MAP BY DAVID LINDROTH.

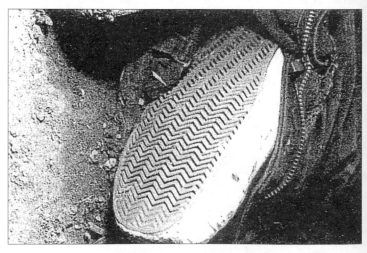

Cassie Riley's shoe, still on her foot, September 25, 1974. Note the tread pattern of wavy lines, typical of girls' Keds. ALAMEDA COUNTY SHERIFF'S DEPARTMENT.

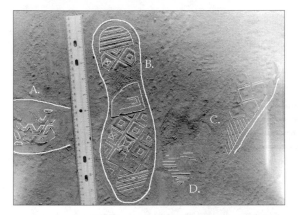

The four unknown shoeprints:

ABOVE: a) A partial print, differing from *b*, *c* or *d*, is well worn. b) A clear print of a relatively new shoe, identified by its tread as a Converse All Star basketball shoe. c) This partial print differs from *a* or *b*—the diagonal grooves are wider apart, the diamond treads are more worn: the center of the diamonds appear round, not pointed as in *b*. Likely an older Converse model. d) A portion of a tread not matching *a*, *b* or *c*.

BELOW: The newer Converse All Star print (*b*) on top of the Keds print (*cr*), evidence that the owner of the Converse All Star was present at the murder site at the same time or after Cassie Riley. Note the possible bicycle track on the lower right (*zz*). PHOTOS COURTESY ALAMEDA COUNTY SHERIFF'S DEPARTMENT. PHOTOS ENHANCED BY CARLTON SMITH.

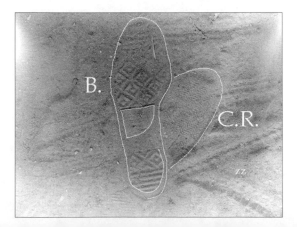

The Anatomy of a Hunt

The exterior of the van driven by Daveggio and Michaud.

The alleged makeshift torture chamber in the back of the van.
WASHOE COUNTY SHERIFF'S DEPARTMENT.

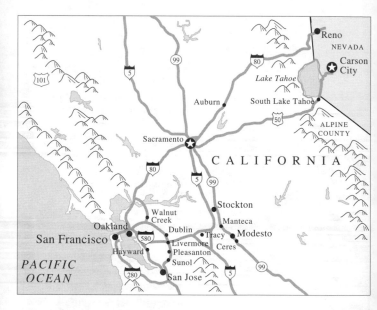

A map of central California and western Nevada, showing the locations of many of Daveggio and Michaud's crimes. MAP BY DAVID LINDROTH.

The Sundowner Motel, where Vanessa Samson was raped and tortured on December 2, 1997. PHOTO BY CARLTON SMITH.

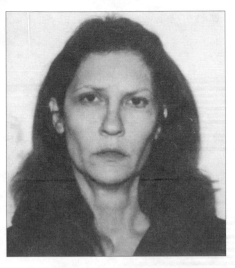

The Hunted

Michelle Michaud as she appeared when she was booked on a charge for writing bad checks in Douglas County, Nevada. DOUGLAS COUNTY SHERIFF'S DEPARTMENT.

The Lakeside Inn. Daveggio and Michaud checked into the Lakeside Inn on the evening of December 2, 1997, after allegedly killing Vanessa Samson in their Dodge van and disposing of her body over a cliff. FBI agents arrested them there the following day. PHOTO BY CARLTON SMITH.

The Douglas County Courthouse in South Lake Tahoe, directly across U.S. Highway 50 from the Lakeside Inn. Michaud had a previously scheduled court appearance on December 3. Two days later, while jailed here after her arrest, Michaud gave authorities a chilling account of her life with James Daveggio. PHOTO BY CARLTON SMITH.

Then, on September 11, 1997, they drove into Sacramento and broke into the house of Ted and Janet, a couple James had met at Bobby Joe's. Ted was visiting his daughter in Eureka, California; Janet wasn't there. Mickie forced the bathroom window and let James in the front door. They took showers and then James ordered Mickie to find him something to eat. Mickie made him a peanut butter and jelly sandwich and gave him a glass of milk. After watching television for a bit, James broke out some crank, and he and Mickie snorted it. Then James decided to break into several piggy banks Ted and Janet had around the house. He gave the money to Mickie and told her to buy some cigarettes and bring them and *Charlotte, a 12-year-old school friend of Renee's, back to Ted and Janet's house.

Mickie took the van and bought some cigarettes. She drove around awhile, then returned and told James she couldn't find Charlotte. James got mad at her, Mickie said, so she got back into the van and drove over to Charlotte's house, which was in her old neighborhood. Charlotte was Renee's closest friend; she considered Mickie almost a surrogate mother; she'd known Mickie since she was four. Nevertheless, Charlotte and Renee had previously consumed methamphetamine with Mickie and James.[33]

Mickie asked if Charlotte could run some errands with her. Charlotte said she could. Mickie drove back to Ted and Janet's with Charlotte. Charlotte had never been there before. Mickie asked Charlotte to come into the house. Once inside, she saw James. The three sat down at the dining room table, and James provided more methamphetamine to snort. Charlotte didn't want to use it, because she'd just weaned herself off the substance, but Mickie encouraged her. Charlotte relented, saying she would just do it this one last time.

After perhaps 15 minutes, Mickie told Charlotte she wanted to talk to her in the bathroom. Charlotte went into

---

[33] This summary of the events involving Charlotte, James and Mickie is taken from Mickie's extensive interviews with the FBI, and from interviews of Charlotte by the Sacramento police on Dec. 1, 1997.

the bathroom with Mickie. Mickie sat down on the toilet and told Charlotte to take off her shirt. Mickie told her that she'd been thinking of her a lot. She told Charlotte that she and Charlotte were going to "party" with James. Charlotte said she didn't want to. Mickie pulled a flat black .22 automatic from the back of her pants. Charlotte took off her shirt.

Charlotte told Mickie she was scared, and that she didn't want to do anything. Mickie told her she had to. Mickie made her take off the rest of her clothes. Mickie tried to convince Charlotte to fondle her breasts but Charlotte refused. Mickie opened the bathroom door and pushed Charlotte out into the living room.

James had his .38 revolver out. He said he'd thought he'd heard someone in the backyard. Apparently satisfied there was no one there, James pushed Charlotte into the bedroom. James forced Charlotte onto the bed, performed oral sex on her, and then raped her. As far as Charlotte could tell, James did not have an orgasm.

Afterward, Charlotte went into the bathroom. Mickie came after her. Mickie asked her if she knew what would happen to her if she told.

"Yeah," Charlotte said, "I'll be in trouble."

"Yeah," Mickie said. "I'll personally kill you if you tell." Charlotte put her clothes back on.

"Then we sat down," Charlotte said later, "and we watched tv. We all acted like nothing had happened. After an hour of watching tv, James took me in the bedroom and told me to play it cool, that he only did it because he liked me."

Mickie drove Charlotte home, and Charlotte didn't say anything to anyone—at least for a while.

Several days later, James, Janet and James' friend Vickie went to Eureka to meet with Ted, but not before James had sex with Vickie at Ted and Janet's house. For some reason, Mickie got angry at James for this; she said she later felt that Vickie had "betrayed" her. Mickie thought Vickie was trying to steal James away from her on the trip to Eureka. They were gone two days; James made Mickie get her sister Millie's boyfriend *Ralph to wire them $400 so that James could have some cash while he was in Eureka.

Mickie wasn't sure where she spent this time, but she was back at Janet's when Ted, Janet, James and Vickie returned later in the week. One day after they came back, Mickie had gone to get more cigarettes. When she came back, a young woman who was about three or four months pregnant was walking near the house, and asked for a ride. Mickie turned her down, but James struck up a conversation with her. He got in the van, and the three drove around for a while while James broke out the meth, and tried to get the young woman to take her clothes off. At first the young woman resisted, but eventually she gave in. Mickie drove the van into the mountains toward Lake Tahoe while James and the young woman had sex in the back. Later Mickie joined them. Afterward, Mickie gave the woman a ride to her home in Sacramento. The woman didn't seem very upset about what happened, Mickie said later; she gave Mickie her telephone number.

But after this, James grew more restless. He wanted to go back to Lake Tahoe and gamble, he said; so he and Mickie got into the van and drove into the mountains. There, on September 21, Mickie convinced the long-suffering Bert Rand to wire her $60. A few days later, she and James arrived in Reno, Nevada; this time Mickie called Bert and told him the van had broken down, and that she had no place to stay. Rand authorized Mickie to use his credit card at the Circus Circus hotel. Mickie and James checked into a mini-suite at the hotel, and proceeded to think of ways to get more money so that James could gamble. They would be in Reno five days, and when they left, they would be kidnappers.

It didn't take James long to lose the little money that he and Mickie had brought with them to Reno. They stayed in the living room of the mini-suite they had conned out of Bert Rand and watched movies while they tried to think of ways to get more cash. At least food wasn't a problem; they charged all their meals to the room that Bert Rand would have to pay for.

Soon they realized they could charge gifts purchased at the hotel gift shop to Bert's card, so they begin buying small pieces of jewelry, then pawning them for cash. James took this money and lost it as well.

Very early in the morning of September 27, at James' urging, Mickie went to see an old friend at the Cal-Neva casino sports bar: Charles Sanfilippo, formerly of Sacramento massage parlor ill-fame. Mickie told Sanfilippo that she and her boyfriend were staying at the Circus Circus hotel, but needed some money. She wanted to borrow some, but Sanfilippo said he didn't have any to lend. Mickie tried to sell him some gold earrings, but Sanfilippo wasn't interested.

To Sanfilippo, Mickie seemed wired; later he used the word "wild" to describe her demeanor to inquiring FBI agents. Sanfilippo said he warned Mickie about the dangers of walking around late at night by herself in downtown Reno. Mickie said Sanfilippo shouldn't worry, that she could take care of herself. Mickie boasted that a few years before, she had killed a man in Sacramento who had tried to strangle her. Mickie told him that she enjoyed killing the man.[34]

---

34 FBI 302, Interview with Charles Sanfilippo, Jan. 6, 1998.

Mickie asked Sanfilippo about the prospects of going to work at the Mustang Ranch, Joe Conforte's brothel operation outside Reno. Sanfilippo told her she'd need to get a work permit from the authorities, and that seemed to sour Mickie on the idea.

That was the extent of the conversation, according to the recollection Sanfilippo gave to the FBI. But Mickie contended there was more. She said that when Sanfilippo asked what she was up to recently, Mickie said she'd told him, " 'Charles, life has really changed.' I told him where we grabbed girls."[35]

"What'd he say?" Mickie was asked.

"He says, 'It looks like your life's a lot more exciting than mine is.' "

In retrospect, it's difficult to evaluate the veracity of this; on one hand, Mickie was telling the FBI that she'd told somebody in advance that she and James had embarked on a mission to "grab girls," and implied that there had been others before that time.[36] On the other, Sanfilippo never bothered to call anyone to warn that Mickie and James were "grabbing girls," and in his interview with the FBI never brought the subject up, although he confirmed virtually everything else Mickie had said about their conversation.

But whatever the truth of the matter, it wasn't very helpful to Mickie when she later claimed that she had no idea that James was going to kidnap anyone until it happened. The fact that the word "grab" came out of her own mouth gives it *some* weight, because it undercuts her own claim of unawareness. One can only wonder how different things might have been if this actually happened, and if Sanfilippo had made an anonymous call to the Reno police.

Meanwhile, the hotel was getting a bit antsy about all the charges Mickie and James were ringing up on Bert's card.

---

35 FBI interview with Michelle Michaud, Dec. 5, 1997.
36 Michaud told FBI interviewer Campion that while there had been girls before *Alicia Paredes, what she meant was the earlier encounter with Charlotte and the young woman who had been pregnant.

They wanted to know when Bert himself would show up to actually present the card for imprint. Bert drove up to Reno that afternoon from his house near Sacramento. Before he arrived, Mickie was with James and Sanfilippo in the Circus Circus suite. Just before Bert arrived, James and Sanfilippo left. Mickie didn't want Rand to know that she had James with her, and he never saw him, but Rand wasn't stupid: he could see from the bill that two people had checked into the room he was paying for.

Mickie and Bert had "an intimate moment," as Mickie termed it later to the FBI and in court; then she and Bert had dinner together. On the way out, Bert paid the hotel bill.

"And after that," Mickie said, "I walked him outside . . . He had his car parked across the street, and I watched him walk across the street, and then kept waving goodbye to him. And I felt so bad. I wanted to go with him, but I couldn't." Mickie said she'd talked to her mother earlier that day, and Rowena had told her that a strange car was parked near the house. Mickie thought it might be someone from the Devil's Horsemen; for some reason, Mickie seemed to think the bikers were after her as well as James.

The next night, after James had pawned a pair of opal earrings for $30 and thrown that money away as well, the hotel said that she and James would have to leave; apparently Bert had refused to allow any more charges on his credit card.

James was furious. He told Mickie to call Bert and convince him to let them stay at the hotel, but Mickie couldn't reach him. Mickie and James got back into the van and drove around downtown Reno for a while, eventually coming to rest in the parking lot of the Sands Hotel. There they spent the night in the van.

The next morning Mickie convinced her mother to wire them $75; James gambled this away, too. After this Mickie prevailed on Sanfilippo for a $20 "loan" for gas to get out of town. Sanfilippo knew he'd never see the money again, but by now he just wanted to see the backs of Mickie and James. Sanfilippo drove up to the Sands parking lot in his own car and handed the $20 through the window to Mickie while James watched. Mickie tried to tell him they'd pay him back, but Sanfilippo just waved them away.

After this, Mickie and James got back in the van, with James driving, according to Mickie. They drove around Reno for a while, aimlessly. At some point, she said later, she realized that James was looking for someone to kidnap. They drove past one woman James thought might fit the bill, but the woman got into a white truck and drove off before they could stop. James kept driving, burning up the gasoline that was supposed to get them out of town.

Shortly after 10 p.m. that night, *Alicia Paredes, a 20-year-old night student at a Reno business college, was waiting with several other students and a campus security guard near the college entrance in northwest Reno.

Alicia was four feet ten inches tall, and weighed about 120 pounds; she had long dark hair. Alicia had come to the United States with her parents from El Salvador when she was just a little girl. By day Alicia worked for a physician, and at night she attended the business college.

On this night, the 29th of September, the other students were picked up one by one, but Alicia's ride didn't appear. She knew that her boyfriend had gotten a flat tire on his car earlier that day, so she guessed that he wasn't going to make it. Alicia decided to walk home by herself. The security guard offered to make a telephone call for Alicia, but Alicia told her that her parents' home wasn't that far, and that she'd be all right.

Alicia began walking north on Washington Street, approaching the concrete bridge over Interstate 80 where it slices through north Reno, not far from the casinos. It wasn't unusual for prostitutes to use the area as a stroll, but Alicia had learned that as long as she walked with her head pointed forward and didn't make eye contact with the men who drove by in their cars, she would be all right.

As she neared the bridge she sensed a van passing her and going over the bridge. She had no way of knowing that once over the bridge, the van turned around and came back, passing her on the opposite side of the street. The next thing Alicia saw was a pair of headlights coming up behind her; she guessed that it was her boyfriend catching up with her. She glanced over her shoulder and realized it wasn't her boyfriend, but someone in a van. At almost the same instant the van jerked to a stop next to her, the side door slid open, and Alicia saw a "man with a big stomach" coming after her.

"What did I do? What did I do?" Alicia tried to say, but the man grabbed her by the hair and threw her to the ground. Then he picked her up and threw her in the van, into the left-side passenger seat behind the driver. The van door slammed, and Alicia was being held down by a man who was cursing at the driver and simultaneously telling her to shut up.

James shouted directions at Mickie to tell her how to get on the freeway, but Mickie made a wrong turn; this infuriated James, who was holding Alicia's head down in his lap. Finally Mickie made it to the onramp, and began driving the van westbound on Interstate 80. Once they were on the freeway, James told Alicia to take her clothes off. Alicia complied.

As the van made its way up the Truckee River canyon, James forced Alicia to fellate him; he began slapping her. He wanted to know if Alicia liked that; Alicia said no, she didn't. He stopped. James got on top of Alicia and forced her; while he was raping her, Alicia managed to grab some of Mickie's hair as she was driving, hoping to get her attention. Alicia thought that perhaps Mickie had been captured, too, and she wanted to establish some sort of contact with her so they could act together. But Mickie ignored her.

Soon they reached the California agricultural inspection station just west of the state line. James pulled Alicia down into his lap once more and covered her with blankets, but not before warning her that he would kill her if she raised an alarm. It took less than a minute to get through the agricultural check. Once they were past, James told her she'd been "a good girl," then resumed his attack on Alicia. Finally he was finished, leaving his ejaculate on Alicia's face and hair. Then he allowed Alicia to put her clothes back on.

By now the van was reaching the pass over the Sierras. Alicia had tried to remain calm throughout the ordeal. Now that the man had finished, however, she began casting about for ways to get out of this alive. She tried to act like she hadn't minded James' attack. She thought the best thing to do was talk to James, both to distract him and to see if she could learn anything about him. If she did live, she knew that any information she could provide might help authorities catch him.

"Am I going to be okay?" she asked.

"Yeah," said James, "you're going to be fine."

Alicia wanted to know if they were going to bring her back to Reno. She said she had to go to work the next day.

"What time?" James asked.

"Eight."

"We have plenty of time," James said.

James wanted to have sex with Alicia again, but Alicia said she was too tired. James seemed to accept this.

James told Alicia that he and the woman driving the van were going to Oregon. Alicia asked if they were going to take her to Oregon, too. James said no.

By this time the van was heading down the Sierra slope toward the foothills. James was smoking a Benson & Hedges cigarette; Mickie had a tape in the cassette player. Johnny Cash's voice sang "Folsom Prison Blues," and James sang along with the lines about a man shooting someone in Reno, and watching him die.

Alicia was now afraid James was going to kill her. She asked if James had ever held a gun.

"Sometimes," James said, "but I've never done what he does."

Alicia asked the man if he was from Reno; James said no, he wasn't, but that he lived in Nevada. He used to be a truck driver, James said, but he no longer worked.

"Now I just do what I want to do," he said.

Mickie told James he was talking too much. She turned her ire on Alicia.

"You're asking too many questions," Mickie snapped, from the driver's seat.

Alicia said she wouldn't ask any more questions. "I don't want to get in trouble," she said.

Mickie asked Alicia if she had any children. Alicia was inspired to lie.

Yes, she said, she had a baby, nine months old.

"What's his name?"

Alicia borrowed a name from one of her relatives. She said her baby and her family would miss her if she didn't come back.

"Won't you let me go?" she asked. "I won't tell." But James wouldn't say anything.

There was a brief discussion between James and Mickie, in which James called Mickie by name. James wanted to know if Mickie was ready to "do what we talked about, the plan." Mickie wasn't sure.

"Are you going to let me go?" Alicia asked.

"Well, it's dangerous," James said, "first of all because we kidnapped you."

"I wasn't hurt," Alicia said. "I won't tell."

"I'm not taking you back to Reno," James said. "You can, you might do something stupid."

"Oh no," Alicia said. "That's fine. You can drop me over here [on the highway]. That's fine, that's fine." She just wanted to get out of the van as soon as possible. In her mind, the man seemed ready to let her go, but the woman called Mickie seemed more reluctant. And there was the talk about "the plan," which made Alicia think that her kidnappers had already discussed murdering her.

"So, Mickie," James said, "what do you think?"

"Let me think about it," Mickie said. A few minutes later, Mickie pulled the van off the freeway on an offramp. She drove across the freeway by way of an overpass. They passed a darkened tractor-trailer rig. Mickie found a dark road and went down it to its dead end. She stopped the van and told Alicia to get out. James got out of the van first.

"I'll drive," he told Mickie.

Mickie looked at Alicia.

"Next time," Mickie said, "don't walk by yourself, or you're going to find people who aren't as nice as we are."

Mickie told Alicia to turn away from the van and count to 20. "I'll be watching you," she said. Mickie got in the van. Alicia started counting. When she finished, the van was gone.

Alicia began walking back up the darkened road toward the freeway. Near the overpass, a car with two men and a woman came by. Alicia got their attention. They gave her a ride to a nearby service station, where Alicia called 911. Within a few minutes, a Placer County sheriff's patrol car arrived. Alicia explained what had happened to her. The deputies notified their department's sexual assault response team, and began driving Alicia to the hospital. When they neared the place where Mickie had turned off the freeway, Alicia grew excited, and explained that this might have been the place where the kidnappers had let her go.

Deputy Sheriff Don Murchison and his partner Jeff Adams followed the darkened road. Alicia was positive that this was the place where she'd been released.

Adams and Murchison inspected the scene with their flashlights. They found a plastic comb, which they collected for evidence, and noticed a long indentation mark from a tire. They took several photographs of the indentation and the general area, then took Alicia to the hospital in Auburn, California. By now Alicia was shaking; the trauma of the ordeal was finally catching up with her.

At the hospital, Alicia met Detective Desiree Carrington of the Placer County Sheriff's Department sexual assault detail. Carrington, a diminutive, dark-haired woman with a calm demeanor, had been a detective for Placer County for about three years, most of that time in the sex crimes detail. She was both meticulous and methodical in preparing her cases. She talked to Alicia briefly before Alicia was examined by a nurse who was trained in treating victims of sexual assaults.

By now, Alicia was thoroughly frightened; she broke into sobs several times while telling her story. The nurse noted numerous scratch marks and bruises. She took samples of material from Alicia's face and hair that later tested positive for semen.

Afterward, Detective Carrington conducted a longer interview with Alicia; Alicia cried throughout the interview.

Alicia described the kidnappers: a woman with dark hair, and a heavy-set man who was unshaven, and who possibly had a mustache, and who smoked a long, white, thin cigarette. He had an earring in his ear, Alicia said; the man had told her it was a horse. He was wearing a buttoned red or purple cowboy shirt, jeans and shoes with heavy black soles. His voice was lighter than the woman's, whose voice was very low. Alicia said she'd asked the man if he was from Reno; the man said he wasn't. Alicia had noticed a rosary hanging from the van's rear-view mirror. Alicia was worried that her parents didn't know where she was.

At about 3:20 Carrington called the Reno Police Department to tell them that a kidnapping had occurred in their jurisdiction, and that the victim was in Auburn. A Reno police officer told her that a car would be sent to Alicia's parents' house to let them know what had happened. A while later the Reno police called Carrington back; Alicia's parents were shocked to discover that she wasn't home in bed sleeping. They were now on their way over the mountains to Auburn to pick her up.

The next morning, Carrington and her partner, Detective Bill Summers, drove up to Reno from Auburn to meet with their Reno police counterparts. That afternoon, she and Summers met with Alicia at her parents' house to put together a composite drawing of the face of the kidnapper. No one was satisfied with the result, especially Alicia. By now Alicia was much calmer, but was discovering areas of injury she hadn't noticed the night before when in the hospital. They went to the Reno Police Department, where Alicia gave another taped interview, and this time an artist was able to prepare a sketch that was a bit better, in Alicia's eyes. This time the kidnapper had a definite mustache.

Once the sketch was completed, Carrington transmitted it to her office back in Auburn so it could be disseminated to other police agencies. A press release showing the composite was also sent out to newspapers and television stations in the hope that someone might recognize the kidnapper and call in. After this, Carrington called the Federal Bureau of Investigation and talked to Special Agent in Charge Jerry Hill. The fact that the kidnappers had taken Alicia across a state line made it a federal case.

After leaving Alicia off on the dead-end road near Auburn, James had driven straight to his ex-wife Diane's house near Modesto. According to Mickie, they arrived in the early morning hours of September 30. James went inside, leaving Mickie to sleep in the van.

All the way to Diane's, James was worried. According to Mickie, he now had second thoughts about letting Alicia go. He was sure that Alicia would tell, and that she probably knew enough to identify him. He was sure that if he was arrested, Alicia would be able to identify him by his distinctive voice.

Mickie told him to calm down. As far as she could tell, James had had his shirt on the entire time; the main thing any victim would notice, she said, would be James' tattoos. "How could you not notice those?" she said later. James seemed to be mollified.

The next day, Mickie drove the van into Sacramento with Brittany so the girl could get some money from her uncle to help pay Diane's rent; Diane was having a tough time making ends meet. James also wanted her to find out what was going on with the Devil's Horsemen.

After spending another day at Diane's, Mickie drove into Sacramento once again, and this time visited Clara, James' supposed "cooker." Clara had clipped an article from the newspaper that told of the Reno kidnapping and rape. The article said that the female driver of the van had been called "Mickie," and included the composite drawing. Clara made it clear to Mickie that she believed James and Mickie had been the kidnappers.

Mickie returned to Diane's and showed the clipping to James. James was furious. He decided that they needed to disguise themselves. He put a silver stripe on the van, shaved his entire head, and told Mickie to start wearing her long hair inside a baseball cap. He began calling her "Dude" and insisted that she call him "Butch." James was paranoid that the police would find them at Diane's, so he insisted that they return to Sacramento. He was again talking about killing Lizzie.

In Sacramento, he and Mickie checked into a cut-rate motel. While James was out, Mickie called her sister Millie and asked her to come over to take her to the storage locker; Millie came and saw that Mickie had a gun. Mickie told her that she needed the gun, because the Devil's Horsemen were after them. After Millie helped her pick up some warm clothing from the storage locker, Mickie told her sister that she and James were going to Oregon to start a new life. Mickie said James wanted the van cleared out so they'd have more room.

After this, Mickie and James drove to Dublin to visit Joanie and Astrid. James removed the two middle seats from the van and put them in Arnelle's shed. Then he and Mickie headed back to Sacramento, and Ted and Janet's house.

At some point during this first week of October—it was after the middle seats had been removed from the van, but before James had ditched the rear bench seat, Mickie could remember that much—James and Mickie ran out of meth. They had checked into a motel in south Sacramento. James told Mickie to see a friend of theirs who dealt crank to replenish their supply. James remembered that Mickie's friend with the crank was also friends with a young woman, *Aggie. He told Mickie that as long as she was getting a new supply of meth, she might as well try to get Aggie, as well.

"So he gave me instructions on how to get her," Mickie said later. "He always wanted to make sure that nobody knew any of them left with me . . . and I always made sure somebody knew. He was always telling me I wasn't doing it right. Well, no, I wasn't."

Mickie went to see her friend with the crank, and Aggie happened to be at the friend's house. Aggie seemed glad to see Mickie; she hugged her and began telling her of her recent troubles, just like the good friend she thought Mickie was.

Mickie backed away and told Aggie not to hug her anymore. Mickie told Aggie that she was exciting her and that she wanted to kiss her. Aggie backed away.

"You're trying to scare me, aren't you?" Aggie asked.

"Don't I scare you when I say that?" Mickie asked.

"No," Aggie said, "you don't scare me."

Mickie shook her head. "Aggie," she said, "I've become something so dark, so ugly, you don't know." But Aggie wouldn't believe her.

After a while Mickie left and returned to James at the motel. James was mad at her for not returning with Aggie, Mickie said later. This time James concocted a plan: Mickie would go get Aggie and bring her into the motel room. James would hide himself behind the curtain in the shower. Once Aggie was in the room, Mickie was supposed to call out the word "Butch," and then James would spring out from behind the shower curtain and attack Aggie from behind.

Mickie returned to her friend's house, and Aggie was still there. After smoking some more methamphetamine and talking with her friends, Mickie asked Aggie if she'd come with her, that she wanted to talk to her. Aggie agreed to go with Mickie.

Mickie led her into the motel room, just as James had planned. He was hiding behind the shower curtain. The lights were off. Aggie and Mickie sat down on the bed and talked. Still Mickie refused to say the word "Butch." Just as Mickie put her head on Aggie's lap James emerged from behind the shower curtain and jumped on Aggie from behind. Aggie screamed. James held her down while Mickie retrieved a pair of handcuffs from under a towel on a nearby table.

"So anyway," Mickie remembered, "he's holding her down. She's face down on the bed and she's like, 'What the hell is going on, what's happening?' He's telling her to shut up and whispering in her ear, 'I'll kill you if you scream,' and all this other stuff . . ."

Mickie tried to handcuff Aggie, but was only able to fit one of the bracelets on. James was shouting at Mickie, telling her she didn't know how to do anything right. He put a blindfold on Aggie, told Mickie to duct-tape Aggie's mouth. Mickie taped Aggie's mouth shut, and told her she had to cooperate or she'd be killed. James asked Mickie if anyone had seen Aggie leave, and Mickie told him yes, and apologized, but said there was no other way, too many people had been around.

Mickie realized that James had hit Aggie in the mouth; blood was running from a cut, and the duct tape wouldn't stick.

"All of a sudden I saw the blood, and it freaked me out for a minute," Mickie said. She stood up; James grabbed her to calm her down. Then he got a wet washcloth and tried to wipe away the blood, but Aggie kept bleeding. James cut off Aggie's clothes, and told Mickie to take them off. Mickie sat on Aggie's back while James forced Aggie to fellate him, even though her mouth was still bleeding. Mickie was holding her head, telling her what to do to "Daddy." Finally James got behind Aggie and sodomized her.

"Then it was over," Mickie said, "and he laid down beside her and got very compassionate, very concerned with her mouth and . . . talking to me like I was a piece of shit, it was my fault, and I needed to get dressed and go get some ice and bring it back for her. It was all my fault that this had happened."

Several days later, Mickie drove the van over to see her mother Rowena, where Renee was staying, along with Mickie's son Rusty. Rowena told Mickie that it wasn't too late, she could ditch James and come back to live with them. But Mickie said it *was* too late, and that she didn't want to bring any more of the mess that was her life into her parents' house. She drove away, crying.

Mickie may have thought that she was leaving Renee and

Rusty in a less risky environment, but that wasn't the way it worked out. Renee had learned that James and Mickie were going to Oregon to see if they wanted to move there; she wanted to come too. But Lamont and Rowena didn't want her to go. Somehow the 12-year-old Renee convinced two of James' friends, Vickie and Larry, to pick her up at her grandparents' house and bring her to Ted and Janet's. Mickie was angry, but Renee was insistent about coming along.

That afternoon, Mickie, James and Renee began driving to Oregon. On the way, Mickie told Renee that she and James had to get out of the state because the police were looking for them; Mickie told her daughter about the Reno kidnapping and rape.

On the road, Renee fell asleep in the rear of the van; she awakened to find James in the back with her, rubbing her leg. Renee moved his hand away, but James replaced it and continued. James tried to put his hand down her jeans. Renee got up and moved to the front of the van, where Mickie was driving. James followed her and started rubbing her shoulders.

After a bit they stopped at a supermarket, and Renee told Mickie what James was doing. Mickie assured her that she would make James stop. But once they began driving again, Mickie began to tell Renee about her "secret lusts," and one of them was Mickie's desire to have sex with her.

Mickie told Renee that she and James had had three adventures: the first one, she said, was Charlotte; the second was something that Renee's later interviewer couldn't quite make out; the third was the Reno rape. The fourth was going to be Mickie's letch for Renee. James was touching Renee, Mickie said, because Mickie wanted him to.

When it got dark, Mickie pulled off the freeway and went onto a dirt road. James flipped the lever on the front seat that Renee was sitting in so she was horizontal. Mickie jumped on top of her daughter while James held her down by her shoulders. Mickie undid Renee's pants. James began to perform oral sex on her. Renee protested, calling Mickie "Mommy," but Mickie told her not to call her that.

This went on for perhaps 30 minutes, and when it was over, Renee crawled to the rear of the van and fell asleep, crying. When she woke up, they had stopped at a motel in Klamath Falls, Oregon; James carried her into the room while Mickie brought her flannel pajamas.

In the morning Renee awoke to find her mother lying next to her. Mickie asked Renee if it was all right if James had sex with her; Renee said no, it wasn't all right. Then next thing she knew, Mickie started rubbing her face, and James pulled the blankets off of her and produced strips of duct tape. James taped her mouth shut, and then taped her hands behind her back while holding her down. James performed oral sex on Renee again; he stopped when Mickie told him to.

By now Renee was in a panic. Mickie removed the duct tape, leaving a reddened area on Renee's face. Mickie tried to calm her down, but Renee didn't want to talk to her.

James now gave Renee a rock of meth. Renee knew how to smoke it. She taught her mother how to do it. Mickie was amazed.

Later that day, they drove to an Indian casino where James gambled some more; afterward, they returned to the motel, where James shaved his head again. By now, Renee just wanted to go home. James wasn't so sure that was a good idea; he was worried that Renee would tell. Mickie got the impression that James wanted to kill Renee, and possibly her. Then she decided that James was only trying to scare her. Somehow Mickie convinced him that they had to go back. They went back to Sacramento the next day.

When they got to Sacramento, they drove to Charlotte's house. For some reason they now decided to go to Santa Cruz. Mickie asked Charlotte if she wanted to go with Renee, James and Mickie to Santa Cruz, and Charlotte agreed. Charlotte asked Renee about the mark on her face, and Renee told her what had happened. Then Charlotte told Renee what had happened to her, and that Mickie had threatened her with a gun. That night the four of them spent the night in the van;

according to Charlotte and Renee, James kept trying to touch Charlotte, but Renee told him to stop.

The next day they arrived in Santa Cruz. By now they were almost broke again; Mickie went to the local welfare office to see if she couldn't get some assistance there. Mickie told the welfare workers that she and her boyfriend James were homeless, and that they were living in a van, along with Mickie's two children. The welfare office qualified them for welfare, and issued a voucher for a motel room. Meanwhile, Mickie had the two girls begin calling people they knew to see if someone would wire money to them. At one point, James called his sister Jodie; Jodie sent him $50.

The next two nights, James and Mickie stayed in the van with Renee and Charlotte. Again James tried to make advances, and again Renee told him to back off. The following day they drove back to Sacramento; James fired off the gun in the mountains on the way back to show how loud it was.

Once back in Sacramento, Mickie dropped James off at a mall. James said he was on his way to kill Lizzie with his gun. Mickie told him to be careful. After that, Mickie dropped Charlotte at her house, then took Renee back to Lamont and Rowena's.

Now began a blank period in the lives of Froggie and Mickie, blank primarily because Mickie later couldn't remember much about it, and by the time she was talking, James wasn't saying anything at all. It appears, however, that Mickie wrote a number of bad checks around the Sacramento area, including one for a $300 portable television set for use in the van that was promptly pawned for $100. Mickie and James slept in the van, or at various friends' houses. The plan to move to Oregon seems to have been put on hold for some reason.

Near the first of November, it appears that Mickie and possibly James drove back to Santa Cruz, where Mickie picked up a welfare check, and notified the office there that she would be moving back to Sacramento. Paperwork transferring her case to Sacramento County was initiated. Then it appears that Mickie and James went to the Pleasanton area to see Joanie and Astrid.

By this time, 17-year-old Joanie was pregnant; James learned that he was going to be a grandfather at the age of 37. Mickie thought James seemed pleased with the news.

Meanwhile, both Mickie and James continued to use methamphetamine—"like other people drink water," as Mickie put it later. On the night of November 3, she and James found themselves in the van outside a Dublin laser-tag amusement center, where *Sidney, one of Joanie and Astrid's friends, worked. It appears that James and Mickie had given or sold Sidney crank to use on earlier occasions, because when they arrived in the van at the laser-tag place, they asked Sidney if she wanted to partake.[37]

Sidney agreed to do a few lines, and when her work break came, she went out to the parking lot. Sidney got in the back of the van with Mickie. As she was bending over the mirror, attempting to snort the drug, Mickie clobbered her from behind.

Sidney let out an exclamation, then tried to elbow Mickie. James came over from the front seat and punched Sidney in the head. The next thing She knew, she had a pair of handcuffs on her, and Mickie was driving the van. James was yelling at Mickie that she had picked a bad place to stop. Mickie was yelling back at James. Then she got on the freeway and started driving eastbound, into the hills just outside of Livermore.

While they were driving, James took off the handcuffs; Sidney was complaining that they hurt her wrists. She said she wouldn't resist.

"I was concerned about my life at that point," she said later.

James made Sidney fellate him. He wasn't happy.

"Act like you enjoy it," he told her.

At that point, Sidney stopped and said she couldn't because it reminded her of her step-father.

That remark seemed to take the starch out of James.

"I think he didn't like that," Sidney said later, "because he wanted somebody who didn't get hurt like that before, so he didn't continue."

With a consummate, probably unconscious sense of James' psychology, Sidney had touched on the one thing that was likely to ruin James' fantasy; it was one thing to make believe that he was with a young girl who was eager and willing, and another thing entirely to be told that he was old

---

[37] This account of the events of Sidney's abduction and rape come from Sidney's testimony before the Alameda County Grand Jury, November 4, 1998, in Alameda County Superior Court case #134147AB, and from Michelle Michaud's interviews with the FBI on December 5, 6 and 8, 1997.

enough to be her father, who should presumably know better.

Mickie brought the van to a halt somewhere in the hills outside Livermore. James was still mad at her, telling her that she'd gotten them lost. At that point, Mickie got out of the van and got into the back. She attempted to perform oral sex on Sidney while James masturbated. When that was over, they took two photographs of Sidney without her clothes, and told her if she told anyone they'd send the pictures around to Sidney's friends.

Mickie and James tried to decide what to do with Sidney; it was obvious they couldn't simply drop her off at the laser-tag place because by now she would have been missed. Sidney began to be afraid they would kill her.

At length, Sidney convinced them that she would lie about what happened. As Sidney put it later, she was Joanie's friend; she didn't want Joanie's father to wind up in jail, especially now that Joanie was pregnant. They drove back into Dublin, and let Sidney out at a service station. Sidney called her boss to come and get her. By then, the boss had reported her missing to the Alameda County sheriff's office, which policed Dublin. When she later told her story to the police, Sidney said that she had been abducted by three young men. The police took the report, but even Sidney could see they didn't entirely believe her. A few days later, Sidney's boss fired her; he didn't believe her at all.

The same night they abducted Sidney, James and Mickie drove back to Sacramento. This time they stopped at Mickie's sister Millie's place, and asked to stay there for a few days. Reluctantly, Millie agreed.

Millie's boyfriend, Ralph, wasn't happy to see either Mickie or James, but most especially James. As far as Ralph could see, James had been nothing but bad news for Mickie ever since she'd met him; in Ralph's view, Mickie had undergone a drastic personality change since the beginning of her relationship with James. Sometimes, in fact, Ralph thought Mickie suffered from multiple personality disorder.

As for James, Ralph saw him as another bigmouth who tried to convince everyone he was tough.

"He liked people to think he was a bad ass," was the way Ralph put it later. Back when James was still a member of the Devil's Horsemen, he liked to flaunt his membership in the gang in front of Ralph, suggesting that the club was a secretive, almost mystic order, and that the members were engaged in ominous business that was too important to be mentioned to the uninitiated like Ralph.

Both James and Mickie were wired on crank when they got to Millie's. Mickie was talking crazy. At one point she boasted of having been a "hit lady" for the Hell's Angels, and talked of a murdered bail bondsman named Leo who had been killed some 15 years before; Mickie said she'd gotten into Leo's house, and then had opened the doors so the bikers could come inside and shoot him, execution-style. She'd also once attended a lynching in a rural county south of Sacramento, Mickie told Ralph. Ralph thought Mickie was just running her mouth, but with Mickie, who knew? So Mickie and James settled in at Millie's for a few days.

Later, Ralph was to tell the FBI[38] that the James he knew was fascinated by serial killers. While James and Mickie were visiting Millie this time, in early November, they watched a broadcast of *The Silence of the Lambs* on television with him. In Ralph's recollection, James had said that he thought serial killers were both very smart and very interesting. James went on to say that he'd been reading about serial killers like Ted Bundy and the Green River killer. James was particularly interested in the Gerald Gallego murder case, Ralph recalled.

The Gallego murders were among the Sacramento area's most notorious; stripped to their essentials, Gerald Gallego and his wife Charlene Gallego had abducted and murdered ten people, mostly young women, in the late 1970s in the Sacramento/Sierra Nevada area. Gerald Gallego was said to be driven by a perverse desire to possess his victims as "sex

---

38 FBI 302, interview with Ralph, Dec. 5, 1997.

slaves," and was assisted in his depredations by his wife, Charlene.

After the Gallegos were arrested (for ironic symmetry, Placer County Detective Carrington's partner, Bill Summers, had helped arrest them), Charlene had testified against him. Gerald was given the death penalty; Charlene was sentenced to serve a term in a Nevada state prison in Carson City. As it happened, for yet more irony, Charlene had been released from prison in August of 1997, just about the time James and Mickie had taken to calling themselves Bonnie and Clyde, and James had begun to think of raping and killing his way to notoriety.

In any event, James had read several books about the Gallegos; to Ralph, James seemed extremely interested in them. He told Ralph that he thought the Gallegos had made a "great team." James told Ralph details about the Gallegos' reign of death. Ralph was repulsed.

"You're a sick motherfucker," he told James.

A few days later, Lamont heard from Millie that James and Mickie were staying at her house. By now Lamont had heard from Renee about the trip to Klamath Falls, despite Mickie's threats. He called James on the telephone and told him he was a child molester. He told Millie to kick them out, and Millie did. It was the day after Mickie's 39th birthday.

After leaving Millie's, James and Mickie drove to Lake Tahoe, arriving that night. There they checked into the Horizon Hotel and Casino, where Mickie wrote a check for lodging. The next night, Mickie wrote another check for $200, and gave the money to James for gambling. A few hours later, Mickie tried to write another $200 check; this time the cashier asked her to wait while he verified that the account had funds. Since the account hadn't had money in it for months, Mickie was nailed.

The hotel's security people soon surrounded Mickie, and she was taken to the security office. She tried to be cool; she said she'd be happy to clear the matter up with the officials.

The security people made another call to the bank, but were given the same information—the account had been closed for more than a month. Mickie expressed surprise that the account was no longer active. She claimed it was all news to her. It turned out that Mickie had also paid a second night's lodging with another rubber check. She told the hotel officials that her boyfriend, James Daveggio, was asleep in the hotel room.

At that point the hotel security people called the Douglas County, Nevada, Sheriff's Department. The Douglas County department had jurisdiction for all the crime committed on the Nevada side of the line in Lake Tahoe, including the hotels and casinos in Stateline, Nevada. The Sheriff's Department dispatched a deputy to take Mickie into custody on a charge of defrauding an innkeeper.

In the meantime, James must have seen what was happening; by the time the security people opened the door to the hotel room, it had been cleaned out of luggage and other personal effects, and James was nowhere to be found.

The Douglas County sheriff arrived, and took possession of the four checks that Mickie had written, and Mickie herself. She was booked into the Douglas County jail that same night, November 9, 1997. Although this was her first overnight stay in jail in her life, it was a place Mickie would—in the very imminent future—get quite used to.

While Mickie languished in jail, James drove the van back to Sacramento. For the first night, James parked in a south Sacramento mall's parking lot; during the night he removed the van's rear bench seat and threw it out in the parking lot so he would have more room to stretch out.

The next day James went to see his friend Clara. Clara contacted a bail bondsman she knew, and arranged for him to bail Mickie out of the Douglas County jail. James headed back up the mountain to Lake Tahoe with two friends of Clara's; it appears he dropped them off someplace in between Sacramento and Tahoe, because James headed for Tahoe by himself. At one point that afternoon, James found himself alone in the van, parked by the side of the road. A school bus came by, and a young girl perhaps ten or twelve years old got off, and began walking by herself. Later Mickie would claim that James became obsessed with kidnapping the schoolgirl; in Mickie's mind—and in fact, this entire event may have been *only* in Mickie's mind—James called the little girl 238, for the time the school bus stopped.

But nothing happened, and James finally arrived back at Lake Tahoe late in the afternoon; it appears that Mickie was released on her bail around 1:30 p.m. James didn't show up to get her until late that afternoon, and it was cold.

The next day, Mickie and James were back in Sacramento, where they picked up a $500 Western Union money order from Rowena; Mickie had called her mother from the jail and asked for help. Rowena in turn had called Bert Rand; the ever-loyal Rand coughed up over $500 to send to Rowena to pay for the money order. Mickie thought the money would be used for restitution on the bad checks she had written; instead James took it for himself to gamble with.

They apparently drove back to Lake Tahoe so Mickie could make a court appearance on November 12; James gave her $40 to make a down payment on the $389 in restitution she owed for the checks. After this they returned to Sacramento, and that was where things were to turn completely weird.

Later, it wasn't possible to sort out exactly what had happened; Mickie tried to explain to the FBI in her interviews, and she may in fact have done so at one point, but if she did, it wasn't on tape.

Briefly, however, it appears that some sort of falling out took place among the meth-cooking and -dealing pals Mickie and James had been hanging out with for the last few months. The way Mickie told it—in her maddening, non-chronological way—suspicion blew up between Fred and Vickie. Fred seemed to think that Vickie was some sort of police plant.

At one point, either while Mickie was in jail or just after, Fred claimed that he had been robbed and his tires had been slashed. He blamed Vickie and her friends. Fred and his friends went looking for Vickie and hers, and apparently caught up with one or more of them near Bobby Joe's. Shots were exchanged and, while it doesn't appear that anyone was hit, feelings were running high.

Into this tornado of suspicions and paranoia came Mickie and James on November 12 or so. There was some discussion about getting rid of some of the guns used in the shootout, and the .38 snubnose that James had been packing went into the pistol laundry, along with, apparently, the black .22 automatic Mickie had been carrying. In return, it appears, James picked up a silver-plated .25-caliber automatic.

Over the next several days there was a great deal of driving around, as the bad blood built up on both sides. At one point, after the shooting near Bobby Joe's, the Sacramento Sheriff's Department was out in force along Stockton Boul-

evard, stopping people in older white cars that were similar
to the model that Clara usually drove.

Clara apparently was furious with Vickie; she seemed to
blame Vickie for the robbery of Fred, and the slashing of his
tires. James sided with Clara. According to Mickie, he offered to kill Vickie and her daughter Nikki for $2,000.

James and Mickie drove to Vickie's house to stake it out.
Early in the morning Vickie returned, along with her boyfriend, followed almost immediately by her daughter Nikki.
While they waited for Vickie and Nikki to arrive, Mickie
said later, James contented himself with describing all the
things he was going to do to Nikki after he'd killed her
mother.

In retrospect, all this talk about stalking and shooting
seems to have largely been fueled by the methamphetamine
everyone was using, which, as noted, has the effect of ratch-
eting up a user's paranoia and aggression to dangerous levels; when the people using the drugs also have guns, just
about anything can happen, whether intended or not.

In any event, Mickie and James followed Nikki to a car
wash; James told Mickie how to park the van so he could
reach out and grab Nikki and yank her into the van. But
Mickie and James were in turn followed by Vickie and her
boyfriend, and they never had a chance to grab Nikki, Mickie
said later.

Frustrated, James and Mickie drove around that evening;
they noticed that the police cars were all still very much in
evidence. But if one believes Mickie's story, James decided
to grab another girl that night.

After cruising around for a while in south Sacramento,
James spotted a young black woman who was walking down
the street; Mickie thought she was a hooker. James got in
the back of the van. Mickie pulled up next to the woman
and rolled down the window. Mickie said it was her boyfriend's birthday, and he wanted to have sex with two women
at the same time. Was the woman open for business?

The woman agreed to a deal, and got in the passenger seat
of the van. Mickie pulled forward, and just then James leaped

up from the rear of the van and released the reclining front passenger seat. He tried to immobilize the woman, but she was much too fast and aggressive for him. Scratching him, she managed to elude James and open the van door. By then Mickie was speeding away. The woman leaped out of the van and escaped, falling on the pavement.

James was furious with Mickie. He told her to get away from the area, because the police would soon be all over them if they waited around. He made Mickie drive back to Clara's. That night, Mickie said later, James beat her fearfully in the van. The next day, James wanted to trade the van to Clara for different transportation; James thought the van would be too hot. But apparently Clara didn't want the van; and by this time, she wasn't too sure she wanted James around, either. It was only later that Clara discovered that either James or Mickie had robbed her of a small black metal box containing a stash of methamphetamine.

Within a day or two, James and Mickie got back in the van, and started for the Pleasanton/Dublin area. The plan was to spend Thanksgiving with Joanie and Astrid, then make the long-awaited trip to Oregon.

But while James and Mickie were driving to Pleasanton, the police in Sacramento were getting their first inkling that something bad had been going on between James, Mickie, Renee and Charlotte.

By this time the rumors about James and Mickie's rape and molestation of Charlotte and Renee had spread throughout Mickie's old neighborhood. It was only a matter of time before Charlotte's father heard the story—or at least a version of the story, one that had James molesting Charlotte in the van while they had been in Santa Cruz. Enraged, Charlotte's father called the Santa Cruz police to complain about James.

The police in Santa Cruz took a report from Charlotte's father over the telephone around 9 p.m. on November 18. The Santa Cruz officer then interviewed Charlotte over the telephone. Charlotte told of the events in Santa Cruz, and said that Mickie's boyfriend James had tried to touch her and her friend, Mickie's daughter Renee.

Then Charlotte told the Santa Cruz officer that before the trip to Santa Cruz, Mickie had threatened her with a gun and had forced her to take off her clothes, after which James had raped her in a house in Sacramento. Charlotte was quite clear about who the suspects were: Michelle Michaud, her friend's mother, and Michelle's boyfriend, "James Deveggio" (sic). Charlotte described them in detail, mentioning James' dis-

tinctive tattoos, and even providing the license plate number
for Mickie's green minivan. Charlotte said both Mickie and
James were armed, and that she believed they'd been involved in other crimes.

With this information in hand, the Santa Cruz officer contacted the Sacramento Police Department. Just before 10 p.m.
on November 18, a Sacramento patrolman named Twilling
went to Charlotte's father's house to find out what all this
was about. At the house, Officer Twilling interviewed both
Charlotte and Renee, who was staying with her temporarily.
The two girls described their experiences with James and
Mickie. Then Renee told Twilling that James and her mother
were wanted by the police for a rape in Reno, Nevada.

It would be nice to be able to say that, armed with this information, Officer Twilling would have been able to rush
back to the precinct house and put out an all-points bulletin
for Michelle Michaud and James Daveggio. If he had, a great
deal of tragedy might have been averted.

But that's not the way police work works; rather, what
happened here is more typical of what actually takes place.[39]

Like most other bureaucracies, police departments have a
chain of command; and they also have specialists. And while
Twilling was apparently quite willing to believe Charlotte
and Renee that James Daveggio and Michelle Michaud had
been up to no good, he wasn't responsible for investigating
the case.

That chore fell to a sex crimes detective, one Pete Willover.

Willover received a copy of Twilling's report on the
morning of Thursday, November 20, 1997; it was the same
day James and Mickie were checking into a motel in the
Pleasanton area.

Willover began his investigation by running records

39 Information here about the Sacramento police investigation of Michelle
Michaud and James Daveggio comes from documents submitted as part of
Sacramento Police Department case #97-921.

checks on James, Mickie, Charlotte and Renee. Willover discovered that James was listed in the Sacramento department's files, and that he was a registered sex offender; James had last registered his address on September 4, 1997. If Willover had immediately checked the address to see if James was home, he would have discovered that Mickie had been evicted more than a month before James' registration date, a sure sign that James was lying about his whereabouts, which in turn was an ominous indicator for any registered sex offender. But there is no record in Willover's log that he checked out the address.

Willover found that Mickie also had an arrest record, from her massage parlor bust in 1991.

Charlotte, too, was in the files: she had been listed as a missing juvenile on August 11, 1997, and as a victim of a lewd act upon a child on July 9, 1997. Willover noted that the lewd act had taken place at Mickie's house. (The lewd act was perpetrated by a teenage boy, unrelated to either Mickie or James, who was eventually placed in juvenile custody.)

Like Charlotte, Renee had also been listed as a missing person, this time in a report filed on September 6, 1997; and she was mentioned in another report taken by the department on January 16, 1997, apparently as a witness.

But it appears that Renee and Charlotte's history of going missing was seen by Willover for what it almost certainly was: two teenaged girls running away from home. And while Willover was thorough in his investigation over the next ten days, it's difficult to avoid the conclusion that he was less than enthusiastic in pursuing it; he got the names mixed up in his initial report, and certainly he was substantially less than speedy at a time when speed might have made all the difference.

The day he received the case, Willover apparently felt Twilling's own work had left something to be desired. He called Patrolman Twilling and grilled him about the information that he had taken from Charlotte and Renee, again confusing their names, and getting Renee mixed up with

Michelle. Willover seemed more concerned with who had legal custody of Renee. Willover questioned Twilling as if he was a suspect himself.

"When asked where Michelle's [sic] mother and the mother's boyfriend were, he [Twilling] stated that they're 'apparently floating around Sacramento because they're wanted by the police in Reno, and possibly for bad checks.' "

Willover told Twilling to go find Renee and arrest her to put her into protective custody until the legal responsibility for her well-being could be straightened out.

Twilling agreed to do that, but told Willover that while he'd been interviewing Charlotte and Renee, Mickie had called to talk to Renee. Renee told him that she'd told Mickie that the police were now asking questions about the rape and molestation of Charlotte and herself. Mickie hung up on her, Renee reported, apparently afraid that the police were taping the call. Renee told Twilling that she thought James and Mickie had fled the state.

The following day, November 21, 1997, the arrested Renee was brought to a Sacramento County social services agency for an interview. The interview was videotaped, and attended by an assistant district attorney, two social workers, and Willover. Willover later summarized the interview.

Renee described the trip to Klamath Falls, and what had happened. She also told of Charlotte's experience with Mickie and James, at least as Charlotte had described it to her. Renee readily admitted to using crank with James and Mickie, and said that James had given it to both her and Charlotte. She'd also done crank with Sidney, Renee said, when she'd gone to visit Joanie. Renee was asked for Sidney's address, but Renee said she'd moved.

When Renee was asked where Mickie was, she provided Fred's name, and an approximate location of Fred's house.

When she was asked whether James and Mickie had done anything like this to anyone else, Renee said she'd heard that they had, to another Sacramento girl. Renee couldn't remember her name; it appears she may have been referring to Aggie, because by now her brother Rusty had heard from

Aggie about the assault in the motel room in early October.

"They also admitted," Renee continued, "about the girl who was on the news who was raped in Reno. This happened right before they came and got me [for the trip to Oregon]. They said they were in the Nevada. They admitted this to me. Charlotte saw it on the news and said that James looked just like the sketch. They said it was a dark green Dodge Caravan."

It's difficult to know what Willover or the Sacramento County assistant district attorney, Ross Huggins, were thinking of when they heard this information on November 21.[40] That Willover and Huggins had probable cause to ask for warrants to arrest James and Mickie after this interview seems beyond dispute.

On the surface of it, they had just heard a witness tell them that not only had James and Mickie committed sexual assault upon—and given illegal drugs to—two 12-year-old girls, but also that they were involved in a crime that had been reported on the news.

It couldn't have been terribly difficult to check the back issues of the newspaper to see if it had printed any information on what Renee was talking about, about a man–woman team of kidnapper/rapists; if it had been on television, it had probably also been in the newspaper. After all, the police department itself should have received the all-points bulletin that had been disseminated by Placer County's Desiree Carrington after Alicia Paredes was kidnapped. In any case, there could not have been very many man–woman kidnap/rape teams operating out of Reno, Nevada.

True, no one seemed to be able to say exactly where

---

40 When contacted by the author, and asked for particulars about what he did with this information, Willover said only, "This sounds like an interview," and terminated the conversation. Significantly, the portion of Officer Twilling's November 20 report recounting the Reno rape allegation—later faxed to the various law enforcement agencies investigating James and Mickie after their arrest—was blacked out.

James and Mickie were *now*, on November 21, but that
wasn't a major problem, either. It would have been simple
to issue a want for Mickie's Dodge minivan. The authorities
had the plate number, and if they had checked, they would
have discovered that it was unregistered.

If the Sacramento police had issued an alert for the van,
they might have enlisted the eyes of the California Highway
Patrol and other law enforcement agencies in a search for it
and its occupants. With all the driving around that James and
Mickie were doing, it's entirely conceivable that a random
check by some patrol officer might have netted them before
they did any more damage.

And finally, Willover and Huggins knew that James was
a registered sex offender; they might have checked with the
state Department of Justice's criminal information index, to
say nothing of its highly computerized (and expensive) Violent Crime Information Network and discovered that James
had ties to the Pleasanton/Dublin area in the form of two ex-
wives and three children who lived there, not to mention the
fact that he'd grown up in the area, and had a documented
criminal history there. With the Thanksgiving holiday approaching, it would have been a logical step to ask the Pleas-
anton/Dublin authorities to drop by Arnelle's house to see if
anyone knew where James and Mickie were. If they had,
they almost certainly would have been able to arrest James
and Mickie based on the information that was then in Willover and Huggins' possession. After all, Arnelle and the
girls knew exactly where James and Mickie were.

Unfortunately, none of these things were done. Instead,
based on Willover's subsequent report, it appears that he
took the weekend off—at least insofar as Daveggio and Michaud were concerned.

The following Monday, November 24, Willover went to see
Lamont; he was still trying to figure out who had legal custody of Renee. Lamont told him that Mickie had given written permission to Renee's boyfriend's mother to have

custody of her. Lamont said Mickie's son was still with him and Rowena.

Lamont said that he and Rowena had seen Mickie on November 18, when she'd come by to pick up some things. At that time, Lamont said, he and Rowena had confronted Mickie about the molestation of Rachel and the rape of Charlotte; Mickie told them the girls were lying. Willover gave Lamont his telephone number, and asked him to have Mickie call the police if she showed up again.

An hour later, Willover was back in his office. He called the Reno Police Department and asked a sexual assault detective there, Rebecca Clark, whether they had any reports of rapes that involved man-and-woman suspects with a dark green minivan. Clark told Willover that she didn't know of any, but would check with her supervisor to make sure.

Next Willover called the Washoe County, Nevada, Sheriff's Department, which had jurisdiction in the area surrounding Reno, and received substantially the same information. The time was just before 11 a.m.

Willover's investigative log doesn't indicate where he was for the rest of the day; it does note that Detective Clark of the Reno Police Department called him back and left a message indicating that the Placer County Sheriff's Department had a case that sounded similar to what Willover had asked about, and giving Placer County Detective Bill Summers as the person to be contacted.

By early the next morning, November 25, Willover had picked up the message that Detective Clark had left on his voice mail. He called Summers in Auburn, and left a voice mail message telling him briefly about Mickie and James, and asking him to call back. Willover did not hear from Summers at all that day.

The next day, November 26, the day before Thanksgiving, Willover received a fax from Summers; it was a copy of Carrington's all-points bulletin. The sketch of Alicia's kidnapper strongly resembled James. Willover called Summers and said it looked to him like they might be seeking the same couple. Summers agreed to meet Willover at Willover's office at noon.

Willover's information must have excited Summers, because Summers came down the freeway from Auburn to Sacramento 45 minutes ahead of schedule. In Willover's office, the two detectives discussed their respective cases; both men thought it was likely that James and Mickie had been responsible for Alicia's kidnapping. When he left, Summers took photographs of James and Mickie to show to Alicia up in Reno that afternoon. For some reason, that did not happen; and still, despite the mounting evidence that James and Mickie were on some sort of crime rampage, no wants or warrants were issued for either one, and no one bothered to contact the Pleasanton/Dublin authorities. It would turn out to be a fatal oversight.

While Willover was waiting to hear back from Summers on Tuesday, November 25, James and Mickie checked into a motel not far from the interchange between I-680 and I-580 in Pleasanton. They seemed to be quarreling with one another, at least judging by Mickie's later recollection. By now both had been consuming methamphetamine for days; James was acting "twitchy," as Mickie later described it, both belligerent and assaultive. He cursed Mickie and called her a whore in front of Joanie and Astrid, and then took the girls to play miniature golf. Mickie stayed at the motel to write a letter to herself that she imagined giving to James:[41]

Why?

I am so confused and so scared. I'm not sure of anything when it concerns us any more. When you talk to me these days it seems like you are belittling me, making jokes about my ignorance . . . the other night in front of Arnelle, I still don't understand why you were putting me down like you were . . . Then to come up those stairs and say the things you did and punch me and twist my arm behind my back . . .

I feel that I'm walking on eggshells around you, if I say or do something it's going to anger you or set you off again. You've never put your hands on me in

---

41 The letter was among the personal effects recovered by Pleasanton police at Arnelle's house; subsequently, the materials seized from Arnelle's were turned over to the FBI pursuant to a search warrant executed in March of 1998 by the Bureau.

an abusive manner, and now that you have I wonder
when it will happen again . . .

Mickie reminded James of her past with Jose, and said
she just couldn't stand to be battered and brutalized again,
no matter how much she loved James.

We have been through so much together, already. I
know you're so frustrated and angry and feeling help-
less right now and your dignity and pride are starting
to wear thin . . . just hang in there a while longer
things will start to come together . . .

Now Mickie wrote that she was touched when James told
her he loved her, and held her hand. She was glad James had
taken her around to show her all the places that had been
meaningful in his life, including the houses he had grown up
in, and

even where your sweet and beautiful friend Cassie was
so cruelly and horribly taken. I know you live with a
lot of guilt behind that, and I wish I knew how to take
that pain away for you, but I can't and all I can do is lis-
ten and be there, and I feel so special and trusted by
you to have you share that deep pain with me . . .

The following day, November 26, even as Willover and
Summers were finally comparing notes, James was on his
way by himself to see a friend in Santa Cruz. He left early
in the afternoon after bringing Joanie and Astrid to the motel
to stay with Mickie. He wouldn't say where he was going,
only that he would probably be gone all night; Mickie
guessed that he was going to be with another woman. Astrid's girlfriend, *Chloe, also came over to the motel. The
inevitable methamphetamine was produced, and everybody
smoked.

Later there would be four different versions of what happened in the motel room: Mickie's, in which she and the

girls watched movies on television and generally acted like the Waltons; Joanie's and Astrid's, who both said that Mickie was acting depressed and weird, and that she had organized a role-playing game in which the girls had to pretend they were on trial for stabbing someone "71 times"; and Chloe's, who apparently took a bad trip on the methamphetamine. Chloe became paranoid under the influence of the drug; she imagined that Mickie and the girls were plotting against her, and saying bad things about her.

While Chloe was wrong about the specifics, she probably picked up some sort of ominous vibe from Mickie. By now, Mickie's weight had dropped so drastically, and her complexion was so waxy, she looked positively witch-like; she could have doubled for Morticia on *The Addams Family*, rather than Ma Walton.

As evening came on, Chloe got more and more freaked out; she wanted to leave. Mickie and the girls tried to talk her into staying, saying she might get hurt, and that James would be mad at her if that happened; but Chloe suddenly had the idea that she was about to be kidnapped. James had gone, but Chloe now believed that James was actually lurking around outside, waiting to kidnap, rape and kill her.

As she twitched along on the drug, Chloe decided to try to get home despite her fears. She left the motel and made her way to a nearby all-night restaurant, where she called someone to come and get her. Suddenly, everyone in the restaurant looked to Chloe as if they were in on the plot; people with beards became bikers; a van in front of the restaurant was where James was hiding. Eventually Chloe's ride came, and she was able to get home; still, she was sure James had been stalking her.

James returned to the motel the following morning, Thanksgiving Day; he and Mickie went over to Arnelle's to have dinner with Arnelle's husband, Joanie, Astrid, and Arnelle's children by her second husband. James was still mad at Mickie, for some reason. Mickie resumed writing her letter:

*Oh boy—well, you did come back and early in the
morning this time. But now of all of a sudden there is
a change you've decided that needs to come about, and
this change of course is all about what you believe the
solution to the problem is. So if I don't like this or I
don't like that or if I don't do this or I don't do that,
then fuck me, I can just get out, hit the road, you don't
really give a fuck . . .*

Mickie, angry that James had stayed away all night with
another woman, reiterated that she felt humiliated when
James had belittled her in front of Arnelle, and then later had
hit her.

*I can't live like that. At first all I wanted to do is get
as far away from you as possible, but I'm glad it didn't
turn out that way. I guess I'll never really get the
chance to tell you how I feel or what I'm really thinking, because I couldn't make you understand anyway.
So I guess it will be just enough that I love you, and
that's that. Happy Thanksgiving James—I will always
love you more.*

M.

James and Mickie ate Thanksgiving dinner with Arnelle. The
way Mickie remembered it, James practically bolted the
food. Afterward, he wanted to take Astrid back to the motel
with them so he could take her to the Department of Motor
Vehicles in the morning to get her first driver's license. But
as it turned out, they would never make it.

That night in the motel room James and Astrid had a long conversation as Mickie listened in. Later, Astrid was to recount much of what was said, both to Pleasanton police, and also before the Alameda County Grand Jury.[42]

James, Astrid and Mickie watched movies on the motel television. But then James began talking.

"He started talking to me like, really weird," Astrid told the Grand Jury later. "He was asking me if I ever killed anyone. And he told me that I would never know if I'd like killing someone unless I had tried. And he asked me if I wanted to go on a hunting with him."

"Did he tell you what that meant?" Astrid was asked.

"Yeah," she said, "it's when you go and you stalk someone to kill."

"Had he ever talked to you like this before?"

"No," said Astrid. "He was starting to scare me."

"Were you familiar with the kinds of books he liked to read?"

"Serial murder books, serial killer books?"

"Okay. So he's talking to you about not knowing what it will feel like to go on a hunting. What else was going on during that conversation?"

"He just kept like talking like, really weird. He wasn't going to tell me if he killed anyone, but he told me like his perfect plan was to rob an armored truck and like—he was asking me all these weird questions, and like—"

_____

42 Pleasanton Police Department, case #97-7609; Report of the Alameda County Grand Jury, case #134147AB.

"What other questions, can you recall, that he asked you?"

"He asked me that if he ever killed someone, would I hide him out."

"What did you tell him?"

"I told him that I didn't know, it depended on the situation. And then he asked me—he asked me, like, if I liked to torture people, and why."

"And what did you tell him?"

"I told him that I had never tortured anyone, but most people like to torture people, like, to watch the fear in their eyes."

"What did he say to that?"

"He liked that. That's what made him start talking to me."

"How do you know he liked that? What did he say?"

"He told me that's the reason why he thought it would be cool to torture people."

"To see the fear in their eyes?"

"Yeah."

"Why don't you keep going? Tell us what happened after that."

"Then, like my dad went to take a shower, and Michelle and I were talking, and she told me that—that he was going to have sex with me."

Astrid began crying as she told this story to the Grand Jury.

"And I didn't know what to do," Astrid continued. "I was all—I didn't believe her at first, just because he's supposed to be my father, he's supposed to love me."

According to Astrid, and Mickie later, James emerged from the bathroom and indicated that he wanted to have sex with his daughter. He sent Mickie into the bathroom by herself. Astrid told James that she didn't want to, but there was no point in her resisting, because James would just do what he wanted to anyway.

James forced her onto the bed and began performing oral sex on Astrid, while penetrating her with his finger. To Astrid it seemed to go on forever—at least an hour, by her later estimate. She lay there, rigid, wishing she was anyplace else. Finally James called to Mickie to come out of the bathroom. He told her to fellate him, and finally it was over.

But there was actually more to this story than what the Grand Jury was told; as it turned out, Astrid told the police—a week after James and Mickie were finally arrested—that James had molested her no fewer than five times over the previous several years: at Diane's house when she was ten or eleven years old, at Lizzie's, and at Mickie's before Mickie was evicted.

She'd first gone to live with Mickie in January of 1997, a few months after James had moved in with her, Astrid told the police; and she'd stayed with Mickie and her father for about three months. James and Mickie rarely slept together, Astrid said; and Mickie was depressed because, while her father kept saying he loved Mickie, he never acted like it. He was often gone for several days at a time. But still, Astrid added, Mickie took good care of the children.

"She was like, the mom role model," Astrid said. "She like took care of us, fed us all, took us all to school. Made sure we had lunch money every day and like . . . Dad was kind of doing whatever. Never saw him. That's one of the reasons I moved back [to Pleasanton]."

Astrid was asked if she knew anything about her father's childhood.

"I know he killed someone when he was thirteen," she said.

"He did? How do you know that?" a Pleasanton Police investigator asked.

"Because he told me. He believed he killed him. He was . . . they were playing with guns when they were thirteen and he shot at a train and a train driver fell down. And like, he'd been hit."

"And where was this? Where was he, when he was thirteen?"

"Uh, he was around a lot when they were kids. Not really a lot, but he was in a . . . they lived somewhere before they lived in Pleasanton."

"And when did he tell you he killed someone when he was thirteen, or thought he did?"

"On Thursday night," Astrid said, the night her father had asked her if she wanted to go on a hunting, and kill someone.

Astrid's police interviewer, Elizabeth Flores, was clearly startled by this information, and Astrid's assertion that her father had wanted to take her on a "hunting."

"Okay," said Flores. "And what is a 'hunting'?"

"It's where you like go out and you look at people and you decide which one you want to kill," Astrid said. "Or who you want killed."

"And do you think he was serious—"

"Yeah."

"—about this, or just—"

"Yeah," said Astrid. "Michelle told me . . . Michelle wanted me to go too." Mickie had said it was a good day to go out and look for someone to kill because everyone was out shopping on the day after Thanksgiving, Astrid added.

After a few more questions, Flores asked Astrid whether her father had said anything else that Astrid thought was weird that night. Some of the conversation was hard to follow because of Astrid's use of the word "like" as a comparitor, a verb and a punctuator.

"That night," Astrid said, "he kept telling me like, there was something about . . . We were talking about torturing people. And he asked me why I would want to torture somebody. And I told him the thrill, or not exactly thrill, but to watch the fear in their eyes. And he like . . ."

"Asked you why?"

"Yeah," Astrid said. "Asked me why I would want to torture somebody. And I told him, 'To watch the fear in their eyes.' Like, he said that, him too, like . . . and like how people who kill people, they have no remorse. They have no regrets. They wouldn't change nothing, you know?

"Like . . . they don't feel guilt. And like, his eyes, he doesn't show emotions through his eyes. Like a lot of people do.

"And he said something about like, serial killers, and like people that like murderers and stuff."

Her father told her he was like a serial killer, Astrid said.

That he was a serial killer? asked the astonished Flores.

Not that he was one, but that he was *like* one, Astrid said.

"That he was *like* a serial killer. 'Cause, like, about the emotions through his eyes. Like he doesn't show feelings through his eyes and he always has the same look on his face and he like, used the example of a janitor who killed like a hundred people or whatever. At the school. And people would see him every day, and they'd like, the occasional smile, and hi to people. And nobody ever knew it, you know?

"And he was talking about that. Like he doesn't show any emotions through his eyes. He doesn't show pain or nothing like that."

And then James asked Astrid: if he ever killed anybody, would she still consider him her father? And Astrid said she would.

Astrid may have told her father what James wanted to hear, but inside, her emotions were roiling. After James had fallen asleep, she wrote her feelings down on stationery from the motel:

> *Life is getting a little too crazy. The family situation is going to take me a little while to get used to it . . . life is a bumpy road, but I feel that everything and anything [will] get worse until I die.*
>
> *Tonight, the only thing that would have made me happy was if I died so he would realize he doesn't love me or I wish I had a gun so I could shoot him in the head and let him know that his love made me feel like that. I am definitely not afraid or scared of him because I know now that if I had a gun and he was in front of me, I would pull the trigger without any hesitation.*
>
> *I have never felt so unprotected in my life. Him and the man who beat me while I was his child [a reference to Astrid's step-father, with whom she had feuded] are*

people I loved and giving their love to me was by hurting me. Both of them caused the exact same amount of pain and they must not have cared because both of them continue to hurt me. My hatred for those two men is still growing and it will never stop.

In the morning, James took Astrid to the DMV, as he had promised. But the office was closed for the holiday. He dropped her off at Arnelle's, then went to see his former brother-in-law, Joe Carter. Joe was selling Christmas trees in Dublin. According to Mickie, James and Joe were thinking of taking some methamphetamine up to Oregon to sell, because the price was much higher there.

Astrid went to her boyfriend's house, where she told him about her father molesting her. She thought about running away from home. She spent all night with her boyfriend, talking with him, and most of Saturday.

On Friday night, after checking out of the motel, James and Mickie went back to Arnelle's, where they learned that Astrid hadn't come home. Arnelle and James stayed up much of the night worrying; the next day James went to see Astrid's boyfriend, but the boyfriend denied seeing Astrid. That night, Astrid decided to come home, and James got mad at her for staying with her boyfriend all night. Several days later, Astrid would tell her mother and Joanie that her father had molested her, but neither would believe her.

James and Mickie stayed at Arnelle's another night; on the following day, Sunday, November 30, they went to a discount department store in Hayward. There Mickie on James' instructions, bought a flashlight, a man's shirt, and two curling irons. When they got back in the van, James used a razor to cut the electric cords from the curling irons. After this they returned to Arnelle's, unloaded some of the stuff in the van—including Mickie's notebook/diary, with its newspaper clipping about the Reno kidnapping—and then

went to another motel to spend the night. According to Astrid, James wanted to stay in a motel because he couldn't
stand the bickering that went on between Arnelle and her
husband, who was also using crank.

The next day, James and Mickie returned to Arnelle's
house, looking for Astrid and Joanie; apparently they wanted
to take them to Sacramento to help Mickie transfer her welfare case there. But Astrid was back at her boyfriend's, and
no one seemed to know where Joanie was, so James and
Mickie left.

James and Mickie now went to the area around Foothill
High School in Pleasanton, which James had attended before
being expelled in the late 1970s. As Mickie put it later, James
"hated that school, because they took his football career away
from him."

James was driving. He parked near the school, and told
Mickie they were going to watch the high school girls as
they left after school.

"He was just sitting there smoking," Mickie said later. He
watched a number of girls, telling Mickie which ones he
preferred. "He's kind of fantasizing or whatever." Mickie
was getting nervous that James was going to try to grab one
of the girls right there in broad daylight. But after a while,
James started the van and drove around the neighborhood,
telling Mickie to pay attention to how the streets were laid
out. He was "tweaking" on methamphetamine, Mickie said.

James now put the van on the freeway and drove to Livermore, the town just to the east that had once been the
nemesis of Marvin Mutch. James took them to "Naughty But
Nice," a store that sold videotapes and sex paraphernalia.
There a counter clerk—a student who would hold the job for
less than a few weeks—saw them come into the store and
go to an area of the store that sold, in the clerk's later words,
"extreme items . . . handcuffs, gagging devices . . . dildoes,
stuff like that."

Mickie and James didn't know it, but the store's security
camera caught them on tape. James bought a green ball with
straps on it; it was a gagging device.

"Do you actually remember that sale?" the clerk was asked later.

"Yes, sir, I do," he said. " 'Cause in the short time that I was there that's the only gagging device I ever sold."

Mickie was doing all the talking. She asked the clerk about Pleasanton, while handing over the money for the gagging device. At that moment James spotted an audio cassette titled "Submissive Young Girls." He picked it off the rack and threw it on the counter, indicating to Mickie that she should buy that as well.

Mickie and James got back in the van. James unwrapped the gag. "He put it in his mouth," Mickie said later, "and tested it out and screamed into it . . . and he says, 'Oh, yeah, I like this, this works.' "

It was just after 6 p.m. on December 1, 1997.

While James and Mickie were driving around Pleasanton, watching high school girls and buying "extreme items" at the Livermore sex shop, Placer County Detectives Carrington and Summers were in Reno.

Late that morning, December 1, Carrington and Summers met with Alicia Paredes and the FBI's Lynn Ferrin, the agent who had been assigned the kidnapping case for the Bureau.

Alicia looked at a photo lineup and picked James as the man who had kidnapped her.

"This one," Alicia said. "It looks like this one." But Alicia wasn't able to identify Mickie; in fact, she picked someone else as the person most like the woman who had been driving the van.

Summers and Carrington now returned to Reno. The next day, just after 11 a.m., December 2, Carrington obtained a warrant for the arrest of James Daveggio and Michelle Michaud. Unknown to her, according to her later testimony, the FBI's Ferrin also obtained a similar federal warrant for the arrest of James Daveggio.

But both warrants were too late to save the life of Vanessa Samson. By the time the warrants were issued, Vanessa had already been kidnapped and was living the last, horrifying day of her life.

VANESSA

After they returned to the Pleasanton motel from the Livermore sex shop, James and Mickie sat up most of the night, consuming methamphetamine.[43]

According to Mickie, James was obsessed with the idea of killing someone—anyone.

" 'Cause all he talked about," she said later, "was wanting to kill somebody. He wanted to kill somebody. He would take that gun and he'd sit there in that room, and he would tweak ["flash" on methamphetamine] and he would rub it, this is him rubbing the gun against his head, talking about who he's going to kill and how he wants to kill somebody, and he's just going like that. And I'd just sit there and watch him. That was toward the end when he started getting really edgy."

James laid out rail after rail of the meth, burning along. Finally, well after three in the morning, he fell asleep. He had told Mickie to be ready to go at six in the morning, but it was not until six-thirty that he woke Mickie up.

"So I figured we were going to be on the hunt," Mickie said. "He called it the hunt, or, our adventure."

Mickie was driving. She'd broken her glasses, and wasn't able to see very well. It was very foggy.

James was mad; he complained that Mickie was driving badly, that he had to tell her where to go, even after he'd

---

43 This version of the events of the abduction and subsequent murder of Vanessa Sampson was recounted by Mickie in interviews with the Federal Bureau of Investigation on December 5, 6, and 8, 1997.

shown her all the streets the day before. James was in the back of the van.

They passed some kids walking to school, and then hit a patch of particularly thick fog. James decided to stay in the fog, because it was good for concealment.

"And then he spots her," Mickie said later. "And we pass her."

Mickie drove the van past Vanessa, coming head on.

"She's walking fast, she's cold," Mickie said. "And she's got her backpack on and she's kind of like walking. And James liked her long hair and the fact that she was small."

James told Mickie to turn the van around.

"I says, 'What?' He says, 'I said fucking turn around, there's—that's the one right there.' And I said, 'Who?'

"And he said, 'The one with the pretty black hair, the small girl.' "

Mickie was trying to act like she didn't see her, she said later.

They turned around and passed Vanessa again, going in the opposite direction. James told Mickie to pull over and shut off the engine and wait for the girl to pass them.

Vanessa came closer.

James told Mickie to start the van.

The engine refused to turn over at first. Mickie looked up and saw a school bus-stop ahead.

Mickie heard the sliding door open.

Vanessa jumped back, startled. James grabbed her by the hair and Vanessa screamed.

"And he got her in the van," Mickie said, "and he just yelled at her, 'Shut up, bitch, shut up, or I'll kill you right now.' And he told me, 'Get out of here.' "

Mickie got the van started, then took her foot off the brake, and eased slowly up the street. James started telling her which way to turn to get onto the freeway.

Mickie couldn't see what James was doing in the back, but guessed that he'd put the ball gag in the girl's mouth and the gun to her head. James had already prepared the floor of the van with ropes through brackets on the floor, and Mickie guessed that James had tied her to the floor as well.

Mickie made a wrong turn and got on the wrong freeway, heading south; James started yelling at Mickie that she was a fuck-up, that she couldn't do anything right. Mickie got off the freeway and got back on, going in the opposite direction so they could head for Sacramento.

As Mickie drove the van, she realized that James was assaulting the girl in the rear of the van while she was still tied down; Mickie could tell because James was praising his victim, crooning over and over what a good sex slave she was going to be.

Mickie drove over the Altamont Pass, where row after row of windmills turned. Mickie liked the windmills, she said later, because "they reminded me of Calvary, [of] crucifixion . . . I always treat it as a sacred place."

She said she had the radio on, and didn't look in the back. But after they came through the pass, James came up to the front of the van and gave her $20 and told her they'd better stop for gasoline. She turned off the freeway and into a gas station.

Mickie got out of the van, leaving James and his victim inside. Mickie pumped the gas, then went inside and bought a large Coke and some candy.

"I didn't know what else to do," Mickie said later, "but go straight in there and pump the gas and get straight in the van. Didn't know what else to do, you know."

Mickie passed the Coke back to James, then got back on the freeway, heading for Sacramento. Today was the day Mickie was supposed to pick up her welfare check. After that, they'd planned to go to Lake Tahoe, where Mickie had to be in court on the bad check charge.

Mickie pulled off the freeway at the Florin Road exit, and called James by name, telling him that they had arrived in Sacramento. As far as Mickie could tell, Vanessa was still tied to the floor, and still had the ball gag in her mouth. James told her to pull into the parking lot of the welfare office. James told her to make sure to park where no one would be able to look into the van. When Mickie looked back, she saw that James had covered Vanessa with the blankets. James told Mickie to leave her purse behind, but take only her welfare identification into the office.

Mickie got out of the van; as she did so, she heard the sliding door open. When she came around the van, she saw James sitting in the open door, lighting a cigarette. James was talking to Vanessa, telling her to be "a good girl," and not to "do anything stupid." Vanessa made some sort of response that satisfied James.

James told Mickie to hurry up. She went into the welfare office, presented her identification and sat down to wait. The welfare worker couldn't find Mickie's file in the computer. Mickie realized that they'd cut off the "M" on Michaud, so it looked like an "N." Once that was straightened out, the welfare worker located Mickie's file, and told her that her check was waiting. Mickie then got a slip of paper with a number on it; she had to wait for her number to come up. She realized it was going to be a few minutes, so she went back out to the van to explain the delay to James.

James told her to go back in and get it over with. Finally the number lit up and Mickie collected her check, her food stamp card, and her mail—the welfare office was holding her mail because she was homeless. The whole thing took about 20 minutes.

"So I get it and go out," Mickie said, "and he looks at the papers and he tells me, 'Sit here with her, 'cause I'm gonna go to the bathroom.' I was like, oh God. That whole time I never heard a word out of her. As soon as he left she started whimpering a little, crying. And as I sat there my eyes got—I was trying not to cry. And for a split second I was wanting to let her go . . ."

But Mickie didn't; she said she was too afraid of James.

"All I was thinking about was untying her and letting her out of there," Mickie said. "She could have ran, she could have ran for help. But James wasn't gone very long at all, not long enough to even do that."

When James returned, he told Mickie to go to the bathroom, because they were going to leave. When she came back, James decided to drive. As far as Mickie could tell, Vanessa was still tied to the floor of the van.

James drove them to a check-cashing outlet that Mickie had used before. He parked so he could watch Mickie through the window when she went in. The people at the outlet took Mickie's thumbprint, checked her ID, then gave her the cash—a bit over $500. Mickie came out and gave James the money. Then they headed for Lake Tahoe.

As they drove up Highway 50 toward Lake Tahoe, Mickie had the feeling that this "adventure" was going to be different from the one with Alicia Paredes. She had the feeling that James was really going to kill someone, this time, "that it wasn't going to be a good ending."

Mickie was by now in the rear of the van. She removed the ball gag. Vanessa asked Mickie for a cigarette. She gave her one. Vanessa's arms were still tied down, so Mickie held the cigarette for her.

James drove the van higher into the hills. Just before noon they reached a campground near a place called Pollock Pines. James pulled off at a small store near the campground, and went inside to buy a soft drink. He left Mickie and Vanessa in the van. Mickie saw one of the curling irons in the back. It looked as if it had blood and feces on it. When James emerged, he drove the van into the campground and picked a spot close to the bathrooms. He told Mickie to untie Vanessa and let her use the facility if she wanted. Mickie went with her.

When they came out, James put his arm around Vanessa and escorted her back to the van. Mickie got in the back with her. James drove out of the campground. They drove around in the hills for a while, aimlessly. Then James returned to the campground; he wanted to check the bathroom, to make sure Vanessa hadn't left a note behind.

While Mickie was using the bathroom, she heard another car drive up. When she came out she saw a white truck a short distance away. Mickie ran to the van and got in. James decided to drive to Lake Tahoe, less than an hour away. The white truck had spooked him.

James stopped at one of the first motels on the outside of South Lake Tahoe, but no one was there. He got back in the van and drove on. They came to another motel, but there was no clerk at this one, either.

A few minutes later, James spotted another motel offering cheap rooms for the young ski crowd. The sign said "Sundowner," and advertised a room for the whole weekend for $25. He pulled in and parked. James went in to register, leaving Mickie and Vanessa in the van. After signing in, James went directly to the room and beckoned to Mickie. Mickie and Vanessa got out of the van and went into the room. James turned the heater on. It was very cold.

James asked Vanessa if she was hungry, and Vanessa said she was. He told Mickie to take the van and drive to a McDonald's that was just down the highway. Mickie went through the drive-through, giving three orders—Vanessa had said she wanted a Happy Meal—then went next door to a service station, and bought some soft drinks and cigarettes.

Mickie drove back to the motel, worried that a cop might stop her because of the unregistered plates. She was thinking that if she didn't come back, James might shoot Vanessa. Or himself. She got back to the motel room without incident, and brought in the food, and the black box used to keep the methamphetamine.

James told Vanessa to eat her Happy Meal. Vanessa took one bite, and threw up. She said she couldn't eat it. She asked if she could save it for later. James said sure, and turned the television on.

After the room got warmed up, James told Vanessa to take a shower. After she came out, he took a shower himself.

After James came out, Mickie used the bathroom. Then she came out and sat on a chair.

Then, Mickie said later, "we had sex."

Well, it wasn't actually sex, at least not in the conventional sense. How can anyone have sex with someone who doesn't want to be there, who's so scared she can't eat more than a bite of a Happy Meal without throwing up, who doesn't know if she's going to live or die? That isn't sex, it's control. It's about terrorizing someone so you can see the fear in their eyes, as Astrid had so aptly put it. And for the most part, there weren't any sex organs involved; James had his two curling irons to stand in for his unresponsive organ, which apparently knew better than he did that it wasn't sex.

But eventually James had his fill of torture. He told Vanessa to take another shower. When she came out, James told her to get dressed. Mickie got dressed too. She had an idea that things were coming to a head.

James wanted to put air in one of the van's tires. He left the room to take the van to a service station. Mickie sat in the chair between Vanessa and the door while they waited. Outside, the motel owner, working on the place's hot tub for happy skiers, saw James leave. He noticed that the window of the room was all steamed up, and guessed that someone had been taking a lot of showers.

Mickie told Vanessa that things were going to be okay, that James was going to drop her off on the highway. But even Mickie didn't believe it.

Mickie didn't use the telephone and neither did Vanessa. "And she doesn't make a move for the door," Mickie said later. "I wouldn't have stopped her if she did, [but] she didn't make a move for the door."

"Why don't you think she did that?" Mickie was asked.

"She's scared to death," Mickie said.

James came back in ten minutes. He told them to get in the van. James took the key to the room. Mickie got in the back of the van with Vanessa, with James driving. He left the main highway and started going uphill. They passed a Highway Patrol officer. Some distance up the road, they pulled into a small parking lot for the snowplows. James wanted to wait until the Highway Patrol officer left. After a while, they went back on the road, heading downhill this time. James passed the Highway Patrol officer again. He was upset. They stopped, turned around, headed uphill once more. James passed the Highway Patrol officer a third time.

They drove on until they came to another turnout. They waited for a while, then James drove back to the snowplow lot. James got out of the van and told Mickie to drive back up the mountain. The "Submissive Young Girls" tape was playing in the cassette player. James got in the back with Vanessa.

Mickie continued to drive up the mountain. James was making noises in the back. Mickie couldn't see exactly what he was doing. James told her to stop. He told Mickie to come back into the rear of the van. Vanessa was lying on the floor of the van. She wasn't moving. A rope was around her neck. James took Mickie's right hand and put it on the rope, and did the same with her left. They pulled. Mickie couldn't tell if Vanessa was dead or alive.

"There," James said, "now we're bonded—forever."

Afterward, James got into the driver's seat and headed farther into the mountains. Mickie wasn't sure if Vanessa was dead, but thought she was. She wasn't moving at all. Farther up the highway, James pulled off to the side of the road. He opened the sliding door and took Vanessa out of the van. He threw her over the embankment. Someone, either James or Mickie, threw the backpack and Vanessa's lunchbag over as well.

They got back in the van. Vanessa's gloves were still in the back. Mickie collected them. James told her to throw them out as they were descending the mountain. Mickie did it.

Down at the bottom, James returned to the Sundowner. Now he and Mickie cleaned the room thoroughly, wiping down every place that conceivably might have had their fingerprints, and looking for hairs and fibers. When that was done, James drove farther into South Lake Tahoe, then across the line into Stateline, Nevada. He pulled in at the Lakeside Inn and Casino, directly across the highway from the Douglas County Courthouse. Mickie had a court appearance scheduled for the next morning, and James didn't want her to miss it.

Now that they had their warrants, the law enforcement people were finally ready to arrest James and Mickie. They still had the problem of finding out where they were, however.

To that end, a number of FBI agents, accompanied by Summers and Carrington, fanned out across Sacramento early on the morning of Wednesday, December 3.

Although Vanessa Samson had been reported missing by her family the previous evening, police in Pleasanton were just getting organized in trying to investigate her disappearance. That evening, they sent out a teletype to all law enforcement agencies reporting her disappearance. The FBI agents and the two Placer County detectives, of course, had no way of knowing that Vanessa's disappearance was in any way related to what they were doing as they began their search for James and Mickie, and in fact, probably never saw the teletype. Not that it would have made any difference now.

Relying on information supplied by Detective Willover and other information in its possession, the FBI compiled a list of names and addresses of people who might be expected to know where James and Mickie were.

About 1:30 p.m., Summers and FBI Agent Dave Williams went to Lamont and Rowena's house. Rowena told them that Mickie had called a few days before and had told her she and James were in Los Angeles. But Rowena said she thought Mickie had been lying because not enough coins dropped into the telephone. Rowena said Mickie and James were both armed. She said Mickie had a court appearance scheduled at Lake Tahoe that day. Mickie still had the green van, Rowena told them.

Williams called this information into his Sacramento office. Someone there passed the information on to the Bureau's supervising agent in the South Lake Tahoe/Stateline, Nevada office, Chris Campion, and sent him the particulars on James and Mickie just after 4 p.m.

Campion got on the telephone and started making calls to the local courts; on his second call, he hit paydirt: Mickie had been in Douglas County District Court that morning. Campion called the Douglas County Sheriff's Office and the South Lake Tahoe Police Department and asked them to start checking area hotels and motels to see if the green van could be located. The first place checked was the Lakeside Inn, just across the highway from the courthouse. The van was there in the parking lot. Someone checked with the front desk and confirmed it: James, at least, was registered at the hotel.

Campion called the FBI's Reno office, and told them that it looked as if James and Mickie were in Stateline. Ferrin and other FBI agents in Reno started driving up the mountain to Lake Tahoe. Someone at the Reno office called Summers and Carrington in Sacramento; the Placer County detectives dropped what they were doing and started driving to Lake Tahoe, too.

Campion now drove to the Lakeside Inn and met with the hotel's security supervisor, who provided a schematic of the hotel layout, and a copy of the registration slip James had signed. While another agent went out to the parking lot to make sure no one drove the van away while they were waiting, a detective from the South Lake Tahoe Police Department went into the room next to Mickie and James' to see if anyone was in there. The detective established that Mickie was in the room by herself. Then Campion waited for the Reno agents to arrive.

Two of the Reno agents found James in the main casino at the Lakeside just after 6:30 p.m., playing a slot machine. He did nothing to resist. They took him to the hotel's security office and told him he was under arrest on a federal warrant. But beyond confirming that he was James Anthony Daveggio, he kept quiet.

That left Mickie. No one really knew what might happen when an arrest attempt was made. The agents knew that she had access to a gun, if she wasn't actually packing one herself. Would Mickie come out shooting? It didn't seem very likely, but no one was willing to bet their life on it. Campion devised a plan: he would pose as a member of the hotel staff and try to induce Mickie to open the door of the room by using a pretext.

Campion borrowed a hotel blazer from one of the security staff. Accompanied by Ferrin and several other agents, he went to the room James and Mickie had rented.

Campion knocked on the door of the room.

Mrs. Daveggio? he called out. Mrs. Daveggio, your husband has had a medical problem in the casino.

Mickie called out that she wasn't Mrs. Daveggio. Campion asked her to open the door. When she did, Campion pulled her outside the room and turned her over to the FBI's Lynn Ferrin, who had just arrived with the rest of the Reno FBI contingent. Ferrin handcuffed Mickie and told her she was under arrest on a Placer County warrant, while Campion quickly searched the room.

Mickie was cooperative from the start. When Ferrin asked her where the gun was, she told them it was in the little black metal box on the table. An agent checked the box and removed the .25-caliber silver-plated automatic, along with a quantity of methamphetamine. Mickie was taken to a room down the hall to be questioned. Ferrin asked if she would give consent to searching the van. Mickie readily agreed, and signed the form. Next Ferrin handed her a form to waive her Miranda rights. Mickie signed that too.

After finishing his search, Campion figured his part was done. He returned the blazer to the hotel staffer, and then went into the room where Mickie was being held. He had been struck by Mickie's resemblance to a composite drawing made six years earlier in connection with a child abduction case in his jurisdiction. In June of 1991, a man and a woman had taken an eight-year-old South Lake Tahoe girl from the street near a school bus stop not far from her home, even as the girl's horrified step-father watched. The Jaycee Lee Dugard case haunted Campion. Jaycee Lee had never been found. Now they had arrested a man–woman team of kidnappers, and the woman half of the team closely resembled the drawing of the woman in the Dugard kidnapping. Campion decided to hang around for a bit to see if he might get a chance to ask Mickie some questions of his own.

A little after 8 p.m., after arriving from Sacramento, Carrington and Summers came into the room where Mickie was being held. Carrington got out her tape recorder. The way things had happened, James had been arrested on the FBI's warrant, and he was a federal prisoner; Mickie was in custody on the Placer County warrant, and was being held on state kidnapping charges, which meant she would be Carrington and Summers' prisoner. That both warrants arose out of the same set of facts was immaterial; but the difference between being arrested by the federal government and being arrested by a state government was significant, and worked considerably to the authorities' advantage, even though they later steadfastly denied that they had planned it that way.

At this point, of course, no one involved in the arrests of Mickie and James realized that Vanessa Samson had just been murdered, or even that she was missing, or that Mickie was hiding a secret even bigger than the kidnapping of Alicia Paredes.

After introducing herself, Summers, and Mickie for the purposes of identifying the tape, Carrington asked if Mickie objected to answering questions.

Mickie gave a mumbled answer that Carrington took as an agreement to be interviewed.[44]

---

44 Transcript of interview of Michelle Michaud by Placer County Detectives Carrington and Summers, Dec. 3, 1997, exhibit in the federal case against Michelle Michaud, USDC for Nevada, #97-00125.

"Okay," said Carrington, "and you understand why we're here and what we want to talk about?"

"I am not having a real clear understanding," Mickie said, probably thinking that somehow the police had already linked her to the murder of Vanessa. "But I guess something . . . with some young lady and . . ."

"Okay, why don't you tell me a little bit about yourself? Where do you live?" Carrington asked.

"Actually, in a van right now, for the last three months," said Mickie.

Carrington asked a series of questions about the van: who owned it, when the silver stripe was put on the side. Mickie said they'd put the stripe on because "James was having trouble with a motorcycle club . . ."

"How long has he been in trouble with this motorcycle club?" Carrington asked.

"It was just before I lost my home in August."

So she put the stripe on the van after that? Mickie said she wasn't sure.

"Okay," said Carrington, "and what is your relationship with James?"

"He's my boyfriend."

"And how long?"

"About a year."

After a few more background questions, Carrington zeroed in on the topic she'd come to find out about.

"Okay, were you in Reno, Nevada, in September of this year?"

Mickie said she'd already told Ferrin that she had been in Reno, and that she and James had seen Charles Sanfilippo. Mickie said she'd been looking for a job. Mickie said her friend Bert Rand had let her use his credit card at the Circus Circus hotel.

She told Carrington how they'd run out of money, and how Rowena had wired them $75; after that, she said, they'd left.

"I noticed you have a rosary," Carrington said. "Is that your rosary?" Carrington was comparing Mickie's rosary with the one described by Alicia Paredes. Carrington wanted to know if Mickie ever hung it from the rear-view mirror. Mickie said she didn't.

"Never?"

Mickie mumbled again.

"[As long as] we're talking," Carrington said, "it's important to tell the truth."

"I have absolutely nothing to hide," Mickie said.

"Okay," Carrington said, "you may have nothing to hide, but I want you to think carefully before you answer my questions. Okay?"

Mickie said it was her rosary, and that she kept it in the car. She'd had another rosary, but James had ripped it from the mirror and thrown it out on the freeway on their way back from visiting his mother in Manteca.

After a seemingly interminable discussion of Mickie's rosaries, Carrington tried to get back to the subject.

"Michelle," she said, "there was a young girl kidnapped in September of 1997 from Reno."

"Okay," Mickie said.

"Can you tell me about that?"

"And, and they're thinking that we did it, is that what you're saying?"

"Why don't you tell me about it?"

"I can't tell you anything about something I don't know about at all," Mickie said.

"This is the time to deal with it, Michelle."

"I have not been involved in any kidnapping. I have not been involved in any other crime."

"Okay."

"Than prostitution."

"You know . . ." Carrington began.

"And writing of the check," Mickie amended.

Carrington tried another approach. She thought if she could get Mickie to throw all the blame onto James, she might get somewhere.

"I know that James is your boyfriend," Carrington said, "and you obviously must care for him. But sometimes when we're involved in a relationship with people, we sometimes do things we wouldn't do on our own. You know?"

"I'm telling you there's no way."

"Just think of those circumstances," Carrington said.

"There is no way. There is no way," Mickie insisted.

Carrington cajoled her again, but Mickie wouldn't respond.

"I know you use crank, Michelle," Carrington said.

"Sure I do," Mickie said.

"Sometimes when we use drugs they affect you in different ways," Carrington offered. "And sometimes you might do something because you're under the influence of a drug that you wouldn't normally do. Wouldn't you?"

"I use crank not often at all," Mickie said. "Enough to keep the pain away that I have and that's all. And I'm going to tell you right now there's no way. There's no way I did this."

"You or James?"

"No, no, there's no way."

"Tell me about your daughter," Carrington said. "Your daughter is twelve years old, is that right?"

Carrington had tried the bad-love-made-me-do-it gambit, the drugs-made-me-do-it gambit, and now the think-of-your-kids approach.

After Mickie talked for a while about Renee, Carrington asked why Renee wasn't with her. Mickie explained that since she'd been homeless and living in the van with James, she thought it was better for Renee to have a more stable environment where she could continue to go to school.

"Recently," Mickie added, "there have been some rumors that I talked to her about."

Carrington pounced.

"What rumors are those?"

"I don't want to discuss those now," Mickie said.

"This is the time to do it, Michelle. What kind of rumors? This is your chance."

"Rumors that don't mean anything," Mickie said.

"This is your chance, Michelle, to tell your side of the

story. That's why I'm here. I want to hear your side of the story."

"But there's no side of the story to tell."

"Michelle," Carrington said, "we both know there's two sides to every story."

"Have you talked to my daughter?" Mickie asked.

"I'd like to hear your side of the story."

Mickie got a little upset for the first time. "May I ask a question and have you answer me? Have you talked to my daughter?"

"Personally, no," said Carrington.

"Have you talked to my family?"

"Yes," Bill Summers interjected.

"Yes," Carrington agreed, "we have, Michelle."

"So you know what's going on with my daughter."

"What I'd like to hear is your side of the story, Michelle," Carrington said.

"Renee," said Mickie. "I won't say things against my daughter except that what she's saying didn't happen. I know that she hates James and I know that if she thought James and I weren't together, that we could all be together and have that home again. But that's gone and it's not coming back. You know? I'm thirty-nine years old. I can't go back again, and I've lost that because of . . ."

Carrington pressed harder, but Mickie wasn't going for it, sparring with Carrington over Renee, Charlotte, and the trip to Santa Cruz. Carrington then abruptly switched topics:

"James," she asked, "how long have you known him?"

Mickie began mumbling again.

"Do you know anything about his history?" Carrington asked. "Do you know anything about his background? Does he have a criminal history?"

"Oh," said Mickie, "that registered thing."

Carrington pulled from Mickie an admission that she knew James was a registered sex offender.

"What *is* this?" Carrington asked. "You've got a daughter and her friend with your boyfriend who is a registered sex offender and you're trying to tell me that what your daughter is saying, there's no truth to it?"

"James didn't do that to Renee and Charlotte," Mickie insisted. "How can a man that comes into your life and for the first time in your life demands respect for you from your family, stands up to your family and doesn't let them chase him out of your life . . ."

"Well," Carrington said, "we all have our weaknesses."

"James has been nothing but good to me," Mickie said.

Carrington now asked about the trip to Oregon with Renee.

"James did not touch that child," Mickie said.

"What about you?"

"No," Mickie said. "Was she saying I touched her?"

Mickie admitted that she and James and Renee had done crank together.

Carrington continued pressing Mickie on a variety of descriptive items, checking to see whether Mickie would admit to James or her having items that would match with Alicia's description of her kidnappers. The discussion led nowhere productive.

At a brief break in the interview, Campion came into the room and asked to take some photographs of Mickie; he wanted to show them to his witnesses in the Jaycee Dugard case. He still wasn't sure whether Mickie was a suspect in his case, but knew he needed to consider the possibility. At one point, Campion suggested that he didn't believe that Mickie was the driving force in whatever had happened; it was his experience that the truly malignant miscreant was the man in man-woman teams. Mickie said nothing to this.

Carrington now returned to her attempt to get Mickie to confess. "You denied that you know about any of these things. That they ever happened. That James had any part of it, that you had any part of it, but I know you did and that James did and that these things happened. I know that and you know that. And this game that we're playing can't go on forever. Okay? Tell me."

"There's nothing I can do."

"Michelle, Michelle," Carrington said. "No, I don't want to hear those words anymore. I want you to tell me the truth now about the girl in Reno. I want to hear it, and I don't want you to deny anymore. No more denials. I've had enough of that. That's not going to work. Tell me what happened."

Nothing happened, Mickie insisted, but Carrington wouldn't let it stand. She bore down on Mickie, asking why.

"Why were you a part of it? Tell me. I know, I know."

"Nothing happened," Mickie said, again and again.

"There's no way out of this one," Carrington said. "It's done. You've been caught, Michelle."

"I haven't done anything."

"You're her mother," Carrington said. "This is the time to do what you need to do, which is tell the truth. Don't put your child through any more of this misery and this heartache, Michelle. Tell the truth, now."

When Mickie persisted in her denials, Summers took a hand, playing the bad cop.

"We're talking about the gal in Reno," Summers said. "Now listen."

"Yes, sir," Mickie said.

"We're not sitting here listening to you tell us a story of denial, okay? We know that you were driving the van when that gal was raped as well as kidnapped from downtown Reno. I know the route that you took. You were seen going through the quarantine station. Now tell us the truth. We know where you dumped her. Tell us what took place. Stop playing these games. Now tell us what happened, because I'll tell you what, lady, you are in a lot of trouble."

Mickie didn't say anything.

"I'm waiting," Summers said. "You were driving the van . . ."

Mickie mumbled again.

"No, no, no," Summers said. "We're not playing this game, that you didn't know anything. Listen, there's other officers who've already talked to James, okay? I just got done talking with one of the officers a couple of minutes ago. You were driving the van. Now, did you touch the girl or not?"

"You can call Western Union, and they'll tell you they saw ..."

"No, no, no, no, no," Summers said. "You didn't hear me. Now listen. We want to hear what your side of the story is. Did you get involved in the rape at all or did you touch her in any way?"

Mickie rallied under Summers' onslaught.

"I told you I've done nothing wrong."

"Michelle," Summers said, "you're looking at some very serious charges here. Now, this girl was kidnapped and transported across a state line ... We know you were in Reno. We got that confirmed. We got the dates. We know when you left. We know what you were wearing. Listen, girl. If you want to play this game, that's fine. But I'll tell you what, there's always a different side. Don't play this game with me. I'm not stupid."

"I've told you I've done nothing wrong," Mickie persisted.

After another ten minutes of trying to pressure Mickie, Carrington went back to James.

"Michelle," she said, "they've already talked to James."

"And what did James say?" Mickie asked.

"Don't worry about what James has got to say," Summers told her.

"He has to say the same thing I'm saying," Mickie said.

"He's not saying the same thing you're saying, girl," Summers said, although in reality James wasn't saying anything at all.

"You're naive," Carrington offered.

Mickie started to weaken, finally. She said she couldn't remember, and stuck to that for a minute or two.

"Well," Summers said, "you don't forget kidnapping gals off the street. Did James tell you to pull over and to slow down and pick her up, or was it your idea? We already know what he's going"—Summers amended himself in mid-sentence—"what he has said. What is your story, girl? Whose idea was it? And you better start answering some questions and telling us the truth."

Mickie stuck fast to her idea: that she hadn't done anything wrong. Summers saw that she was clinging to this notion like a rock in a storm, and that maybe she even believed it.

"Why did he pick up the girl?" Summers persisted. "Maybe you were driving, maybe you didn't do anything wrong, but why did he pick up the girl? Tell me, Michelle. I'm not saying you did anything wrong." If he could show Mickie some daylight, Summers thought, maybe she'd go for it.

"I have nothing more to say," Mickie said.

Despite this effort to end the conversation, Summers and Carrington continued to pepper Mickie with questions. Mickie steadfastly maintained her denials, and reiterated that she wasn't going to say anything else.

Finally Mickie struck back, in her own way.

"You keep getting mad at me," she told Summers. "I have nothing more to say. I want a lawyer or something because I've done nothing wrong, and I give you my word of honor on that. I've done nothing wrong."

"All right," Summers said. For the record, Summers noted that they were ending the interview. He told Mickie that she would be booked into the Douglas County jail. He told her that if she changed her mind and wanted to talk, she could call Carrington or him, but since she'd asked to talk to a lawyer, they had to stop questioning her at that point.

"How do I get in touch with an attorney?" Mickie asked. "I have no money, so how am I going to get an attorney?"

Summers told her she'd be provided with a public defender. But first, he said, she'd have to appear before a judge to be arraigned, and then she'd have to be extradited back to California.

Mickie said she didn't understand.

Summers explained that Mickie had been arrested on a California warrant from Placer County, and that she'd have to go back to California before she could be arraigned. He didn't explain that she wouldn't be allowed to consult a lawyer until the extradition process was begun, or that, if she waived extradition, extradition might take as long as ten days or two weeks, and that in that case, she might not see a lawyer until all that time had passed, and then, only in Placer County. If that happened, Mickie wouldn't be provided with a lawyer at all during that period of time.

Mickie wanted to know where James was.

"He's in Reno," Summers said. And with that, the Placer County detectives and the FBI succeeded not only in breaking Mickie away from James, they were able to make sure she was right where they wanted her, without a lawyer, in case she finally caved in on her denials.

Mickie was taken to the Douglas County jail, the same place where she'd spent two nights in November after writing the bad checks. The jail people made Mickie strip over a clean white sheet; the idea was to collect her clothes and any hairs or fibers that might be potential evidence. One of the jailers found a length of nylon rope in Mickie's pocket.

Meanwhile, Lynn Ferrin and a team of specialists from the Washoe County, Nevada, Sheriff's Department, were going through the green minivan looking for evidence to tie Mickie and James to Alicia's kidnapping. The van had been towed to Reno.

The search would take most of the night; Ferrin and the team finished just after 3 a.m. Even then, there were things that they missed—items that would tie Mickie and James to the torture and killing of Vanessa Samson. But one thing Ferrin noticed was a receipt from a Pleasanton motel for November 30 through December 2. He passed this information onto Chris Campion up at Lake Tahoe.

Once in the women's unit of the jail, Mickie was glad to see an acquaintance from her earlier stay, a 32-year-old Nevadan named Teresa. Teresa was serving time for a probation violation. During Mickie's first stay in the jail, Teresa had given her a pair of socks because her feet were cold. Mickie considered Teresa a friend for her kindness.

Now, almost as soon as she saw Teresa on Dec. 4, Mickie began to cry. She told Teresa she and James had been arrested for kidnapping and rape, but that she hadn't done it.

Then, according to Teresa, Mickie told her, "That's not the half of it."

And with that, Mickie proceeded to tell Teresa most of the story.

At just about this same moment, a man driving over the Sierras on California Highway 88 spotted what looked like someone lying in the snow off the right side of the highway, some 30 feet down an embankment. Rather than disturb the scene, the man drove on to a nearby telephone, and contacted the Alpine County Sheriff's Office. The man, an employee of a Nevada mining company who'd only stopped because he had to relieve himself, said he wasn't sure if the person was dead or alive.

Alpine County, with just over 1,100 full-time residents, was California's smallest county in terms of population, even though it covered over 700 square miles of territory—most of it up and down, as its name suggested. It lay athwart the Sierras, with Nevada's Carson Valley to the immediate east, and South Lake Tahoe, in El Dorado County, to the north. Highway 88 was the county's major thoroughfare, linking the Nevada town of Minden, south of Reno and Carson City, with Jackson in Amador County, California—scene of Michael Patrick Ihde's first arrest in 1978, and James' drunk driving arrest in 1995.

Besides Highway 88, there was also a road over Luther Pass, linking the area to US 50, the main road into South Lake Tahoe. The Alpine County seat was the small town of Markleeville, tucked away in the Sierras about seven miles south of Highway 88.

Because the caller wasn't sure whether the person in the snow was alive or dead, the local fire department went to the area, along with Alpine County Sheriff Skip Veatch, and one of his deputies, Everett Brakensiek. The caller hadn't been too specific about the location, so it took about 15 minutes of searching each side of the road before the figure was spotted.

Two firemen clambered down to the body and found no

pulse; the body was, in fact, partially frozen. Veatch and Brakensiek noted that there were no fresh footprints around the body, only a slide mark down from the roadway above.

At first, the firemen and the two deputies guessed that the body might have come from a possible car mishap on the road above; but one look at the victim's neck showed that wasn't the case: there was an indentation around the neck that Brakensiek and Veatch immediately recognized as a ligature mark, a sure sign that the victim had been strangled. Just down the slope from the victim, the deputies retrieved a Jansport backpack; inside the backpack was a wallet containing a driver's license for Vanessa Lei Samson. Next to the backpack was Vanessa's lunch bag, still packed with the items she never got to eat.

In Pleasanton, meanwhile, the police department had been gearing up for a large-scale investigation into Vanessa's disappearance the day before.

When Vanessa had failed to turn up for work at the insurance office, her supervisor called the Samson house asking why Vanessa hadn't come in. Vanessa's family members tried to contact Vanessa on her pager, but the calls had gone unanswered. That evening a Pleasanton police officer came to the Samson house and took a missing persons report.

The following morning, December 3, Sergeant Joe Buckovic, the Pleasanton department's investigations supervisor, asked Detective Gary McCloud to look into the matter.

By the end of the afternoon, it seemed pretty clear that something serious had befallen Vanessa; the fact that she hadn't answered the pages, and that none of her friends or family members knew where she might be, was ominous. At 4 p.m. that afternoon—just about the same time the FBI was learning that James and Mickie were at the Lakeside Inn— the Pleasanton police assigned a tracking dog to check Vanessa's normal route for any scent of Vanessa. The dog found nothing.

At 7 p.m., McCloud checked, and found that while some computer records had been searched for Vanessa's history,

no teletype had been sent out alerting other area law enforcement agencies to the circumstances of her disappearance.
McCloud then issued such a teletype, which described Vanessa, listed December 2 as the day she was last seen, and
asked any department with any information to call McCloud.
That was just about the time that James and Mickie were
being arrested, although nobody in Pleasanton had any idea
of that.

The next morning, December 4, Buckovic assigned two
detectives to go to the Samson family house, and after that,
her job; a third detective to find a helicopter for use in an
aerial search; a fourth and fifth detective to check local busi-
nesses along Vanessa's route that might have security cam-
eras, in case she might have passed their unblinking eyes;
and drafted two patrol officers to actually walk the route
Vanessa usually took to work while they interviewed people
along the way and passed out fliers. Buckovic also used a
new piece of computer equipment that was pre-loaded with
all the telephone numbers of every person in the city; by
selecting an area from a map, the computer would automat-
ically dial every number in the area, leave pre-recorded mes-
sages, and accept responses.

Buckovic also contacted the Federal Bureau of Investigation to ask their advice for how to handle a possible kidnapping case. All this was going on when, just after 2 p.m.,
Buckovic received a call from the Alpine County Sheriff's
Department. The Alpine department had entered Vanessa's
name into their computer, and it almost immediately coughed
up the fact that Vanessa was a missing person in Pleasanton,
California.

Buckovic sent a photograph of Vanessa to Brakensiek just
before 4 p.m. Half an hour later Brakensiek called back with
the bad news: the body they'd found off Highway 88 was,
in fact, Vanessa's.

The detectives sent out by Buckovic began to come in as
the afternoon progressed; the only thing that seemed anything like a possible lead had come from two men working
on a roof on Singletree Lane near Kern Court. They'd seen

one of the fliers passed out by the police. After reading the
flier, David Elola and David Valentine remembered the green
minivan they'd seen, along with the scream they'd heard on
the foggy morning two days before. This time they called in,
and spoke to Detective McCloud.

At 8:45 that night, Buckovic cancelled his missing persons bulletin on Vanessa; instead he sent out a request that
any agency that had contact with either Vanessa Samson or
a dark green van to call the Pleasanton police.

The following day, Mickie was watching television in the
day room of the women's unit at the Douglas County jail
when a local television station broadcast the news: a
woman's body had been found the day before, off the side
of Highway 88. Mickie immediately went to see her friend
Teresa.

According to Teresa's later statement to the Douglas
County Sheriff's Department, Mickie woke her up and told
her that they'd found "the body of the girl James killed."

"I started crying," Teresa wrote later, "and I told her we
have to tell Deputy Conrad. I told her he could help her do
the right thing. So I asked if Michelle and I could see him
at the gate and he said yes. When we got out there I said,
Conrad, she has told me she knows what happened to the
girl they just found . . ."

Deputy Douglas Conrad then contacted his superior at the
jail, and a call was made to the FBI's Campion, informing
Campion that Mickie wanted to talk to him. Campion then
came to the jail.

On the surface of it, this seems to be a fairly straightforward sequence of events: the news of the discovery of Vanessa's body, followed by Mickie's friend putting her in
touch with the authorities so she could tell what she knew.
But in actuality, the events seem to have been much more
complex than this, and were fraught with potential problems
for any later prosecutors of Mickie and James. And indeed,
the somewhat contradictory sequence was to form the foundation for Mickie's later federal appeal.

What actually happened may never be known, despite a lengthy hearing on the subject that took place in federal court almost a year later. Based on the record, however, it seems possible that Campion knew that Mickie wanted to talk even before Deputy Conrad did.

Teresa and Conrad both testified that Teresa and Mickie had buzzed the intercom and asked to talk to "Deputy Conrad" at the jail gate around noon; yet, another report of the Douglas County Sheriff's Department indicates that Agent Campion called *them* to set up an interview with Mickie at 11:45 a.m.[45]

At that time, Campion told the sheriff's department that James and Mickie were suspects in a murder case. This, of course, was a full 15 to 20 minutes before Mickie herself had come forward. Why was Campion so sure he could get an interview with Mickie, particularly since she'd refused to answer any more questions without talking to a lawyer, two days before?

Later, Campion was to testify that he had never known that Mickie had asked to speak to a lawyer on the evening of December 3, after her talk with Carrington and Summers; that should have ended all the questioning, and probably would have, if Mickie had been provided with a lawyer immediately—as she would have been had she been arrested on *federal* charges.

Instead, because she was being held on state charges and faced extradition, no lawyer had yet been provided to her. The setup, whether intentional or not, was perfect: as a submissive woman, in the power of the police, prevented by legal technicalities from consulting with counsel, Mickie was ripe to talk. The fact that she'd previously asked to see a lawyer didn't arise under the circumstances; and indeed, no

---

45 Investigation report of Sgt. Tim Minister, Douglas County Sheriff's Department, DCSO case #97-7633T. Minister wrote: "On Friday, December 5, 1997 at approximately 11:45 a.m., I received a call from FBI Agent Chris Campion. He informed me he would be enroute to the Lake Tahoe substation to conduct an interview with inmate Michelle Michaud . . ."

one but Carrington and Summers seemed to know this, including the Douglas County Sheriff's Department people, who had custody of her, at least according to their later testimony.

It thus does seem possible that not only had Teresa already told someone about her Dec. 4 conversation with Mickie, in which Mickie told about the murder, and that someone made sure that Conrad, a familiar face to Teresa, was on the gate when Teresa brought Mickie forward; it also seems possible that someone had put a listening device in Teresa's cell to monitor Mickie's conversations, once she was booked, and thus overheard Mickie's initial soul-cleansing to her friend Teresa on Dec. 4.

By the time he arrived at the jail, Campion had already been in contact with Pleasanton's Buckovic. He had informed the sergeant of the arrest of Mickie and James in the Alicia Paredes case, and suggested to Buckovic that Mickie and James might have been responsible for Vanessa's murder, as well. Campion told Buckovic that the FBI had recovered a motel receipt from the Pleasanton area that was dated November 30 to December 2.

Buckovic asked around, and people in the department told him that James was a former resident of Pleasanton. Buckovic passed this information back to Campion, along with the fact that witnesses had identified a green minivan in the area about the time of Vanessa's abduction. Campion already knew that Mickie and James had been driving a green van because he'd seen it at the Lakeside.

Campion arrived at the jail to find that Mickie had been segregated from the other prisoners. He and Douglas County Sergeant Tim Minister, the head of the Douglas County investigations unit, now prepared to interview her.

MICHELLE

Mickie was waiting in a conference room just outside the women's section of the jail. She seemed nervous and somewhat diffident. Based on Teresa's account—she was busy writing it up even then for the Douglas County people— Campion believed that Mickie was ready to give it all up. He moved quickly to take advantage of her apparent remorse.

Noting that something was "obviously bothering" Mickie, Campion suggested that Mickie had something she wanted to "get off your chest. Is that true?"

"I have some information about the young lady who was killed a couple of days ago, yes," Mickie said.

Now Campion read Mickie her Miranda rights, and had her sign a form waiving the rights. Mickie did it; later she was to contend that when she asked to talk to a lawyer, Campion put her off—although the tapes of the interview never backed up that contention.

Mickie began easing into the subject of Vanessa, describing her vaguely, but concentrating on her clothing and her backpack.

"I was supposed to get rid of that thing but didn't," Mickie said. "I left it on her so they'd find it."

Mickey seemed to be suggesting that she hadn't been responsible, that she'd left the backpack with Vanessa's identification behind in order to help the police.

"So they would know who she was, so her parents would know where she was and what happened," Campion said, trying to encourage Mickie. "Okay, remember when we talked the other night . . . and I told you that I didn't think that you were responsible, 'cause I don't think it was your idea. Remember when I told you that?"

Mickie seemed discouraged. Just because she'd left all the evidence behind, she suggested, wouldn't prevent people from thinking she was some sort of monster.

"Who's gonna know that?" she asked. "Who's gonna care, who's gonna believe that? . . . It's over, it's hopeless."

Campion didn't want to encourage that kind of thinking, not when Mickie was just starting to open up.

"I did, right then, Michelle," he said, "as soon as I saw you."

"He changed so much," Mickey said. "I fell in love . . ."

"Who are we talking about?"

"James has changed so much. I don't know what happened to him."

"We're talking about James, James Daveggio."

"Daveggio."

Mickie told Campion about the pact James had imposed.

"You're sealed together with him, is that what he told you? Why is that?"

"Together forever, 'cause you know why."

"Because why?"

"Because of love."

Campion pressed harder, but Mickie began to wobble.

"Look," she said, "I want to tell you everything, I do."

"Okay."

"I'm just scared. All the way around, I don't know."

"People will understand," Campion told her. "And the reason they will understand, because what they know is, people don't do things—people do things for all sorts of different reasons."

"I couldn't save her," Mickie said. "Hell, I couldn't save her. I saved the other victims. She got out of there. She . . . but I couldn't save her and they won't let . . . Do *you* understand that I couldn't save her?"

"Yeah," said Campion.

*   *   *

The interview progressed, with Campion doing most of the questioning, and Minister taking handwritten notes. Interviewing Mickie was like trying to get a rusty pump going again. There were a lot of fits and starts, as Mickie's voice trailed off, as she started down one path of thought, only to end up on another. There was no sense of sequence to any of her ramblings; it was as if Mickie was providing a running commentary on a movie only she could see.

Campion and Minister tried to sort through the barrage of non sequiturs to impose some sort of coherence on Mickie's recollections. Most maddening was Mickie's almost complete lack of calendar awareness; she often had no idea of what day or even what month something had happened. Because Campion and Minister were hearing much of this material for the first time, they didn't have a clue either.

Repeatedly they tried to get Mickie to impose some sort of order on the events, by asking her whether something she was talking about had happened before or after another event. But Mickie often couldn't recall; this was one of the effects of months of repeated methamphetamine use, a sense of time that was completely shot.

Campion was most interested in getting the details abut Vanessa's murder down as fast as possible. That way, in case Mickie had another mood swing and began refusing to say anything else, Campion would at least have something.

Mickie kept coming back to the fact that she'd saved Alicia Paredes.

" 'Cause I told her, 'Don't turn around, don't even look at the van either, you gonna get shot, don't look at the van, start walking up the hill.' "

"Okay," Campion said. "See, you saved her. People will understand, Michelle, you have a heart."

"Then they would think," Mickie said, "why didn't I do anything to stop him in the beginning? But they weren't in the van, you don't know."

"Exactly," Campion said. "So what I wanted to do, and when, I know this is really the biggest thing that's happened in your life, but when you calm down a bit, I want you to tell me what happened and how you got to be there, and what led to all this, okay? Look at me, I really want to know how this all happened."

Mickie said she still had a hard time understanding what had happened herself.

"It's horrible," she said. "How can that happen? I'm sorry. I'm so, so sorry. I don't know how we got, me, to this. I don't know how he can belittle me so much . . . how he can make me feel so . . . worthless . . . so . . . Do you know, I was an esteemed member of my church. I've owned a home. I was making payments on another home with this elderly gentleman's help . . . [my child] was going to Catholic school. I had to earn so much in my life and when I met him, slowly but surely it all got taken away."

"Everybody's worth something," Campion said.

"How weak can a person be?" Mickie asked. "I went through something like this long ago with my daughter's father. I was . . . with him for eight years, I had no idea . . ."

Campion tried to reinforce Mickie's notion that she wasn't as culpable as Froggie, that she'd proved that by helping Alicia escape. He prompted Mickie to say her name, but Mickie either didn't know it or couldn't remember.

Campion prodded her gently for details about Alicia's kidnapping. Mickie's recollection was spotty, but she got most of the basics right. Mickie remembered passing Alicia in the van, then James telling her to turn around to draw abreast of Alicia.

"He wanted me to stop, and I kept telling him, 'James, don't,' you know . . ."

"So you had a little idea of what might happen, huh?" Campion asked.

"He told me to shut the fuck up. When he went to open the door, I kept going. But he jumped out the damn door."

"Out the side door of the van?"

"Then he grabbed her and she started screaming, and he yelled at me, 'Bitch, you'd better come back,' and I backed up. I thought if I kept going . . . he'd just yell at me because he couldn't grab her, he jumped out of the van."

Mickie explained how she was afraid of James and the .38.

"Well, you tried," Campion said. "But what I need you to do—look at me now. Can I trust you . . . everything you gonna tell me is the truth, and you're not gonna leave anything out?"

Campion by now had seized on the key to Mickie: her pathological need to subordinate herself to someone with authority. All Campion had to do from here on in was crack the whip whenever Mickie began to show signs of getting out of line; that was Mickie's reward, and no less than what she expected.

"Whatever you need for me to do," said Mickie, "all you [gotta do is] ask and I'll do it."

Campion wanted to know the whereabouts of the .38 revolver. Mickie tried to explain that they'd given it to someone at Clara's in exchange for the smaller .25 automatic after the shootout near Bobby Joe's. This was all news to Campion, and Mickie wasn't making it much clearer.

"See," she said, "I'm trying to tell you this whole big thing," Mickie said. It was complicated, she added, and it had to do with Clara and Fred and Froggie and Vickie and Nikki . . .

Campion's head began to spin. He decided to leave this stuff about the shooting, whatever it was, until later.

Campion guided Mickie back to the Alicia kidnapping, making Mickie go over the details once more.

After describing what happened in Reno again, and ending with their arrival at Diane's near Modesto, Mickie brought Campion up short.

"You see," she said, "he's been reading these books, and I have these books too, on uhm, serial killers."

"Uh-huh."

"And he was telling everyone about these."

"He was reading these books?"

"Yeah," Mickie said. "He had a thing about the Charlene and Gerald Gallego book."

"Oh really?"

"Yeah," Mickie said. "Now do you understand?"

"Uh-huh," Campion said.

"I kept thinking that Charlene was just a little bitch, that she rolled over and had gotten away with it. Kept saying that she went with him, that she had to enjoy [it] somehow."

Campion had to be wondering who was playing whom, at this point. Wasn't what Charlene had done exactly what Mickie was doing? Wasn't she rolling over on Froggie, and claiming that, like Charlene had with Gerald Gallego, she'd *had* to do what Froggie demanded if she wanted to live herself?

Campion went back to the whip.

"What's the real story, Michelle?"

"That's what he was saying."

"What's the real story, Michelle?"

"Oh, you're asking *me* that, now?"

"Uh huh."

"I give you my word. I give you my word that anything you want me to do to prove my word, I'll do."

"What we have to do here, you and me together," Campion said, "is we have to show people, tell people what happened and how this happened and how it unfolded. Okay? I'll help you."

"If I could have saved her maybe it would have made a big difference," Mickie said.

"Well, you saved the first girl. So let's talk about the second one, okay?"

Just trying to describe it, Mickie said, was almost impossible.

"It's so unreal, it's like it's not happening to your body, it was like I was outside of myself and I could see . . . to have that, go into your head, somebody very detrimentally telling you what's gonna happen and very matter-of-factly and it's very precise and there's no deviation in his voice, you know, [he's] going to do that and you know he's going to *do* what he says, and then five minutes later holds you and tells you how much he loves you."

And with that, Mickie began to describe the last hours of Vanessa Samson.

Mickie talked for nearly an hour more, then Campion ordered a break. An hour later, she resumed, describing all of the events of Dec. 2, including the stop at the welfare office in Sacramento, the stop at the campground, and finally the events at the Sundowner Motel, leading up to James' momentary departure to go to the gas station to take care of the van's tire.

Mickie described the nighttime ride up the side of the mountain, passing the California Highway Patrol officer several times, then James driving the van to where there was an embankment.

"Anyway," Mickie concluded, "there was an embankment and that's where she was thrown and . . . I know, the very important part you need to hear, I left out."

"Yup, you're right," Campion said.

"But it's so hard."

"I know it's hard, Michelle."

"No, you don't, no, you have no idea, no idea."

"I can see it on your face, so just take your time because we need to go through it."

Mickie said she couldn't. She'd been having nightmares still thinking about it. She wanted to put it in writing.

"Look," she said. "He made me stop the van. When he got out of the van I was driving the van. Then he stopped the van again, she was just laying there when I got in the back. She was just laying there. Then the rope, he had the rope, stopped the van again. He straddled her and he had the rope and my hand was there and his hand was there and my other hand was there and his hand was there and together

and she wasn't . . . you know . . . and then it was, he was . . .
she was dead."

Mickie was crying as she tried to explain what had happened.

"And then it was done?" Campion asked.

"I didn't get to protect her," Mickie cried. "I didn't get
to help her."

"Okay."

"And then he said, 'Now we're bound together.' "

"That's when he told you, 'Now we're bound together.' "

"Yup," Mickie said. "No matter what I do, no matter what
happens, my life is over, and he's right."

"He's not right, Michelle."

"He's right."

"And I'll tell you why," Campion added.

"I just told you," Mickie said.

"I know why it looks like it's over, but it's not, because
you did tell us," Campion said. "People will understand."

"I can't ask anyone to understand what *I* don't understand," said Mickie. "How can I do that, how can I ask
mercy, how can I ask forgiveness?"

"Well," Campion said, "you know the One that can have
mercy and give forgiveness, it's not either one of us."

"He was supposed to let her go," Mickie said. "She didn't
do anything. She didn't do *anything*. I'm so afraid. But I'm
so sorry."

Campion knew he still had to get something nailed down.
Mickie sensed it:

"Did it . . ." she asked, ". . . was she gone before? Is that
possible?" Mickie was suggesting the possibility that Vanessa had been dead before Froggie made her put her hands
on the rope, that Froggie alone had been directly responsible
for her death.

"Okay," said Campion, "so you're not sure whether she
was already dead when you and he were holding her down
and strangling her neck with the rope?"

"Not sure," Mickie said.

"You don't know, you're unsure?"

"No movement. Not sure."

"She wasn't moving, but you couldn't tell, okay?" Campion asked.

"I'm sorry, so sorry, so sorry, I'm so sorry. She cooperated with him, she didn't . . . I knew and I had to do something. I got sick and then I had to . . ." Mickie indicated she was sick with guilt, that's why she'd asked to talk to someone.

"Had a hard time sleeping," Mickie said. "I couldn't go to sleep."

"What was going through your mind, Michelle?"

"How she was out there in the cold and her parents didn't know where she was . . . So maybe in talking to you guys, at least it helped. Not take so long to finalize things for her, help her rest with God. I pray to her, I pray for her. That's all I know to say now. And he told me how, he told me anyway . . ."

"He told you what?"

"We're bound forever, no matter what I do. But you know what, he shouldn't have had me read those books."

"Why's that?"

" 'Cause I know what to leave behind . . . It's all there. He bragged on those books so much. I couldn't believe he was telling his family. The girls were looking at him like, 'God, Dad, why are you reading this stuff?' you know, but . . ."

"So what did you leave behind for us, Michelle?"

"The gagging apparatus."

"And where is that?"

"It's got her saliva on it because I didn't wipe it off and throw it away. It's in the van. The iron with her feces and her blood, I didn't clean it, didn't throw it away and it wasn't used on me and I didn't clean it and I didn't throw it away. And there's a cloth in there that was used as a blindfold a couple of times."

With this statement, Mickie gave the authorities everything they needed to find physical evidence linking her and James to the murder of Vanessa Samson.

*   *   *

Campion continued pressing Mickie for details: what she did, what James did, what Vanessa did, over and over. Mickie kept trying to tell them, trying to remember things the police could check to verify her story. She told again about the trip up the mountain, about getting in back with Vanessa's body, while James drove. About throwing Vanessa's mittens out of the van as they went, after James had gotten rid of the body. About going back to the Sundowner to clean up, to make sure there were no fingerprints, no hairs or fibers. About throwing out the trash at the nearby McDonald's. About the piece of the rope, which she'd put in her pocket, trying to keep James from knowing about it.

Campion ordered another break just before 7 p.m. They resumed just after nine. So far, Mickie had been talking for about six hours.

When they resumed, Campion asked Mickie to talk about getting together with James, back in the beginning, trying to find out more about James' background. He eased into Renee's story about the trip to Oregon.

"We were . . . on the way to Idaho to see his uncle . . . We stopped there," Mickie said.

"You're looking pretty disgusted about that," Campion observed.

"Yeah," Mickie said, "I don't wanna . . ."

"What's going on here?" Campion asked.

"I don't wanna talk about that right now," Mickie said. "I don't. My daughter, I have—I won't go against my daughter."

"Go against your daughter?"

"Yeah," Mickie said. "She's a good kid. So whatever she says is okay, whatever she says is okay."

"Whatever she says is okay. What do you think she said?"

"I know. I couldn't tell you anything about that."

"Why not?" Campion asked. "This is a pattern here, Michelle. You've obviously figured that out now."

"Yeah."

"It's real clear to me, so let's not have any secrets. I know this is the—"

"I don't know no secrets, I just don't know. Whatever Renee says."

"All right," Campion said. "Okay. If we need to come back to that, can we come back to that?"

Mickie agreed. She added that everything that had gone wrong had begun with James and the Devil's Horsemen. James had freaked out, because of the shootings. He'd wanted to kill Lizzie, Mickie added.

"Kill Liz?"

"Yes."

"Or Renee?"

"No, Liz."

"Oh, really?"

"Oh, yeah. Liz betrayed him."

"To whom?"

"To the club."

"What did she tell 'em, the club?"

"That he stole the safe."

"The safe out of the clubhouse? Oh, man," Campion said.

"Yeah," said Mickie.

"Did he?"

"I don't know for sure."

"What do you think?"

"In the beginning I didn't think he did. I don't know."

Campion tried to wrest the conversation back away from the club to Topic A, which was whether James had killed anyone else.

"Okay," he said. "Michelle, I think that James has . . . done this before, kidnapped girls, taken girls, and I think you can help us."

"If there . . ." Mickie started, then began again. "Wait a minute, so help me God, if there's other girls, I swear I don't know anything about it, so help me God. If I did I'd tell ya in a minute."

" 'Cause you realize . . ." said Campion.

"Daddy [Lamont] told me that [James had] been under

investigation long before I lost my house and he couldn't tell me why."

"James told you he was under investigation?"

"Daddy did. My dad."

"Your dad."

"Told me on the phone the other day."

Mickie slid into a brief discussion about methamphetamine, saying she had never used the drug until she'd met James. She recalled the visits to the house made by the Sacramento Police in the spring, when they'd told James to find a new place to live.

Campion tried to get Mickie to describe James' vehicles, looking for information that might match with any known abductions. Mickie was getting tired.

"We're looking for anything, Michelle, that you can help us [with]," Campion told her. " 'Cause there's a lot of kids like this girl from this week who are out there and we don't know where they are, their parents don't know where they are, we don't know what's happened. And they need to know, they deserve to know."

Mickie said she didn't know of any other victims. That led Campion back to Renee's story. Now Mickie told about James having duct-taped Renee.

"Up in Klamath Falls, on the way there," Mickie explained, "it was raining real hard and . . . We stayed there in that hotel. But he, he didn't penetrate or anything like that, you know. I wouldn't let him do that. When he put the duct tape on her mouth and put her hands behind her back and tied her up I got freaked about it. 'Cause I didn't want him to do that to her. So I took that duct tape off her mouth, told her to calm down, it's gonna be okay, gonna be okay. But she kept saying, 'Mom, you used to tell me about people like this, I never thought it would be *you*.' I kept telling her, 'It's not me, Renee, it's not me.' "

Mickie continued:

"The next day she got up and she wouldn't talk to me, you know. What're you gonna do? Couldn't stop him. I stopped as much as I could, though. And then, he gave her some crank, and she ended up teachin' me how to smoke off foil." Mickie laughed.

"Renee did?"

"Renee," Mickie said, "my own daughter."

"Kids are amazing these days, aren't they?" Campion said.

After the duct-taping, Mickie continued, Renee wanted to go back to Sacramento, so they all got back in the van and headed south.

"I told James," Mickie said, " 'Renee promised not to say nothing, she wants to go back home, let her go back home.' He was talkin' about doing us. [I said] 'No, that's my daughter, and so help me God, you're not doing anything to her.' "

"He talked about doing what?"

"Does he think it's safe to let her go. I didn't think he was serious. Jesus, how could he be serious? That's my daughter. If he loved me, how could he be serious? But something inside tells ya, this is serious."

"So he, he suggested that you couldn't let her."

"That we'd keep her with us to go see his uncle and she'd have to stay with us or, and he never finished the or, and I told him, 'You're not serious.' If she wants to go back home, she's going back home, 'cause I'm gonna take her back home one way or the other. The only time I've ever really stood up to him, you know?"

"Okay."

"But he talked to Renee, and Renee convinced him. Like she said, 'Who am I gonna tell?' You know, 'It's my mother, look what my mother's done, [look at] what she's done.' You know, I allowed it, is the way she's talking."

It was getting late, but Campion kept pushing. He wanted to try to get a track on Froggie's movements during the late summer and fall to see whether he'd been any place where there was an unsolved murder.

Mickie tried to reconstruct their movements, but wasn't entirely successful. But, she said, there were various documents, motel receipts and the like, stashed in various places that would show where they'd been.

Mickie explained about the fight at Lizzie's, and the confrontation with the Devil's Horsemen at the Stockton Boulevard motel.

Campion asked again whether there had been any abductions between Alicia Paredes and Vanessa Samson. Mickie said there hadn't.

"So help me God, I'd tell ya, so help me God," Mickie said. "I'll swear on a stack of Bibles, anything. Please believe me, if I knew, I'd tell ya. You don't know how it feels to be away from him, to know I don't have to hear his voice. I don't need to look in his eyes, but he can't make me do things. I'm very, very scared. You do not—I don't trust this place, 'cause I know he can get to me, and there's nothing you can do . . ."

"Well, we'll see about that," Campion said. He wanted to know if Mickie had made any telephone calls after being arrested at the Lakeside Inn.

She'd called Rowena, Mickie said, and Bert Rand. She'd tried to call her social worker. She'd also tried to call Lynn Ferrin, but hadn't been able to reach him. Ferrin, of course, had been busy searching Mickie's van.

At one point, Mickie added, she considered calling a local television station, but thought better of it.

"I just wanted to reach out," Mickie said. "I felt very, very . . . and I still do. I pray for her, believe it or not, I do."

"You've got a lot on your chest that needs to get off," Campion said.

"I pray for her. You try not to think about it. I thought about the other ones for a long time. I thought that was hard on me. Thought the kids were hard on me. But this, I can't stop throwing up. I can't stop crying, and I can't, my body won't calm down, and I can't, I can't accept it. I keep thinking . . . that'd be fine. Then I keep looking at my own pathetic . . . weakness is being scared. There's a part of me that's very logical and a part of me that's very intimidated. Very scared. I mean, I told my mom tonight all I want to do is just be held. I need my mother . . ."

Mickie was crying.

"I need to feel her arms around me so bad."

After Mickie had calmed down, Campion had her describe more of her background, touching on Jose and her two children. Then Campion produced a picture of Jaycee Dugard.

"I wanna show you a picture of a little girl," he said.

"A little girl."

"Well," Campion said, "she's your daughter's age. And I want you to help me with this. Her name's Jaycee Dugard."

"I remember hearing about her," Mickie said.

"What do you remember hearing about her?"

"No, on the news," Mickie said. "Big stuff."

"Uh-huh."

"But he's never said anything about her."

"James has never said anything about her?"

"No. Huh-uh."

"I talk to her mom every week," Campion said.

Campion showed Mickie a picture of a car similar to the one in the Dugard abduction, and asked if she'd ever been with anyone who'd had a car like it. Mickie said she thought it looked like James' old Thunderbird, the one he'd sold to Clara.

Now Campion showed Mickie the composite of the woman in the Dugard kidnapping.

"Okay," Mickie said.

"All right. Do you know who that is?"

"No," Mickie said. "But I know the only woman who has dark hair and long like that. You thought that was me, huh?" Mickie said she'd had a scar on the side of her face since 1980.

"Okay. Is it you?"

"No," said Mickie. "Swear to God."

"Okay."

"So help me God, no."

"I wanna help you, Michelle, but I need to know right now—" Campion said.

"I know you do."

"—if that is you."

"I swear to God," Mickie said. "Look at me. It's not me. It's not me."

"Okay," Campion said. "You're not lying to me, are ya?"

"Touch my hand," Mickie said. "Okay. That's not me, I swear to ya. I swear on everything that's holy, I swear. That's not me."

"Okay. And you would tell me if James ever said anything to you about this case?"

"I swear to you. I'd tell you faster than . . ."

"Okay."

"I promise."

"All right."

"I don't know what else to say."

"Okay."

"But look at me," Mickie said.

"I believe you," Campion said.

After only a few more questions, mostly about articles Mickie had with her when she was booked, Campion decided to close down for the night. It was nearing 11 p.m.

The next day, he told Mickie, several other investigators would come and ask her questions.

"They're gonna ask you some questions," he said. "About each of the cases, and they might be hard questions sometimes, all right? But I want you to know that what they're lookin' for and what I'm lookin' for is the truth, that's the only thing. And wherever that takes us, wherever it takes you, that's what you gotta tell us."

" 'Kay," Mickie said.

" 'Cause that's, you've made a great first step here today. And we've talked about a lot of things. And this, if you keep with it and stick with it, is the biggest step you'll have ever taken in your life, because it's the first step to putting everything that's bad in your life behind you."

The following afternoon, Campion returned to the jail. This time he was met by Desiree Carrington. Over the morning, discussions had been held amongst the various law enforcement officers, and a decision was made to put Carrington into the interview mix, both because of her familiarity with the Alicia Paredes kidnapping and because, as a woman, some thought she might be more effective with Mickie.

Besides, Carrington had read Willover's reports about Renee and Charlotte. Comparing those accounts with Mickie's would be one way to make sure she wasn't lying.

Almost from the outset, Campion tried to put Mickie on the defensive. He told her that the police did not believe she'd been entirely truthful the day before.

The problem, Campion explained, was that Mickie had neglected to say that she had actively participated in James' assault on her daughter.

"All right," Campion said. "Let's just forget about yesterday for now, and have you tell me and Detective Carrington what happened with you and James and your daughter."

Mickie said she'd told exactly what happened: that James had never penetrated Renee. "I wouldn't allow that," Mickie added.

"Him and I argued about some things, I told you," Mickie added. "Some things I'm lucky that he didn't do and when he duct-taped her, it was the hardest part, and when I took it off her mouth, then I kept telling her, 'Calm down, calm down, you can breathe,' he got mad 'cause I took that off her mouth, but he ended up calming down, and he ended up taking it off her wrist, and then, you know, she was okay."

Mickie admitted that she'd touched her daughter's breast and had her hand down her pants while they were driving to Klamath Falls. But Mickie said she'd only done that to prepare Renee, that she knew Renee was going to have to submit to James.

"And Renee kept saying, 'No, Mom,' you know, 'I don't want to do that,' and I kept telling her, 'Well, you're gonna do it, you know, one way or the other, I don't know no way out.'"

Mickie described James performing oral sex on Renee in the van the night before they'd stopped in Klamath Falls.

"What made you think he was going to [do], that you stepped in?" Campion asked.

"He told me," Mickie said.

The subject came up when Renee told her that James was trying to put his hands in her pants, and asked her to stop him, Mickie said.

"So that's where it began," Mickie said. "There was no talking him out of it."

"Did you even try at that time?"

"Yeah," said Mickie, "but . . . you don't talk James out of anything."

"What did you say to him?"

"I just told him, 'Not Renee,' you know."

Renee hadn't heard her say that to James, Mickie added. When James persisted, Renee thought that Mickie had let her down.

"What I'm telling you," Campion said, "is you can't leave anything out."

"I'm not trying to leave anything out," Mickie said.

"I understand and this one is particularly hard, I know," Campion said. "Because it's your daughter. But if you want to make things right, if you want to do what you can do to make things right, we need to have everything."

"I'll try," Mickie said.

"Even if it makes you not look very pretty."

Mickie said that Renee had been smart after the events in the motel room, because she'd stripped the bed of its sheets and bedspread, and took them with her when they left to go back to Sacramento.

Campion had Mickie go through the events in the motel room in detail.

"Let's hear what happened," he said.

"He duct-taped her," Mickie said. "And she started to panic, I took the duct tape off her mouth."

Campion pressed her. Mickie said that she'd had no idea that James was going to put duct tape on Renee until he emerged from the motel bathroom with the tape in his hand.

Carrington shook her head.

"Michelle, there's a couple of things I don't understand," she said. "You said he came out of the bathroom when you and your daughter were talking and he put the duct tape on her. How did that happen, your daughter's twelve years old? Who held her down?"

"Nobody held her down," Mickie said. "She wasn't held down. She wasn't held down at all." James had already prepared the strips of tape, Mickie said. He grabbed Renee's hands and put the tape on, telling her not to move.

Mickie described the scene in more detail, but Carrington still was skeptical.

"I think there's a little bit you're not telling me," Carrington said. "You have to remember, I've talked to detectives who've talked to your daughter. Did you have sex with James while he was having sex with your daughter?"

"No," Mickie said.

Carrington was trying to establish whether Mickie had committed a criminal act; the way the law read, if Mickie was stimulating James while James was assaulting Renee, she would have been culpable for abetting the assault.

"Did you have a conversation with your daughter about what was going to happen before James put the duct tape on her?"

"I don't know," Mickie said. "I might've tried to prepare her for something, I don't know. I prepared Astrid. I, I was always preparing them. No, because maybe I knew, but because I knew, you know what I mean? Not because he told me that this was the minute he was gonna do it or this was what he was gonna do, because I knew somewhere along the line it was gonna happen sooner or later."

Mickie said she'd known that James was going to go after Renee even before they'd left Sacramento. James had told her that he was going to force sex on Renee, and maybe kill her, but Mickie thought he was only trying to scare her, "keep me in line," she said.

After more discussion about Renee, Campion turned to the topic of Charlotte. Here again, Mickie admitted, she'd known ahead of time that James intended to make a sexual assault.

Mickie explained how they'd broken into Ted and Janet's house in Sacramento, while Ted and Janet were away. They'd run out of cigarettes, Mickie said, so Frog had broken into one of the piggy banks to get money. Then he sent Mickie to get cigarettes and Charlotte.

When Mickie returned without Charlotte, she said, James had gotten mad at her.

"He was mad," Mickie said. "Started calling me a piece of shit, you know, and told me I was worthless, trying to push me around a little bit. And I didn't want him to get violent, so I, I went back in the van again and went over to Charlotte's house, and I got her. Real good friend, ha. She had no idea, called me 'Mom,' felt just like a second mom to her. She was just glad to see me, you know. We all used to hang out at my house when it used to be, the one the kids would come and talk to, I was the one they trusted . . ." Mickie began to cry again.

"It's okay," said Campion.

"No, it's not," Mickie said.

"It's done. There's nothing you can do to undo it."

"Just say it's okay."

"You'll, you'll be okay. They'll be okay."

Mickie went on to describe the events at Ted and Janet's house with Charlotte. Afterward, Mickie continued, Charlotte promised not to tell anyone.

"Why did she promise?" Carrington asked.

"Because I told her what James told me to tell her."

"Which was what?" Campion asked.

"I threatened her life," Mickie said. "Because I threatened her life, that's why she was scared. Yup. Didn't need to threaten her life, but I did. I told her what he told me to tell her." Mickie was crying again.

"You said the words 'cause you had to," Campion said.

"Yeah," said Mickie.

"I know this is hard," Campion said.

"Don't worry about me," said Mickie.

"I am," Campion said.

"It's hard," said Mickie, "but it's harder for them, and I feel worse than them. I don't feel anything for me, really, as much as I do them. They all trusted me, I trusted him. What do you do?"

"What are you gonna do?" Campion asked. "What's past is past. The only thing that anybody expects you to do, Michelle, is to acknowledge it, say, 'Yeah, I did it,' and then move on. That's the only way anybody's ever gonna understand."

When the rumors began in October about Renee and Charlotte, Mickie said, James got mad again, pointing out that no one was saying that Mickie had been part of it, only James.

"He said, 'You see, they're implicating me, they're not implicating you, they're saying, "James did it," they're not saying "James and Michelle did it." ' But he wanted to make sure that I was gonna be implicated with him in something."

"Okay," Campion said. "Well, and that happened."

"Yeah, it did."

"And the only difference between you and him is that you have a heart," Campion said, "and you could cry about it and he can't. He's only crying 'cause he got caught."

Now Mickie described the rape of Aggie in the motel room in early October. Mickie said she'd tried to make sure someone knew Aggie was with her before returning with her to

James. Mickie thought that was the only reason Aggie was still alive.

"And no more was done," Mickie said, after telling the story. "Aggie was cold, shaking, crying and James just got real cold after that, just kinda like he hated me, you know? A sick kinda hate like I was worthless, just garbage, but nothing I could ever do was good enough, up to his specifications."

"Did he take the handcuffs off, or did you?"

"Yeah, he took them off her because then he always became a compassionate and caring person to the person he just did all that to and then I became, you know . . ."

"You became what?"

"The whipping post."

Mickie said she'd kept part of Aggie's clothing.

"Why did you keep that one piece?" Campion asked. "Did he ask you to?"

"No, I did that because, I don't know, I just figured if anything ever came down I'd need it somehow. You know, when you think about things that incriminate yourself and you also think about, I was thinking more of how he always told me all the time, if he goes down, I go down with him, together forever, and he was angry because he always thought, 'You see, Michelle, they're not saying, "Michelle and James did it," ' they're saying, "*James* did it," "Frog did it," 'you know?"

Campion asked Mickie why she thought James had begun going after women and girls he didn't know, or who weren't connected to Mickie.

"That weren't easy access," Mickie observed.

"Yeah," said Campion, "that he had to go and hunt."

"I don't know," Mickie said. "I don't think I understood any of that until he started reading those books."

The conversation wandered around as the afternoon turned into evening. Campion was still trying to get the events into some sort of coherent order, but Mickie's mind was wandering. Concentrating was difficult. It had now been a little over three days since she'd had any methamphetamine, and her crash was just over the horizon. Already she had a splitting headache.

"I mean," she said, "everything I've said is true, but honest, I'm having a hard time remembering right now for some things."

"Okay," said Campion.

"But," Mickie continued, "can I tell you about Astrid before I forget?"

Mickie told about Astrid's overnight stay at the motel in Pleasanton on Thanksgiving night, and how, the next morning, Astrid ran away from home.

"Only I knew why she wasn't coming home," Mickie said. "Her parents [Arnelle and her husband] were angry at her because they didn't understand."

"Did she talk to you afterward? What did she say?"

"She talked to me . . . She's going to kill him one day. She's going to take that man's life. She has it in her right now. She needs help. She has so much hatred in her. She's such a beautiful person inside. I worry that she will kill him, and then what will happen to her? She has a lot of anger because, when they were little, he was never around."

Mickie believed that she was responsible for what happened to Astrid because she had encouraged her, along with Joanie, to renew their ties to their father.

"I tried to get all the family together," she said, "because he thought he needed a family and they needed him."

Mickie racked her brain trying to think of what else to say. She said that James had been using the computer to cultivate relations with young girls; she thought there might be information on the computer that would lead the investigators to their identities. Mickie said the computer was at Diane's, and that Diana's daughter Brittany might be using it. She thought James had tried to have sex with Brittany after they'd returned from Reno, but that Brittany had resisted. Diane probably knew nothing about it, Mickie added.

Mickie described the chaotic period between leaving Diane's house after the Alicia Paredes kidnapping and the twin trips to Klamath Falls and Santa Cruz. It was sometime during this period that their friend Clara showed her the newspaper article about the Reno attack, she said, the one with the composite of James, and a reference to "Mickie." That was when James decided they should make changes to their appearances, she added.

Mickie was fading fast, losing her ability to concentrate. Campion and Carrington pressed her, however, and she managed to get through a description of the crazy events in November, when Fred had been robbed, the shooting had taken place at Bobby Joe's, James had offered to kill Vickie and her daughter for $2,000, and the hooker had managed to get away.

It was late by now, and Mickie was definitely crashing. Campion asked if it would be all right if they returned the next day to resume questioning.

"No problem," Mickie said. "If I remember anything else I'll write it down."

"Exactly," Campion said. "Now, what I want you to think about is, we've talked a lot between when you and James got back together, and when you got arrested the other night. I want you to go back in your mind, fill in anything else you can, in your mind, of things you and he did, you know what we're looking for now. And anything that happened before your break-up with James [before Mickie lost her house], I wanna go in, tomorrow, into depth about how he went from being a nice guy to . . .”

“To this,” said Mickie.

Mickie had already told Campion that James had stalked the 10-year-old girl at the school bus on the way to Lake Tahoe around the time of her arrest on the bad check charges. Now Campion and Carrington showed her several maps, trying to find out just where this occurred. Mickie had no idea, because she hadn’t been there, James had only told her about it.

“Is there anything else?” Mickie asked.

“No,” Carrington said.

“Can I ask you a question?”

“Sure,” said Campion.

“James has done this before me?”

“Uh-huh,” Campion said.

“You know that,” Mickie said. “Why didn’t anybody stop him?”

“We didn’t know, we didn’t,” Campion said. “We weren’t able to stop him for all this.”

“How did you know he did it before?”

“ ’Cause he was caught.”

“He was caught doing this before?” Mickie asked. “The same . . . I’m in?”

“Yup.”

“Neither one of us was gonna be able to help that girl, were we? Nobody . . . You’ll never know, you’ll never know.” Mickie began to cry again.

“Well, I don’t think we will know like you know, Michelle,” said Campion, “but we were talking about it earlier today, if we had gotten to James a day earlier, don’t think we don’t realize that.”

“If I would have had more guts, if I was stronger.”

“There’s a lot of ifs in this.”

“You know, he’s not even, he’s not even caring. He’s not shedding any tears for her. He’s not having any remorse. He doesn’t care. It doesn’t keep him up at night. It doesn’t make him feel like he's garbage. He doesn't . . . Thinkin' about her and her family. That's not right. How can he not?"

Maybe it was because James had done it before, Campion suggested.

"I don't know," Mickie said. "I don't know and I don't want to know. Because I can't handle this. I can't live with it. I can't live with it. I'm not living with it. I can't . . . I wish it was me. And then I get scared, 'cause it could have been me. And I don't wanna die. And I don't have a right to feel that way, do I?"

"Of course you do," Campion said.

"No, I don't."

"You're a human being. You have the right to feel that way."

"Oh, God, God, God, please don't say that, okay? Just don't say that, I don't know anymore, I don't know anymore, I don't know anymore. I'm full of so much pain and remorse and hurt and I wish so much, I wish, I wish, I just wish . . ."

"I wish we could go back, too, Michelle," Campion told her. "We could see the pain on your face. Remember what we talked about before, though, about asking for forgiveness."

"I was there," Mickie said. "Can you imagine how horrible that is, how helpless, scared? How it is to be all alone?"

"Yup," Campion said. "But what's done is done and what you're doing is bringing that deed out of the darkness and into this light for us, for her parents, her family, and for her. She's looking down on all of us and she's saying, 'Thanks, Michelle,' so people will know."

"I can't talk about this no more right now," Mickie said.

"Okay," said Campion.

But before they could resume the following day, Mickie collapsed in her cell and had to be taken to the hospital. Her crash from the methamphetamine had arrived.

Just before lunch the next day, December 7, Teresa went into Mickie's cell and found her unconscious on the floor. Teresa called for help; a jail guard came in as Mickie came to. Together they helped her onto the bed. An EMT unit arrived at the jail and transported Mickie to a local hospital.

There, doctors determined that Mickie had collapsed in part because of her sudden cessation of methamphetamine, coupled with the fact that she hadn't taken any of her hormone medication for several months; she said James wouldn't allow it.

Campion and Carrington came to the hospital. After examination including a cat scan, and treatment, Mickie seemed somewhat improved. She was still nervous about the Devil's Horsemen, however, and talked for perhaps an hour about the club and her fears; Carrington took notes, but the interview was not recorded.

The next day, Mickie was returned to the jail. Campion and Carrington began their interview anew. Both saw a different Mickie: a woman who seemed far more coherent, even a little feisty.

Campion began, as promised, by asking Mickie how she and James had gotten together. Mickie told the story of meeting Frog, and how she was going to beat the Mexican kid's head in with the baseball bat. She sounded tough, aggressive, Campion and Carrington both noticed. They guessed it might be the effect of the hormone medication, or the fact that Mickie was finally down from the meth.

"Actually," Mickie said, "one part of me right now, the

strength is starting to come back, who I used to be, and it feels good to have it back."

"Yeah," Campion said. "I can hear it in your voice, see it just sitting here talking to you."

"Feels good to have it back," Mickie said. "Make darn sure I don't ever lose it again."

Campion and Carrington led Mickie through a long discussion of her relationship with James, including her fantasy about the Waltons, leading up to her eviction and James' dispute with the Devil's Horsemen over the clubhouse safe.

Carefully, Campion led Mickie into a discussion of her own past, suggesting that people who have had sexual experiences at a very young age often carry a lot of guilt "that can affect a person through their whole life."

"Have you ever heard that before?"

Mickie asked them to turn off the tape, and a discussion took place that lasted just over half an hour; from comments made by Campion later in the interview, it seems clear that Mickie told of having been sexually molested at a young age.

By this time, Campion had heard from Ferrin; based on Mickie's first two interviews, a new search warrant had been issued for the van, and the search was even then in progress. But by now Ferrin had recovered the ball gag and the curling irons. To nail this down, Campion asked Mickie to describe the gag, and tell the story of its purchase at the sex toys store in Livermore. Mickie told where James had purchased the rope and the curling irons. Mickie said she knew what James intended to use the items for; she just didn't know when it was going to happen.

Mickie was suggesting that these preparations were all James' idea. Carrington had her doubts.

"Let's go over it one by one," Carrington said. "When he bought the gag . . . when you and he went into the store and bought the gag . . . did you know what he was going to use it for?"

"Yeah, I knew what he was gonna use it for, but I didn't know how long before."

"Tell me what—"

"Or how long before."

"Tell me what he was going to—what you knew he was going to use it for," Carrington demanded.

"Well," Mickie said, "there's only one thing he can use it for . . ." Mickie described the use of the gag. "I mean," she ended, "I'd be a liar if I said I didn't know."

The same thing with the rope, Mickie said: James wanted the rope to tie someone up with. After the hooker had scratched him, James was furious, Mickie said; he wanted to make sure no one else was able to do that to him.

Carrington asked if Mickie knew what James was going to do with the curling irons.

Not at first, Mickie said, but when James cut the electric cords off with a razor . . . "So," she said, "now I know."

Mickie said that she and James had planned to go to Sacramento with Joanie and Astrid on December 2, but when they couldn't find the girls the day before, decided to skip it. The next morning they got Vanessa, Mickie indicated; if they'd managed to get with the girls instead, they would've been on their way to Sacramento, and Vanessa would never have been taken.

Mickie described Vanessa's abduction in detail, as well as the trip to the welfare office in Sacramento and James' trip to the bathroom, when he left her alone with Vanessa. Campion and Carrington wanted to find out if Mickie had bypassed chances to turn Vanessa loose, or get help; that was a double-edged topic, because while it tended to increase Mickie's potential culpability, to the extent she implicated herself, it also increased her credibility.

"Did he give you the gun?"

"No. Yes."

"He did give you the gun? To watch her while she was gone?"

Mickie said she couldn't remember. Campion wasn't satisfied, but let it go.

Carrington wanted to know if the keys were still in the

ignition. Mickie didn't know, but said James usually took the ignition keys with him.

While she was sitting next to Vanessa, still tied up and gagged, Mickie said, "My mind's just racing. I'm thinking of scenarios. And just at a point where I'm getting the guts, where I think I'm gonna turn around and tell her, you know, 'I'm gonna let you out of here,' here he comes. It's like he knew I was thinking it. He didn't trust me, believe me."

Mickie told of driving up toward Lake Tahoe. James had no specific plans, Mickie said; still, she sensed that this time things would be different.

"Did you say to him, 'James,' you know, 'let's just let her go—you've had, you did what you needed to do'?" Campion asked.

"He's not gonna let her go," Mickie said. "It was different."

"Did you really know, Michelle?"

"No. I didn't really think he was going to go this far. I didn't really know. Did I have an idea? Did I think? I'd be a liar if I said I didn't."

"So you had a suspicion," Campion said. But Mickie suggested that she would have to say she did it with James, because if she let James take all the blame, someone might retaliate against her family.

"Yeah, I had a feeling it wasn't going to be a good ending," Mickie said. "By the end of the story I know what I'm gonna have to say, and I'm gonna have to say it because I know that if I don't, something's gonna happen to my family. I'm gonna look you straight in the eye and tell you, I'm gonna tell you I did it. I'm gonna swear to it, I don't have a choice, and I know that as well as I know anything, that's why it's all gonna be so hard."

She would lie if she had to, to do that, she said.

"You can't lie to me to protect anybody," Campion said. "You can't do that. First thing, Michelle, is it won't protect them."

"It'll protect my family."

"No it won't."

Mickie wanted to know if the FBI had gone to see Clara or Fred or Vickie, or any of those she feared.

"We're working on them," Campion said.

For the first time, Mickie began showing some fight with Campion.

" 'Working on it,' " Mickie said, sarcastically.

"Yes."

Mickie said she didn't believe Campion. "You know what brings me to this point, all the thinking in my mind and you all telling me that you knew him, [but] you couldn't stop him any more than I could."

"You can stop him now."

"And I can stop him now . . . I can stop him from hurting my family."

"No, you can't. We'll stop him from hurting your family, Michelle. No matter what you say or do right now, it's us— up to us to stop him from hurting her family and you."

"Is anybody watching my family?"

"We've got people on it, yes," Campion said. "Your family is safe. They are not gonna be harmed. He cannot get to them, he cannot have anybody get to them. And you're not gonna lie to me to protect somebody, because you've been doing that your whole life. It's not gonna be today. You're gonna tell me the truth, Michelle. Now, whether that's [that] you did it or you didn't do it, it's gonna be the truth, and you're not gonna lie to me because you've been doing that your whole God damn life. And we agreed—"

"I had to do it for my mom and dad, for Jose," Mickie said.

"—and you're gonna start living like a human being now. Do we agree on that? We need the truth from you, Michelle."

Campion told Mickie that no one would believe anything she said if she started lying again at that point.

"You can't lie to me about what happened," Campion told her, "otherwise this will never end. These nightmares will never end, Michelle."

"Never gonna end anyway, Chris."

"Yes they are. You gotta tell—You know what confession is?"

"Yes." Mickie's momentary resistance collapsed again.

"From the church?"

"Yes."

"You gotta tell your sins."

"Yes."

"To get the forgiveness. It's very basic. If you leave things out, you don't get forgiveness for that."

"No."

"You're a human being and you deserve forgiveness," Campion said. "We went through that a hundred times."

"I know."

"You gotta say what happened. I'm not your judge. Des [Carrington] is not your judge."

"I know. I know."

Mickie said she was afraid because she'd heard that some of the prisoners at Folsom had been giving her brother a hard time because of her. She thought it was James' influence in the prison, but Campion said that wasn't it.

"Do you think those . . . are gonna stick your brother if they know Frog is a baby raper? Baby rapers do not do well in prison, Michelle."

Campion told her they were going to keep her safe.

"I wish to God I'd never met this man," she said.

"Well," said Campion, "we wish that, too."

Now Campion and Carrington wanted the details: just how did Vanessa Samson die?

Mickie was reluctant; but with pressure, the picture gradually came into focus, and it was horrifying: according to Mickie, she watched in the rear-view mirror as James raped Vanessa even as he strangled her.

"And you saw that?" Campion asked.

She had, Mickie indicated. Campion made her act out the positions, with Carrington playing the role of Vanessa. James had pulled Vanessa up into the air by the rope around her neck, Mickie said, while she watched in the mirror.

"He lifted his head and then he went—he was like, clicking his teeth, like that, and he was dribbling, you know . . ."

That didn't satisfy Campion and Carrington; they wanted more. Was Vanessa moving while this was going on? They wanted to know exactly what Mickie saw so they could determine whether she had later helped kill Vanessa when James made her grab the rope and pull. But Mickie said she believed that Vanessa had probably been murdered at that moment.

Mickie said James made her change places with him, so he was driving and she was in the back. As she lay next to Vanessa, Mickie said, Vanessa didn't move. James drove for a while, and then he stopped the van and came back.

"I was scared to death," Mickie said. "I could smell her even more then. I knew medical enough to know what that was, what was going on."

Mickie said she didn't look at Vanessa's body. James told her, "Don't be a sniveling bitch," Mickie said.

Mickie said James then straddled Vanessa's body. He took Mickie's hands, and put them on the rope, intertwined with his. James pulled the rope taut and "then he looks at me, and then he tells me, tells me to look at him, and I do," Mickie said.

"He said, 'Together forever.' "

Campion nodded. " 'Together forever,' " he said.

"We're bonded," Mickie said.

"All right," Campion said.

"That's what he did."

"Okay," said Campion. "It's gonna be all right. You're free of him now."

"God."

"Michelle," Campion said, "look at me. Look at me. Do you swear that's the way it really happened?"

"I swear. I swear," Mickie said.

"Your nightmares will continue forever if that's not the way it happened," Campion warned.

"I swear. I swear. I swear it is. I swear," said Mickie.

Mickie talked about some other things, including the attack she and James had made on Sidney, Joanie's friend in the Dublin area. It was now very late, nearly midnight. Everyone was tired, drained. But Campion wasn't quite ready to quit.

"I'm just really trying to get inside your head," he told Mickie, "and find out how this goes."

Campion said he didn't understand how Mickie could have gone from being upset with James for bringing women to her house at the beginning of their relationship to later helping him commit rape and murder.

" 'Cause you go from those things, and those things are things that happen between men and women," Campion said, referring to James' fooling around. "Especially asshole men and women who really love those asshole men. How does the next step come? Where does that—how does a guy like James bring up the idea that you're gonna go grab girls that you don't know and go and rape 'em?"

"I think," Mickie said, "as I'm sitting here talking to you, telling these stories, I'm thinking about those things, too. My mind is very full. I wanna give logic. I wanna give it mostly to me. . . .

"I've been a hooker. I've seen a lot of things, I've done a lot of things for money. I'm desensitized to a lot of things. I can shut parts of me off, but they come back to me later, when I'm alone, and the pain comes with it. I . . . know men. I've seen men come in, [who have] been married twenty-five years, show me pictures of their children, their wife, they love their family, there's nothing they wouldn't do for their wife.

" 'What the fuck are you doing here seeing me?' That angers me. 'Why are you here if you love her so much? Why are you betraying her? Why are you here betraying the children? Why are you here being a pig?' You see what I'm saying?"

Campion nodded.

"Those thoughts are in my heart," Mickie continued. "And I know men that way. But I also know that men have this sexual nature . . .

"Uh, these are all things that I try to be and let go of myself through the years, and those are some of the answers I can give you. I think most men are pigs. I know what their minds are harboring. To have a man of your own, there is no man ever is going to be with a woman like me and accept who I was. There's no man ever that's going to come into my life and take me out of that world because he thinks I'm good enough, or he loves me enough. I've waited a long time for a man like that to come along, that would seize my heart, probably the most pathetic stupid thing I can ever think. I'm a whore and that's the way it is, a whore is a whore. And that's what gets proven to me over and over again."

James had come into her life, Mickie said, and made her think that her prince had finally come.

But instead of kissing a frog into a prince, Mickie had discovered that Frog had always been a frog, and nothing, not even the most perverse kind of love, had the power to change him.

JUSTICE

This was apparently the last exchange between Mickie and Chris Campion. The very next day, the FBI's Ferrin obtained a federal warrant for Mickie's arrest, and she was transferred to federal custody. That meant she was assigned a lawyer, and the lawyer, Mary Boetsch of Reno, advised her to clam up forthwith, which Mickie did.

Despite the FBI's search of the van, there was comparatively little physical evidence to link either James or Mickie to the attack on Alicia Paredes. The semen found in Alicia's hair and on her face could not be definitively matched to James. The van had been cleaned numerous times between the September kidnapping and rape and the arrest in December. Outside of Alicia's identification of James, and certain items in the van, such as the rosary around the rear-view mirror, the rape case was substantially a circumstantial one.

A far different situation existed in the Vanessa Samson case, however. The gag and one of the curling irons both contained traces of DNA that belonged to Vanessa; a number of items recovered by Ferrin and the Washoe County forensics team from the van contained fingerprints that matched James, Mickie and Vanessa, proving beyond any doubt that Vanessa had been in Mickie's van after she was kidnapped, and that one of the curling irons had been used to rape her.

The United States Attorney's Office in Reno elected to try Mickie and James for the Alicia Paredes kidnapping as a federal crime, even though similar charges had been filed in Placer County, based on Carrington and Summers' investigation. Approximately six months went by while laboratories in both Nevada and California examined the bits of evidence recovered from the van, and while the lawyers for the government assembled the thousand pages of documents the investigation had spawned, including Mickie's lengthy interviews with Campion and Carrington; indeed, the heart of the federal case against Mickie and James was contained in Mickie's admissions to Campion, Minister and Carrington.

At length, the lawyer appointed to represent James, Michael Kennedy of the Federal Public Defender's Office, asked that the government be required to try James separately from Mickie; the law required separate trials if the government intended to use Mickie's statements against James, because in that case James' lawyer would have the right to cross-examine her, while Mickie herself would have the right to remain silent. The only solution was two separate trials, with Mickie going first, Kennedy contended.

The government didn't directly oppose James' bid for a separate trial, but provided copies of Mickie's statements to the Judge, James W. Hagen, as court exhibits—in all, approximately 500 pages of transcribed material.[46]

Judge Hagen read the material and decided to grant James' motion for a separate trial.

Meanwhile, Mickie's attorney, Mary Boetsch, asked the judge to suppress all of Mickie's statements to Campion and Carrington on the grounds that the Placer County detectives and the FBI agents had "colluded" to prevent Mickie from seeing a lawyer immediately after her arrest. Had Mickie been taken into custody on a federal warrant, she would have been assigned a lawyer within a few hours, Boetsch contended; by arresting her on the Placer County warrant instead, the authorities were able to maneuver Mickie into a

---

46 The government wanted Judge Hagen to order the material sealed. Hagen did so. Following Hagen's ruling on the severance motion, the author filed a motion in U.S. District Court for the unsealing of the Michaud transcripts. The government and the attorneys for the two defendants, Kennedy and Boetsch, opposed the unsealing on the grounds that publicity from the contents might jeopardize the defendants' rights to a fair trial. Judge Hagen agreed, and ordered the seal maintained. The author nevertheless obtained the transcripts from a confidential source.

vulnerable position they soon took advantage of. Judge Hagen ruled that there was no such collusion.

Following the judge's ruling, Mickie agreed to enter a conditional plea of guilty to one count of kidnapping for the purpose of assisting James Daveggio in the sexual assault of Alicia Paredes; the government agreed to allow Mickie to withdraw her plea of guilty if, sometime in the future, the Ninth Circuit Court of Appeals agreed that there was collusion between federal and state authorities to deny Mickie an opportunity to consult with an attorney before she agreed to talk to Campion.

After her conditional plea of guilty, Mickie agreed to testify against James Daveggio at his trial. She did so in May of 1999, nearly two and a half years after the kidnapping of Alicia Paredes. In June of 1999, James was found guilty of kidnapping for purposes of sexual assault after his jury deliberated less than two hours.

Mickie was then sentenced to a term of 12 years in prison, while James drew 22 years. Like Mickie, James also appealed.

Subsequently, both James and Mickie were delivered to the authorities in Alameda County, where a grand jury had indicted them for the kidnapping and murder of Vanessa Samson, and for the sexual assaults of Sidney and Astrid. As of this writing, charges against both James and Mickie are still pending in Alameda County, more than three years after Vanessa was abducted on her way to work. Similarly, sexual assault charges are pending against James and Mickie in Sacramento County for the rapes of Charlotte and Renee.

Finally, there remains the possibility that James and Mickie may still be tried in Placer County on rape charges stemming from the attack on Alicia Paredes; as noted, while the underlying facts there are the same as in the federal case, the crimes are slightly different, making them potentially liable to criminal charges in that county as well.

So we now come to the end, so far, of the sordid tale of Daveggio and Michaud. And while it's tempting—certainly it's easy—to toss away someone like James, as Campion did, as one of the "asshole men," it should be clear to everyone by now that there was far more going on with the devolution of a mind and soul of a man like James Anthony Daveggio.

How did James come to such evil? The keys are there for anyone to see, and indeed were evident in his personality even to the very end: his soul was filled with rage and fear. Rage at the way his life had unfolded, from the time his inconstant father abandoned him as a toddler, rage at his mother for her failure to prevent the loss. Fear of abandonment that went on, even to a dark night on a California mountain road, where he told his final woman that she was "bound" to him, "forever," through the death of another human being.

It was the same rage and fear which drove James, again and again throughout his life, to demand control over those who had power over him: women. Rage and fear which drove James into an ever-darkening fantasy world, where he could stop the pain only by giving it to others, even his own children.

And as for Mickie: hers was a world in which it soon became impossible to distinguish between the boundaries of herself and the wants of another. Her entire life she had survived by fitting, chameleon-like, into whatever surroundings she found herself in, and trying hard to make the unacceptable become acceptable; and to Mickie, that way was power, the only kind of power she had ever known. It was how she made it, how she lived—being what others wanted her to be: from call girl to fellow sadist with James to prize informant for Campion.

That Mickie had numerous chances to save Vanessa Samson's life was beyond dispute: at the welfare office, for example, where she might have alerted someone to Vanessa's plight; or when she left the motel to get Vanessa's last meal from McDonald's; or most of all, when James left her alone with Vanessa, when a simple telephone call might have saved everyone from the heartache that was to come. But it was the most debilitating aspect of Mickie's personality to become so caught up in her role as James' willing assistant that even when those chances presented themselves, she was unable to act on them, or even to see them as the sort of thing one should do.

And if James' tragedy was that he never found a way to deal with his rage and his fear, Mickie's was that she never had a chance to be herself; it was everyone else's tragedy that no one understood either of them until it was too late.

And finally, what of Marvin Mutch, the putative killer of James' one-time girlfriend, Cassie Riley, back in Union City, when James was just 14? Did James himself kill Cassie? Was that why he felt so guilty, so many years later? Was that what he was hinting at to his daughter Astrid, or to Mickie? Only James knows that for sure, at this late date. That Marvin did not seems incontrovertible, even from the evidence that was presented against him so long ago—evidence that was never made known to James' haunted sister, Jodie, who could still recall, so many years later, the brand of sneaker worn those days by her brother in Union City—yes, Converse All Stars.

As of this writing, Mutch remains incarcerated behind the guarded barricades of San Quentin State Prison, turned down for parole time after time, while others guilty of far more heinous offenses have been set free; Marvin has refused to admit his guilt, probably because he simply isn't guilty.

Over the past quarter-century, Marvin has done the time he was handed, quietly. According to his one-time lawyer, James McWilliams, Marvin has even received awards from the state for his help with some of the state's computer systems, and stands as a model prisoner.

If there are such things as ghosts, surely the ghost of Cassie Riley must be watching all this: watching James, to see what becomes of him; watching Mickie, who loved at least her fantasy about James, and literally to death; watching Marvin, imprisoned for something he never did.

And watching the Alameda County District Attorney's Office—the same people now about to ask a jury to give James A. Daveggio the death penalty—which, 25 years ago, used every trick in the book to convict a man for a crime he almost certainly did not commit, and which now holds the power to undo that aging wrong. Whether they will do justice depends on their sense of justice; we know this, because by now, we also know one thing with certainty: all that is necessary for evil to prevail is for good people to do nothing.